INTIMATE PARTNER VIOLENCE

ISSUES IN WOMEN'S HEALTH

Series Editors: Ralph J. DiClemente and Gina M. Wingood
Emory University
Rollins School of Public Health
Atlanta, Georgia

INTIMATE PARTNER VIOLENCE
Societal, Medical, Legal, and Individual Responses
Sana Loue

INTIMATE PARTNER VIOLENCE

VIOLENCE

Societal, Medical, Legal, and Individual Responses

Sana Loue

Case Western Reserve University
Cleveland, Ohio

SPRINGER SCIENCE+BUSINESS MEDIA, LLC

Library of Congress Cataloging-in-Publication Data

Loue, Sana.
  Intimate partner violence: societal, medical, legal, and individual responses/Sana Loue.
    p.   ; cm. — (Issues in women's health (Kluwer Academic Publishers))
  Includes bibliographical references and index.
  ISBN 978-1-4757-7436-8   ISBN 978-0-306-47586-3 (eBook)
  DOI 10.1007/978-0-306-47586-3
    1. Conjugal violence.   2. Conjugal violence—United States.   3. Conjugal
  violence—United States—Prevention.   I. Title.   II. Series.

HV6626 .L677 2000
362.82'92—dc21

00-049772

ISBN 978-1-4757-7436-8

©2001 Springer Science+Business Media New York
Originally published by Kluwer Academic / Plenum Publishers, New York in 2002
Softcover reprint of the hardcover 1st edition 2002

http://www.wkap.nl/

10 9 8 7 6 5 4 3 2 1

A C.I.P. record for this book is available from the Library of Congress

It has taken us long years to part.
Now at last there's no more to be said:
They are mine—freedom's chill in my heart
And a silvery crown on my head.

No more treachery, no more betrayal.
You no longer must listen all night
To me volubly follow the trail
Of the ultimate proof I was right.

Anna Akhmatova, *Rupture 1*, 1940

PREFACE

It is clear from the pages that follow that the physical abuse of one individual by another, or by both individuals of each other, is an integral component of some intimate relationships, perhaps many intimate relationships. This book is not about the violence as much as it is a reflection on our responses to—or our lack of responses to—that violation of physical integrity and the accompanying emotional and mental trauma. As these next pages indicate, we all too often fail to recognize the signs of physical violence. On those occasions when we are able to perceive clearly the situation of a friend or relative or neighbor, or even ourselves, we may feel compelled to turn away, not to see what we do not know how to address or what is too embarrassing for ourselves or the other to acknowledge.

How we respond to partner violence, individually and collectively, may well determine whether the violence can be prevented before it is ever effectuated, or whether it will cease once begun. Theory postulates that intimate partner violence occurs because we collectively permit it to occur, because of how we view women, because of our failure as a legal system to address and punish the violence when it does occur, and through the inability and/or unwillingness of many of our helping professions to recognize its signs and to intervene. Empirical research has demonstrated the complexity of the interplay between individual and systemic response in allowing the violence to occur and recur. As an example, the response of the assaultive partner may mediate the potential response of the police officer who responds to the emergency call; in turn, the response of the police officer may determine, at least in part, whether that violence will recur.

It is this emphasis on the response and the range of potential responses, rather than the violence itself, that distinguishes this text from others that relate to partner violence. Although the text is U.S.-focused, relevant examples and research from other countries is incorporated throughout. Additionally, the discussions recognize, where known, differences across culture, place, and time.

Chapter 1 provides a background for this discussion by focusing on how intimate partner violence is defined across various cultures and in different contexts, such as the legal and the social science perspectives. Chapter 2 examines a number of the major theories as to why intimate partner violence occurs and why it continues. Chapter 3 presents empirical research relating to how individuals define partner violence and how those definitions relate to their choice of individual and collective response to such situations: what they believe could or should be done in situations they define as partner violence.

Chapter 4 begins an in-depth review of the literature pertaining to responses to partner violence, focusing on societal response to partner violence by examining that response within the framework of deviance. Is it the behavior of the assailant that is deviant in its violence or in its target? Or is it the behavior of the victim of that assault that is deviant, thereby provoking the violence? Or is it the failure of the victim to leave the violent situation that is deviant? How have our views of what constitutes deviance in the context of partner violence changed over time?

Chapter 5 addresses the response and the potential for response of various helping professions to intimate partner violence: health care professionals, the clergy, and, yes, even veterinarians. Chapter 6 extends the inquiry to the justice and law enforcement systems, examining the response of the police, the prosecution, the legislature, and the judiciary to partner violence in the United States. Chapter 7 examines both the range of responses of the batterer to his or her own conduct, such as his or her account of how and why the incident occurred, and the responses that the batterer may offer in response to others' responses, such as court-ordered treatment. Chapter 8 explores the range of responses that have been utilized and are potentially available to individuals who have been subjected to violence in the context of intimate partner violence, while Chapter 9 focuses on both the short- and long-term responses of children who have been exposed to partner violence. Chapter 10 provides an integration of this material and suggests possible avenues for research, intervention, and the provision of services.

This text is intended to serve as a basic resource for students, clinicians, and researchers who are concerned about intimate partner violence. As such, it both provides a summary of how we have responded to such violence in the past and presents potential future directions for research and prevention efforts.   The ultimate success of such efforts necessarily rests on our ability and willingness to address partner violence as both an individual and a community issue and to see what we wish not to see.

ACKNOWLEDGMENTS

The author gratefully acknowledges the helpful review and critique of earlier versions of this manuscript by Drs. Beth Quill and Siran Karoukian. Several students deserve praise and thanks for their time and diligence in locating needed materials: Sandy Ferber, Jay Fiedler, Stephanie Stewart, and Fatoumata Traore. Gina Wingood and Ralph DiClemente, the editors of this series, are to be thanked for their wonderful sense of humor, and Mariclaire Cloutier, the editor of this volume, deserves praise for her patience and support.

CONTENTS

LIST OF TABLES

1

THE DEFINITION AND EPIDEMIOLOGY OF INTIMATE PARTNER VIOLENCE

"[T]o speak a true word is to transform the world."
(Freire, 1978: 60)

IDENTIFYING INTIMATE PARTNER VIOLENCE

Defining Intimate Partner Violence

How one defines a problem may determine how one conceives of its resolution. Some of the difficulties in conducting research and in formulating responses to intimate partner violence stem from the variation in definition of intimate partner violence and its component elements. Consider the following examples. Siann (1985) defined "aggression" as involving an intent to inflict hurt or appear superior to others. Such behavior does not necessarily involve physical injury and is not always negatively sanctioned. Gelles and Straus (1979) have defined violence as "an act carried out with the intention or perceived intention of physically hurting another person." Reiss and Roth (1993) defined violence as "behavior by persons against persons that intentionally threatens, attempts, or actually inflicts physical harm." This definition specifically excludes intense criticism, verbal harassment, a restraint of normal activities, and a denial of resources, which may often accompany intimate partner violence (Murty and Roebuck, 1992; NIH, 1992; Walker, 1979). Denzin (1984: 483-484) defined domestic violence as "situated, emotional, and cognitive activity involving negative symbolic interaction between intimates, usually in the family home...." Acts encompassed by this definition include marital rape, sadomasochistic rituals, spouse abuse, inflicted emotionality, threats of murder, physical torture, harassment, acts of striking, and mock, pretended, or playful violence (Denzin, 1984). Kornblit (1994: 1181) has distinguished between abuse and violence:

> The former refers to actions which are harmful for the victim, both physically as well as mentally, committed or resulting from omission, carried out intentionally or not.
> Violence in a limited sense is used to refer to physical aggression.
> Maltreatment includes abuse (physical, sexual, and/or emotional) and neglect (physical, educational, and/or affective.)

Brown (1992: 1), addressing intimate partner violence directed to women specifically, has defined "wife-beating" as

> a man intentionally inflicting pain on a woman, within a non-transient, male-female relationship, whether or not the partners are officially married. The subject is further restricted to physical aggression....

Brown further distinguishes between wife-beating and wife battering. The former refers to a "physical reprimand," that is often culturally expected, tolerated by the recipient female partners, and not at all seen as deviant. Wife battering, by contrast, refers to extraordinary behavior that is neither usual nor acceptable within the society and that may result in serious injury, disability, or death.

The one element common to these definitions is that of physical aggression. Although these definitions are not uniform in their requirement of intentionality, legal definitions often incorporate intentionality as a critical element. Ohio law, for instance, defines domestic violence as

> (a) Attempting to cause or recklessly causing bodily injury;
> (b) Placing another person by the threat of force in fear of imminent serious physical harm...;
> (c) Committing any act with respect to a child that would result in the child being an abused child....(O.R.C. 3113.31).

Emic and etic definitions of partner violence or domestic injury may vary, however, and definitions may vary between groups. A study of the attitudes of 50 women in Ghana found, for instance, that over 60 percent did not believe that the beating of a husband by his wife constitutes domestic violence, although all 50 indicated that domestic violence encompasses a husband's beating of his wife, including hitting, slapping, and whipping (Ofei-Oboagye, 1994). Mexican-American women in the United States have been found less likely than others to classify slapping, pushing, shoving, grabbing, and throwing things as physical abuse (Torres, 1991), although such acts are often encompassed in laws prohibiting domestic violence.

Emotional and physical abuse are often intimately related. Dutton and Golant (1995: 23-24) have observed that incidents of physical violence may occur only sporadically, although emotional abuse may be used by the batterer to effectuate control during the interim periods. They offer as an example the situation of one of Dutton's clients, who had beaten his wife once in 1985, with a warning that the next violent event would be worse. She recognized a particular expression on his face and thereafter "toed the line" whenever she detected that same expression. In effect, the husband was able to control her behavior through emotional abuse; the next violent incident did not occur until 6 years after the first one.

The issue of intimate partner violence not only calls into question the nature of the acts that constitute such violence, but the nature of the partner relationship that constitutes "intimate partner." Murdock (1949: 1) has defined a family as a "social group characterized by common residence, economic cooperation, and reproduction..." thereby eliminating the requirement of marriage as a basis for defining an intimate partnership. It is unclear, however, whether reproduction is seen as an essential element of "family;" if it were, it would eliminate many household units that, in fact, perceive themselves and are perceived by others as families. Many state laws reflect an awareness that neither marriage nor reproduction are prerequisites for intimate partner violence. Ohio's statute relating to domestic violence, for instance, refers to "family or household member[s]," which includes a "spouse, a person living as a spouse or a former spouse of the respondent." In turn, a "person living as a spouse" is defined as

> a person who is living or has lived with the respondent in a common law marital relationship, who otherwise is cohabiting with the respondent, who otherwise has cohabited with the respondent within one year prior to the date of the alleged occurrence of the act in question.... (O.R.C. 3113.31).

This provision has been interpreted to encompass both heterosexual and homosexual relationships.

The Battering Incident: Forms and Context

What is startling is the range of circumstances across which intimate partner violence affecting women occurs and the forms that it may assume. Intimate partner violence has been committed by men against female partners; by women against male partners (Fiebert, 1996; Balakrishnan et al., 1995; Straus, 1993; Bergman and Brismar, 1993, 1992; Duminy and Hudson, 1993); by one same-sex intimate partner against the other (Coleman, 1994; Letellier, 1994); and by partners against each other (Cook and Harris, 1995; Vivian and Langhinrichsen-Rohling, 1994). Intimate partner violence may take numerous forms including battering or beating (Levinson, 1989), stalking (Kurt, 1995), rape (Whatley, 1993), murder, or forced suicide (Levinson, 1989). The violence may be effectuated through the use of fists, feet (Straus, 1994), sexual organs, as in the case of rape (Whatley, 1993; Hanneke et al., 1986), poison, hanging, drowning, fire (Balakrishnan et al., 1995; Prasad, 1994; Shamim, 1992), electrical shocks (Prasad, 1994), knives or guns (Bates et al., 1995), or another individual, pursuant to the request of the assaultive partner or his or her consent or acquiescence (Chin, 1994; Prasad, 1994; Shamim, 1992). The violence may be perpetrated for any number of proffered reasons, including economic considerations, such as the tendering of an inadequate dowry (Prasad, 1994; Shamim, 1992), religious or spiritual beliefs (Harlan, 1994; Narasimhan, 1990), or dissatisfaction with the actions/behavior of one's partner (Koss et al., 1994), including extramarital affairs (Chimbos, 1998).

Nayala (1997: 25), a woman who was battered for years during her marriage, described the importance of the emotional context in which partner violence occurs:

> [C]ontext is everything. Emotional context, for instance, mattered greatly. When Kevin was angry, laundry was often a cause for a beating: if it was already done, he would throw it around the house, stomp through it, and then order me to clean it up; if it was being

done, he would do the same; if it was undone, he simply beat me immediately and tossed the clothes nowhere because he hated unclean things and refused to touch them.

Two forms of intimate partner violence illustrate particularly aptly the complexity of motivation, means, and consequences: dowry-associated violence and *sati*, the burning of a widow on the funeral pyre with her deceased husband. Each of these acts has been documented in India.

Initially, the dowry payment by a bride's family to the groom was said to derive from Hindu scriptures (Sarkar, 1993). Gradually, it became a means of promoting social mobility for the bride, albeit a voluntary means. Although illegal as of 1961, the offering and acceptance of dowries has become a socially mandated practice. The dowry has been seen as compensation to the husband's family for the cost of maintaining an economically unproductive human being (Divale and Harris, 1976). The dowry brings economic benefits not only to the family receiving it, but to the Indian economy in general. It has been estimated that the total annual consumer budget for dowries approximates Rs 100 billion, or almost $320 million (Sarkar, 1993).

However, where the dowry is deemed inadequate or is paid to the groom's family too slowly, the bride may become the target of violence. The violence may occur shortly after the wedding, or years later (Sarkar, 1993). Such violence is not uncommon and, in fact, may be accepted in course. Narasimhan (1990: 51) notes that even proverbs reinforce the acceptability of violence against a wife: "The drum, the village fool, the shudra, animals and woman, all these are fit to be beaten."

Dowry was reported as the chief motive in 6.9 percent of all 1990 murder cases; a total of 4,656 dowry deaths were reported in the same year (Prasad, 1994). Unlike domestic violence in the United States, where we tend to equate it with intimate partner violence, the assailants involved in dowry violence may include not only the husband, but also his parents, siblings, and other relatives (Willigen and Channa, 1991). The woman's death is often effectuated by setting her on fire after dousing her with kerosene, but may also be brought about through hanging, drowning, poisoning, or beheading (Prasad, 1994).

Sati refers to the Hindu ritual whereby a wife follows her deceased husband to death by joining him on his funeral pyre (Hawley, 1994). The ritual itself derives from various Hindu epics, many of which stress the mythical and mystical powers of women (Courtright, 1994). Although few women now end their lives in this manner, and although the practice is now legally prohibited, the woman who ends her life as a *sati* ("good woman") continues to be venerated (Harlan, 1994). However, whether women who die in this manner have chosen to do so willingly remains an open question.

One of the most well-known instances of *sati* occurred on September 5, 1987 in Jaipur. An 18-year old widow, Roop Kanwar, died on her husband's funeral pyre. Witness accounts of the event varied. Some claimed that Roop wished to die in this manner and had done so with dignity. Other claimed that she was drugged by her husband's family, forced to mount the pyre, and was pushed back following an unsuccessful attempt to escape. Critics charged that the husband's family had been acting on the basis of economic motives, noting that they had arranged for the immolation near their own home, rather than on the town cremation grounds, so as to reap the benefits of any offerings placed at the site (Hawley, 1994; Oldenburg, 1994). Other critics charged that the three most powerful castes, the Rajputs, the Brahmins, and Marwaris, had deliberately orchestrated the revival of this custom in order to revitalize their image, their priestly role, and their commercial interests from donations to the site, respectively (Tully, 1991). The police noted that Roop had brought a substantial dowry to the marriage which, according to local custom, would have reverted to her family when she returned to them as a young childless widow. These possessions could remain with the husband's family only if she, too, died (Oldenburg, 1994).

The death of Roop prompted significant outcries from women's groups and ultimately resulted in the passage of legislation prohibiting the practice of *sati* (Oldenburg, 1994). (See Responses, below, for a discussion of varying responses to intimate partner violence, including social organization.)

Nandy (1994) has examined the circumstances that appear to give rise to *sati* in recent times. Nandy concluded that *sati* is more likely to occur when the noneconomic powers of women have declined or been devalued; when the "market value" of women is low; and when women have access to economic power within the family but the family relationships have become interest-based because of a breakdown in cultural values. Some widows may have chosen *sati*, or had *sati* chosen for them, as a means of alleviating the economic drain that they caused on the family's limited resources (Narasimhan, 1990). These hypothesized bases for sati reflect several of the theories relating to the causation of intimate partner violence that are discussed in chapter 2, notably patriarchy theory and, less obviously, resource theory.

Mahatma Gandhi, commenting on a 1931 *sati* incident, attributed its origin to male domination:

> If the wife has to prove her loyalty and undivided devotion to her husband, so has the husband to prove his allegiance and devotion to his wife. Yet, we have never heard of a husband mounting the funeral pyre of his deceased wife. It may therefore be taken for granted that the practice of the widow immolating herself at the death of the husband had its origins in superstitions, ignorance, and blind egotism of man (Narasimhan, 1990: 57).

THE EPIDEMIOLOGY OF INTIMATE PARTNER VIOLENCE

Intimate Partner Violence Committed by Men

Male-Female Violence in Heterosexual Relationships

Incidence and Prevalence. Estimates of the incidence and prevalence of intimate partner violence vary, due to differences in the definitions and the sampling procedures that are used. However, it is clear that the occurrence of intimate partner violence is not infrequent. In the United States, approximately 1 of every 5 couples experiences at least one episode of intimate partner violence during a one year period (Schafer, Caetano, and Clark, 1998). It has been estimated that in the United

States alone, each year approximately 1.8 million women (3.4%) to 4 million women are physically assaulted by their intimate partners (Sorenson et al., 1996; Novello et al., 1992; Straus and Gelles, 1990). One United States-based study, which utilized a multistage probability design to conduct interviews with 1,635 couples in the contiguous 48 states, estimated that the prevalence of any intimate partner violence during the previous year was between 7.8 and 21.5 percent. Surprisingly, the estimate for female-to-male violence was higher than that for male-to-female violence (5.2% to 13.6%, compared to 6.2% to 18.2%). A study in Melbourne, Australia found that approximately 22 percent of the 2,181 women surveyed through general practitioners' offices and clinics reported that they had been physically assaulted by their intimate partner during the previous 12 months (Mazza et al., 1996). Thirteen percent of the women assaulted indicated that they had never disclosed the assault to others. Results from a telephone survey of women in Toronto, Canada indicated an annual incidence of intimate partner violence of 14.4 percent and a prevalence rate of approximately 25 percent (Smith, 1987). A study of 1,000 women aged 22 through 55 in Santiago, Chile found that over 60 percent had experienced intimate partner violence and more than one quarter had experienced severe violence in their relationship during the previous 2 years (Larrain, 1993). In Malaysia, 39 percent of the 713 women participating in a study reported having been physically beaten by their intimate male partner during 1989 (Malaysia Women's AID Organization, 1992). The Metropolitan London Police in 1985 received nearly 1,500 calls per week from women experiencing violence in their homes (Edwards, 1986) and it was estimated in 1986 that there were over 750,000 incidents of domestic violence in London alone (Smith, 1989).

Definitional differences also create difficulty in estimating the prevalence and incidence of date rape. Despite such methodological difficulties, it appears that violence between dating individuals, including those who have not been intimate in the past, is not uncommon. In the United States, approximately 50% of all college campus rapes are committed on dates (Abbey, 1991). In one study, it was found that just over 21 percent of college-age participants had either committed or sustained violence during their dating relationships (Makepeace, 1981).

Perhaps what is most striking is the widespread occurrence of intimate partner violence, across societies, cultures, and religions. Intimate partner violence has been documented across ethnic groups and socioeconomic strata (Straus and Gelles, 1990; Straus et al., 1980; Schulman, 1979) and in both developed (Statistics Canada, 1993; Bernard and Schlaffer, 1992; Kim and Cho, 1992; Knight and Hatty, 1992; Bruynooghe et al., 1989; Schei and Bakketeig, 1989; Mullen et al., 1988) and developing countries (Morley, 1994; Prasad, 1994; Counts et al., 1992; Shamim, 1992; Women's AID Organization, 1992; PROFAMILIA, 1990).

Despite the widespread occurrence of intimate partner violence, its frequency appears to vary across cultures. Wife beating has been shown to be infrequent among families in the rural areas of northern Thailand (Potter, 1977) and the Mundurucu of South America (Murphy and Murphy, 1974). Wife beating among the !Kung, however, appears to be more frequent (Shostak, 183), although it is surpassed in both frequency and severity in rural Taiwanese families (Wolf, 1972) and among the Yanomamo of northern Brazil (Chagnon, 1968). Researchers examining intimate partner violence at the societal level have found that the prevalence of "wife beating" tends to be higher in societies in which there is greater tolerance of homosexual relationships and where homosexual behavior is more frequent. Intimate partner violence tends to be less frequent, however, in societies in which a double standard exists with respect to premarital sexual relations (Erchak and Rosenfeld, 1994) and in societies where the need for affiliation is high (Lester, 1987).

Risk Factors for Intimate Partner Violence by Men Against Women. A number of factors have been associated with an increased risk of assault by intimate partners. Sorenson and colleagues found that women at highest risk of assault by intimate partners are those who are younger, urban dwellers, African Americans, and those with lesser education and lower incomes (Sorenson, Upchurch, and Shen, 1996). Peipert and Domagalstei (1994) found in their study of adolescent sexual assault that women under the age of 20 were more likely to be assaulted by an acquaintance than were older women. A study conducted by the Joint Center for Poverty Research and Institute for Policy Research (cited in Corlett, 1999) found that women who were receiving Aid to Families with Dependent Children (AFDC) were three times as likely to have experienced physical aggression during the previous year than were non-AFDC women.

Similar findings have resulted from studies in other countries. A recent study of domestic violence in northern India found that domestic violence was associated with the husband having a lower level of education, the husband being young when he first lived with his wife, poverty, and stresses related to having multiple children (Martin, Tsui, Maitra, and Marinshaw, 1999).

A number of studies have indicated that partner violence may begin or escalate during pregnancy (Gillespie, 1988). Pregnant women especially at risk for violence during their pregnancies are those who have been battered prior to pregnancy (McFarlane, Parker, Soeken, and Bullock, 1992). A study of AFDC women in Massachusetts suggested an increased risk of abuse directed towards women who bore and cared for a disabled child (Anon., 1996, cited in Corlett, 1999). Physical abuse of pregnant Hispanic women has been associated with symbolic violence and threats of violence by their male partner (McFarlane, Wiist, and Watson, 1998).

Studies that have specifically focused on premarital violence between intimates have identified similar risk factors. Female victims tend to be younger than those who are married or divorced, and are more often African-American (Erez, 1986). As with violence directed against wives and divorced partners, violence is more likely to occur on the weekend (Erez, 1986). Although women who report having more liberal attitudes are more likely to report violence during dating (McKinney, 1986), it is not clear that more liberal women are more likely to experience dating violence. Sigelman and colleagues (1984) have theorized that dating violence is more likely to occur if the dating individuals' attitudes towards sex roles are highly divergent. And, although the research has yielded inconsistent findings, there are some data that lend support to the hypothesis that dating violence is more likely to occur in the context of a serious or steady dating relationship, as compared with a more infrequent or casual relationship (Billingham, 1987; Deal and Wampler, 1986; Laner, 1989; Roscoe and Kelsey, 1986; Sigelman, Berry and Wiles, 1984). In general, men have been found to display higher rates of violence as the level of commitment in an relationship increases, as measured by the length of time in the relationship and/or the number of dates (Arias, Samios, and O'Leary, 1987; Burke, Stets, and Pirog-Good, 1989; Marshall and Rose, 1987; Rouse, Breen, and Howell, 1988).

Female victims of intimate partner violence have been found more likely to use multiple substances (cigarettes, alcohol, and illegal drugs) than are nonvictims (Martin et al., 1996). This association has also been found in the context of dating violence (Makepeace, 1981). Homicide has been found to be more likely to occur among couples of lower socioeconomic status (Chimbos, 1998) and those in which the wife is substantially younger than the husband (Chimbos, 1998; Cohen, Llorente, and Eisdorfer, 1998). Assaultive men have been found to be more likely than assaultive women to take their own lives after killing their partners (Chimbos, 1998). There is also evidence to indicate an association between intimate partner violence and the commission of "suicide by cop," whereby the assaultive individual purposely disobeys the instructions of police officers to lay down weapons, etc., intentionally escalates the potential for a lethal encounter, and forces the police to use deadly force to protect other civilians (Hutson, Anglin, Yarbrough, Hardaway, Russell, Strote, Canter, and Blum, 1998). Research on violence also suggests that violence may be more intense if third parties present during an incident are supportive of the violence (Felson, Ribner, and Siegel, 1984).

Dutton and Golant (1995) have enumerated characteristics of male assaultive partners that on an individual level may be risk factors for partner violence. These include the partner's descriptions of his parents' rejecting or shaming behavior, recollections of physical assaults directed against him or his mother, personality characteristics such as an intense fear of abandonment or frequent anger, trauma symptoms such as sleep disturbances and memory losses for specific events, reliance on alcohol or drugs to ward off pain, a tendency to blame others, and cyclical mood swings. The characteristics of batterers are addressed in greater detail below. Schwartz (2000) has identified, based upon her own experiences as a battered wife, "warning characteristics" of women who may be particularly susceptible to abuse: the need to rescue the male, self-hatred, an acceptance of abuse, the ability to lie to oneself, a family history of dysfunctionality, and a fear of being alone.

Characteristics of Male Batterers. Stereotypes of abusive men depict such individuals as crude, uneducated, neurotic, macho misogynists—in short, "pigs" (Dutton and Golant, 1995). However, research reveals a surprisingly different portrait.

Research on batterers has frequently focused on their personality characteristics finding, for instance, that batterers may have borderline antisocial personality traits and act out their hostility (Else, Wonderlich, Beatty, Christie, and Staton, 1993). Dutton and Golant (1995: xi) have explained the basis for such an approach:

> Rather than focus on battering as an isolated behavior, [it can be viewed] as the product of an entire personality constellation. Assaultiveness exists…to maintain this personality. The acting out of abuse serves a necessary function—the abuser needs to maintain his sense of feeling whole. And… this personality has its origins in early

development, in the vagaries of attachment and a father's shaming and violent behavior.

Abusiveness is not, however, just a copied behavior but rather a learned means of self-maintenance. The abusive man is addicted to brutality to keep his shaky self-concept intact. The only time he feels powerful and whole is when he is engaged in violence...It is an arduous process to find the inner voice of abusive men. The lifelong silencing of that voice contributes to the acting out of rage in place of grief or longing. The origins of that grief or longing are very early in the childhood development of the man who will be an abusive adult.

It appears from the writings of various researchers that the battering behavior arises not from dominance, but from tremendous insecurity . For instance, men who batter have been described in clinical reports as exhibiting extreme dependence on their wives or girlfriends; they may use threats and abuse to forestall their partner's separation from the relationship (Vaselle-Augenstein and Ehrlich, 1992). They may be fearful of intimate relationships and have been found to be highly jealous and possessive (Dutton and Golant, 19965; Wodarski, 1987). The extreme jealousy has been referred to as "conjugal paranoia" or "morbid jealousy," and has been described as follows:

Escalating their abuse when they sensed an imagined abandonment, many abusive men...would drive their women away. Often this "sense" was based on a fiction, a misreading of signals. They created, in effect, the self-fulfilling prophecy of their worst nightmare. Others, having already been left by their wives, put them under surveillance, instigating a nightwatch on their residence or the transition house where they sought temporary shelter. Such men became a type of a "stalker" and are potentially dangerous...[There were] strong sexual themes in these abandonment fantasies...The men never framed the abandonment in terms of needing the woman and depending on her and her emotional support. Instead, they always reduced the scenario to a sexual triad: She was seeing someone else. (Dutton and Golant, 1995: 15)

Jealousy has also been identified as one of the primary factors in the occurrence of dating violence (Makepeace, 1981; Mathews, 1984; Roscoe and Kelsey, 1986). The violence was often instrumental in obtaining sex.

Men who batter have also been found to have low self-esteem and an excessive need for control (Wodarski, 1987). Dutton and Golant (1995: 13) have described how such personality traits relate to the battering behavior:

[I]ntimate abuse was not just about hits and punches. It was about psychologically and physically trying to control [the batterers'] victims' use of time and space in order to isolate them from all social connection, both past and present. It was an all-out attempt to enslave them psychologically. *And it was performed repeatedly*

> *in order to maintain and inflate the damaged self-identity of the abuser.* (Emphasis added.)

As Fromm (1973: 322) has observed, "The passion to have absolute and unrestricted control over a living being is the transformation of impotence into omnipotence."

The male batterer's insecurity and low self-esteem often surface during adolescence. During this time, the fear of abandonment is transformed to incorporate sexual content and is expressed as sexual jealousy. Feelings of anxiety, dependence, and fear are unacceptable and must be negated. Dutton and Golant (1995: 139) explain how this occurs:

> In order to act in the world—to be agentic—some men believe that one must be fearless (as fear can hamper action), insensitive (as sensitivity can impede action), egocentric (as egocentricity convinces one of the rightness of one's actions), and invulnerable (as insecurity can undermine action). But invulnerability requires a gradual dulling of those emotions that are inconsistent with agency: anxiety, dependency, and fear. These "weaker emotions" are converted and subsumed by role-consistent actions: anger and sexual predation.

The "honeymoon period" which often follows a batterer's act of abuse has been attributed not to a feeling of remorse, but to the batterer's attempt to ward off the departure of the intimate partner (Vaselle-Augenstein and Ehrlich, 1992). The honeymoon period is the last of three phases typically seen in any incident of intimate partner violence:

> The first or tension-building phase may include assaults but is marked chiefly by angry threats and insults. Victims typically react to it by trying to calm or avoid offenders. Such efforts may work initially but become less effective with time. Early successes often mislead victims into thinking they can defuse men's anger.
>
> Unchecked tension grows and finally bursts into a phase of uncontrolled verbal and physical abuse that stuns and confuses victims. Injuries, when they occur, are usually inflicted at this time. The last phase [the "honeymoon period"] is one of contrition. Expressing surprise at their behavior, offenders apologize, express their love, and try to convince victims that they will stop being violent (Steinman, 1990: 124).

Men who abuse in this cyclical fashion are characterized by "the repetitive aspect of their lives and relationships, the emotional poverty of their thought and speech, their flat affect, and noncommittal responses" (Dutton and Golant, 1995: 44). They are likely to "obsess on [a] thought pattern of blame, bad feelings, and fantasized recrimination," known as rumination (Dutton and Golant, 1995: 44). These ruminations may result in an escalation of the violence, with an alteration in the batterer's consciousness and a reduction of social constraints, resulting in "deindividuated violence," in which the assailant is unaware of and unresponsive to cues from his victim, and is the sole individual able to stop the violence once it has begun (Dutton and Golant, 1995: 47).

During the honeymoon phase, the batterer may enlist the assistance of others, such as the children of the relationship, to plead his case for forgiveness for him. During this phase, the assailant's contrition, gifts, and, not infrequently, threats of suicide, may convince the battered victim not to leave, that the relationship really is salvageable with enough effort and love. The honeymoon phase tends to last until the assaultive partner is again feeling vulnerable (Dutton and Golant, 1995).

Surprisingly, batterers may appear to function well in superficial relationships, in contrast to their abusiveness in the context of more intimate relations (Vaselle-Augenstein and Ehrlich, 1992). Consequently, clinicians have characterized batterers as having a "Jekyll and Hyde" personality (Vaselle-Augenstein and Ehrlich, 1992). It has been postulated that such individuals may, in fact, be suffering from a borderline personality disorder (Dutton and Golant, 1995). Defining criteria of this disorder include unstable interpersonal relationships characterized by manipulation, masked dependency, and dissatisfaction, regardless of who the partner may be; abandonment anxiety; intense anger; and impulsivity (Dutton and Golant, 1995; Gunderson, 1984). Goetting (1999: 145) described one such relationship:

> Annette describes Billy as a...man of extremes, a "Dr. Jekyll/Mr. Hyde." On the one hand he was charming and fun to be around; on the other he was brutal. She remembers especially the small gatherings in their apartment. Billy would greet guests at the door, offer them something to drink, and chat pleasantly. Then, after closing the door behind them, he would rant on and on... [T]he stated reasons for Billy's rages centered primarily on his fear of Annette's adultery or her leaving him....

Consistent with this theory, wife-battering men have been found to be more likely to abuse their children (Straus, 1983; Washburn and Frieze, 1981). Many men who batter have done so in multiple relationships (Vaselle-Augenstein and Ehrlich, 1992).

Smith (1990) has found that men who express attitudes indicating dominance over women with respect to such things as money, sex, and social interactions were more likely to engage in partner violence. The use of alcohol has been found to be associated with husband-wife violence (Gondolf, 1988; Fagan, Stewart, and Hansen, 1983; Kantor and Straus, 1987). It is unclear whether the association between alcohol and assaults is a function of the interaction of personality characteristics with the alcohol (see Hamberger and Hastings, 1988), the batterer's expectations associated with alcohol use (Fagan, 1990), the alteration of cognition and perception resulting from the alcohol (Frieze and Browne, 1989), the batterer's attempt to find a socially acceptable excuse for his behavior (Coleman and Straus, 1983), or the assaultive partner's reliance on alcohol as a "time out" (MacAndrew and Edgerton, 1969. See chapter 3 for a discussion of "time out" and deviant behavior).

Reports of battering by men indicate that batterers generally underreport the frequency of their violent behavior, minimize the harm that ensues from their behavior, or deny its occurrence altogether (Ganley and Harris, 1978; O'Leary and Arias, 1988; Szinovacz, 1983). It is not unusual for the assaultive partner to claim that he was provoked or that the abuse was mutual, although such claims may not be substantiated by the police reports or the witnesses (Sonkin and Durphy, 1985). Men may also excuse their behavior by claiming that they were drunk (Kantor and Straus, 1987). (Such "accounts" by the batterer are discussed in greater detail in chapter 7.)

At least one researcher has characterized batterers on the basis of their behaviors, rather than their personality characteristics. Sociopathic batterers are extremely abusive, inflict the most severe injury, and are often violent both inside and outside of the home. In addition, they may have severe substance abuse problems and high rates of previous arrest (Gondolf, 1988). Antisocial abusers inflict less severe injury than the sociopathic abusers. Chronic abusers tend to batter on at least a weekly basis, but the abuse is less severe than that of either the sociopathic or antisocial abuser. The frequency of battering by sporadic abusers is minimal and is the least severe of the battering. Sporadic abusers tend to be apologetic following an incident of abuse (Gondolf, 1988).

Clinical experience with batterers may offer some support to this typology. Dutton and Golant (1995) have noted that approximately 40 percent of the men who presented to their program for treatment had a history of prior criminal behavior and were likely to have assaulted others in addition to their intimate partners. Unlike individuals who have a conscience and may consequently attempt to minimize the seriousness of their behavior or its consequences, as described above, such individuals may be psychopaths. As psychopaths, they are unable to imagine another individual's pain or fear.

A subgroup of antisocial/psychopathic male batterers have been labeled "vagal reactors" (Dutton and Golant, 1995, citing Jacobson). Contrary to the usual autonomic response to stress, which involves an increase in the rate and shallowness of breathing, vagal reactors demonstrate

> a decline in heart rate during the course of the nonviolent argument. In other words, some of these batterers become calm internally despite their emotionally aggressive behavior. This disconnection between physiology and behavior...makes no intuitive sense. They looked aroused, they act aroused, but on the inside they are getting calmer and calmer.
>
> Furthermore, the batterers who showed this heart rate decrease were the most belligerent and contemptuous towards their wives....The "disconnected" group showed the highest rates of violence outside the marriage, and were the most likely to have reported violence in their family of origin (Jacobson, 1993, quoted in Dutton and Golant, 1995: 29).

Jacobson (quoted in Dutton and Golant, 1995: 28-29) further explained this mechanism:

> [I]nstead of being out of control, our most severe subgroup of batterers were like "autonomic athletes," actively controlling their level of arousal so that they can focus their attention on their wives, presumably so that aggression can have the maximal effect.

Male Violence in Homosexual Relationships

Little research has been conducted on male-male violence in the context of intimate relations. Island and Letellier (1991) have estimated that violence occurs in among 10 to 20 percent of couples. Gay men may lack the awareness of and the language necessary to express their victimization (Letellier, 1994), which is compounded by the relative lack of silence within the gay community with respect to partner abuse (see Szymanksi, 1991). As an example, one gay man who was assaulted by his partner with a lead pipe and was almost killed inquired of his social worker, "Well, do you really think that was domestic violence?" (Snow, 1992: 61).

Intimate Partner Violence Committed by Women

Violence in Heterosexual Relationships

A number of recent studies have found that the rate of violence committed by female partners against their male intimates equals that among men against their female intimates (Stets and Straus, 1993; Straus, 1993; Straus, Gelles, and Steinmetz, 1980). Further, male victims of spousal violence are less likely than women to report their injuries to the police (McLeod, 1984). The extent to which these assaults represent efforts at self-defense remains unclear. At least one study, however, concluded that a self-defense explanation for the female-to-male violence was often unwarranted:

> Regardless of whether the analysis is based on all assaults or is focused on dangerous assaults, about as many women as men attacked spouses who had not hit them, during the one-year referent period. This is inconsistent with the self-defense explanation for the high rate of domestic assault by women.
>
> However, it is possible that, among the couples here both assaulted, all the women were acting in self-defense. Even if that unlikely assumption were correct, it would still be true that 25-30% of violent marriages are violent solely because of attacks by the wife (Straus, 1993: 75).

Despite the apparent equality of rate, however, women are at least 6 times more likely than men to require medical care for injuries resulting from a violence by an intimate (Kaufman, Kantor, and Straus, 1987; Stets and Straus, 1990). Whether the injuries suffered by male victims are more likely to be severe than those suffered by women remains unclear (Cook, 1997).

Not unlike female victims, many men will publicly deny abuse and attribute their injuries, instead, to unintentional accidents (Cook, 1997). Unlike women, though, they will use humor to mask the problem:

> That is protective humor. Perpetrators will point to this reaction, among male victims, and say it shows that it is no big deal, that it is obviously not a traumatic thing. But, how do they know? The humor might just be used as self-protection. The awful truth of it is so dangerous to him that he dares not admit it for his own well-being, his own self-esteem. They cannot treat it any other way (George, 1994, quoted in Cook, 1997: 53).

Shame, a fear of ridicule, and a sense of responsibility often play a part in keeping male victims of partner violence in their situation (Cook, 1997).

Violence in Lesbian Relationships

Lesbian battering has been defined as "a pattern of violence (or) coercive behaviors whereby a lesbian seeks to control the thoughts, beliefs, or conduct of her intimate partner or to punish the intimate for resisting the perpetrator's control" (Hart, 1986: 174). One survey of lesbians found that 59.8 percent of the respondents had been victims of battering by their partner (Bologna, Waterman, and Dawson, 1987), while a somewhat more recent survey found that 52 percent of the lesbian respondents had suffered physical violence by their lesbian partners (Lie and Gentlewarrior, 1991). A survey of 284 lesbians found that approximately one-third were physically abused by their partners (Lockhart, White, Causby, and Isaac, 1994), while another study found that almost half of 90 interviewed lesbian couples experienced violence (Coleman, 1990).

As with heterosexual violence, the violence between lesbian intimates may take many forms. Renzeti (1989) has found that the most common forms of violence involve shoving, hitting with a fist, and throwing objects. However, the assaults may also involve severe aggression and weapons (Lockhart, White, Causby, and Isaac, 1994). As with heterosexual violence, the severity of the incidents tends to increase over time (Farley, 1996; Island and Letellier, 1991; Margolies and Leeder, 1995).

Although battering in the context of lesbian relationships has been identified as a major problem (Lobel, 1986), little research attention has been focused on it. In part, this may result from the fact that the occurrence of female-female violence challenges underlying assumptions about relationships between the sexes and theories of causation based on patriarchy (see chapter 2):

> Many of us saw the absence of services to lesbians within the battered women's movement as an area needing attention...[A] number of questions surfaced. Did it really happen? Could it be as prevalent as male-female battering? The presence of violence deeply affected our vision of ourselves and our relationships....We were surprised and saddened by the magnitude of the problem and the severity of the violence....

> Many women in the broader battered women's movement are affected by the acknowledgment of lesbian violence. This acknowledgment forces a deepening of the analysis of sexism and male/female roles as contributors to violence in relationships. To understand violence in lesbian relationships is to challenge and perhaps rework some of these beliefs (Knollenberg, Douville, and Hammond, in Lobel, 1986, quoted in Cook, 1997: 30-31)

Characteristics of Female Batterers

Not unlike male batterers of women, female batterers have been characterized as seeking control. Unlike heterosexual battering, however, female batterers of their female intimates may utilize the myth of mutual battering and homophobic control in conjunction with the violence, in order to maintain control. In the case of mutual battering between same-sex intimates, it may be difficult to discern who was the aggressor and who was the victim because the combatants are perceived as equal (Island and Letellier, 1991; Renzetti, 1992). Hart (1986: 189) has defined homophobic control to include

> [t]hreatening to tell family, friends, employer, police, church, community, etc. that the victim is a lesbian...; telling the victim she deserves all that she gets because she is a lesbian; assuring her that no one would believe she has been violated because lesbians are not violent' reminding her that she has no options because the homophobic world will not help her.

Renzetti (1992) found in her survey of 100 lesbians who had been battered that almost one-quarter had experienced such threats.

Similar to situations involving male-female battering, alcohol and other substance use has been associated with female-male battering and lesbian battering (Coleman, 1990; Kaufman, Kantor, and Straus, 1987; Kelly and Warshafsky, 1987). Conflicts around autonomy and dependency have been noted in lesbian battering (Renzetti, 1992), a finding that has also been noted in male-female battering situations.

CONSEQUENCES OF INTIMATE PARTNER VIOLENCE

Intimate partner violence may result in serious health consequences and a concomitant need for medical attention. In the United States, one or both partners in approximately 500,000 couples sustain injuries from the violence each year (Sorenson et al., 1996). Women in the United States make almost three times as many visits to medical providers for the treatment of injuries associated with intimate partner violence as they do for injuries related to motor vehicle accidents (National Committee for Injury Prevention and Control, 1989). Outcomes of intimate partner violence include damage to joints, partial loss of vision (Beck et al., 1996; Hartzell et al., 1996) or hearing, burns (Balakrishnan et al., 1995; Prasad, 1994), bites, hematomas, fractures, cuts or abrasions, inflammation, penetrating puncture wounds, dislocation, sprains (Bates et al., 1995), and death (Browne and Williams, 1993). Stark, Flitcraft, and Frazier (1979) found that common locations of injuries resulting from intimate partner violence include the head, face, neck, chest, and abdomen. Women with chronic pelvic pain have been found more likely to have experienced sexual abuse in both childhood and adulthood as compared to women without such pain (Walling, Reiter, O'Hara, et al., 1994). Balakrishnan and colleagues (1995) found that burns of the genitalia were common in male victims of intimate partner violence, such injuries often inflicted while they were sleeping.

Researchers have only recently recognized the link between intimate partner violence and an increased risk of HIV infection. Wingood and DiClemente (1997) found in their study of 165 sexually active African-American women between the ages of 18 and 29 that women in abusive relationships were less likely than others to use condoms and were more likely than others to experience threats of violence from their partners when they discussed condoms.

Initial psychological responses to intimate partner violence often include shock, denial, withdrawal, confusion, numbing, fear, and depression (Dutton, 1992; Browne, 1987; Hilberman, 1980; Symonds, 1979; Walker, 1979). Long-term effects may include fear, anxiety, fatigue, sleeping and eating disorders (Goodman et al., 1993; Herman, 1992), and feelings of loss, betrayal, or hopelessness (Walker, 1979).

Post-traumatic stress disorder (PTSD) is one of the most common consequences to the victim of abuse (Herman, 1997). PTSD is characterized by a re-experiencing of the traumatic event; avoidance of stimuli that is reminiscent of the trauma or, alternatively, numbing; and increased arousal (American Psychiatric Association, 1994). A diagnosis of PTSD requires that an individual have experienced a traumatic event that is outside of the range of usual human experience, that would be a source of distress to almost anyone. The individual must also re-experience that traumatic event in one of the following ways: recurrent, intrusive and distressing recollections of the event; recurrent dreams of the event; hallucinations, flashbacks, or illusions of the event; or intense psychological distress resulting from exposure to events that symbolize or resemble an aspect of the traumatic episode. At least three of the following behaviors must also be present: attempts to avoid thoughts or feelings associated with the trauma; efforts to avoid situations that trigger recall of the trauma; an inability to remember an important aspect of the trauma; diminished interest in activities; a feeling of detachment from others; a restricted range of affect; or a sense of a somehow shortened future. Additionally, the individual must be suffering from at least two of the following symptoms: difficulty falling or remaining asleep; irritability or anger; difficulty concentrating; hypervigilance; an exaggerated startle response; or physiological reactivity. In general, the symptoms must be present for at least one month for the individual to be considered to be suffering from PTSD (American Psychiatric Association, 1994).

Herman (1997: 91) has described the practical import of PTSD:

> Prolonged captivity undermines or destroys the ordinary sense
> of a relatively safe sphere of initiative, in which there is some
> tolerance for trial and error. To the chronically traumatized

person, any action has potentially dire consequences. There is no room for mistakes....

The sense that the perpetrator is still present, even after liberation, signifies a major alteration in the victim's relational world. The enforced relationship during captivity, which of necessity monopolizes the victim's attention, becomes part of the victim's inner life and continues to engross her attention after she is released....In...domestic...prisoners, this continued relationship may take a more ambivalent form: the victim may continue to fear her former captor and to expect that he will eventually hunt her down, but she may also feel empty, confused, and worthless without him.

This description is similar to that of the Stockholm syndrome, a victim response to a violent situation. Stockholm syndrome is discussed in greater detail in conjunction with traumatic bonding theory in chapter 2 and in chapter 8.

Reliance on PTSD as an explanation for a woman's reactions to her abuse has, however, been criticized as providing yet another mechanism by which to reassert and reinforce stereotypes about women as hysterical and/or damaged. Lamb (1999: 112) has explained:

PTSD is seen as involuntary and thus arising from a deep biology of sorts. And recently in our culture, we have begun to invoke biology to avoid tricky questions of social or personal responsibility. But there is a sad consequence for women if the culture adopts this perspective on their reactions to abuse. If we see symptomatology as produced by external sources (e.g., the trauma), if we see it as involuntary, outside a person's control, then we are very close to a notion of a woman as damaged—or "damaged goods" as the older, viler saying used to go. Our new medical conceptions of trauma start sounding very much like older hushed-voice opinions that a girl who is raped or sexually abused is now "damaged" and consequently worthless....While modern-day thinkers may be more sympathetic to a victim, it is clear that her body is no longer a "good" body, one that behaves and follows her wishes. Female passivity is thus re-created and reinforced. (Citations omitted).

Death is clearly the most severe consequence of intimate partner violence. Research indicates that of adult women who are murdered, the majority are killed by an intimate or former intimate; of these, the majority have been battered before their deaths (Campbell, 1992). A study of the homicides of women in New Mexico found that 46% of the deaths that were investigated were attributable to a male intimate (Arbuckle, Olson, Howard, et al., 1996). Studies conducted in New York and Chicago indicate that the leading cause of maternal mortality is trauma; the highest proportion of traumatic deaths is due to homicide (Fildes, Reed, Jones, et al., 1992). Intimate partner violence has been implicated in the commission of suicide by women (Olson, Huyler, Lynch, et al., 1999).

Intimate partner violence may also have serious consequences for third parties. Although the causal pathway is unclear, several studies have suggested an association between abuse of a woman during her pregnancy and low birthweight of the infant (Bullock and McFarlane, 1989; Campbell, Torres, Ryan et al., 1999; Parker, McFarlane, and Soeken, 1994; Sameulson and Bakketeig, 1991). Children who have witnessed the battering of their mother may themselves suffer trauma, manifested through such symptoms and behaviors as anxiety, social withdrawal, depression, preoccupation with aggression, suicidal ideation, truancy, sleep disorders, headaches, bedwetting, and digestive difficulties (Attala, Bauza, Pratt, and Viera, 1995; Holden and Ritchie, 1991; Hughes, 1988; Hughes, 1986; Humphreys, 1993). The responses of children witnessing intimate partner violence is addressed in greater detail in chapter 9.

COMPARISONS ACROSS U.S. ETHNIC AND IMMIGRANT GROUPS

In the United States, concern has been voiced with respect to variation in rates or the nature of intimate partner violence across various ethnic or racial groups. Such differences may be indicative of differential response to different groups, differential access to services, or differences in the definition or perception of intimate partner violence. (It is beyond the scope of this paper to engage in discussion regarding the existence and/or delineation of race/ethnicity; suffice to indicate that this issue exists.) Yet, few studies have examined intimate partner violence in the context of specific ethnic groups. Such an examination would provide a better understanding of the factors that may differentially impact upon a specific group.

In one such study, Cazenave and Straus (1979) compared the rates of intimate partner violence among a nationally representative sample of African-Americans and Caucasians. They found that, after controlling for race, income, and occupation, the rates of intimate partner violence were lower among the African-Americans in 3 of the 4 income strata. They further found that African-American women were less likely to be assaulted if they were part of a strong network of family and friends. Stark (1990), however, found in a study of intimate partner violence among African-Americans and Caucasians that although the incidence of intimate partner violence was similar, the levels of lethal violence were higher among African-Americans. Lockhart and White (1989), in their study of 155 African-American women, found that although a smaller proportion of women in the upper socioeconomic strata reported intimate partner violence than did women in the middle or lower socioeconomic strata, they reported a higher median number of assaults per year.

Gondolf, Fisher, and McFerron (1988), in a secondary data analysis of data obtained from 5,708 women in shelters, found no difference in the frequency of intimate partner violence between Caucasians, African-Americans, and Hispanics. A study conducted by McFarlane and colleagues of 199 abused women also found no difference in the timing or severity of abuse across ethnic groups (McFarlane, Parker, Soeken, Silva, and Reed, 1999). However, such findings are not consistent across studies (Gaffney, Choi, Yi, Jones, Bowman, and Tavangar, 1997). Several studies have found that Hispanic women are more likely to have been the victim of violence for a longer period of time (Gondolf, Fisher, and McFerron, 1988; Torres, 1991). Torres (1991) further found that unlike Caucasian women, Mexican-American women were unlikely to classify such actions as slapping, pushing, shoving, grabbing, and throwing things at them as physical abuse. West, Kantor, and Jasinski (1998) identified several differences between the abused Latina and Anglo women participating in their study. As compared to Anglo women, battered Latina women were significantly younger, less educated, and more likely to be living below the poverty level. Almost twice as many of the Latinas as the Anglos were involved in male-dominated relationship and the prevalence of heavy drinking was significantly higher among the partners of the Latina women as compared to the partners of the Anglo women.

In one of the few studies to recognize within-Hispanic differences, Sorenson and Telles (1991) found that Mexico-born Mexican-Americans reported lower rates of intimate partner violence than either Caucasians or U.S.-born Mexican-Americans (20.0% compared to 21.6% and 30.9%, respectively). Overall rates of sexual assault were lower for Mexican Americans. However, one-third of the most recent incidents that were reported by Mexico-born Mexican American women involved the woman's intimate sexual partner and approximated rape. West, Kantor, and Jasinksi (1998) found that abused Mexican women tended to be less acculturated than either battered Puerto Rican or Mexican American women. Perilla and colleagues (1994) concluded from their study of 60 immigrant Latinas in southern California that stressors related to immigration status, such as prejudice and lack of English proficiency, contributed to the abuse.

In the one study of intimate partner violence in Puerto Rican families that appears to exist, Kantor and colleagues (1994) found that Puerto Rican husbands were about twice as likely as Anglo husbands and 10 times more likely than Cuban husbands to assault their wives. Birth in the United States increased the risk of wife assaults by both Mexican and Puerto Rican husbands. They further found that Puerto Ricans had the highest rate of cultural approval of wife assaults, compared to Anglos, Mexicans, and Cubans.

Ho (1990) conducted one of the few systematic studies of intimate partner violence among Asian (Lao, Khmer, Vietnamese, and Chinese) women in the United States. Using focus group data, she found that physical violence by intimate partners was common and generally tolerated among the Lao, Khmer, and Vietnamese women. The problem of intimate partner violence is more acute and complex among first generation Asians, compared to later generations. Ho attributed this finding to women's lack of English language ability, their often tenuous immigration status, and a lack of emotional support resulting from separation for their extended families. In one of the few studies which specifically enumerated Native American women, Arbuckle and colleagues (1996) found that the rate of domestic violence-associated homicide was significantly higher among Native American women, as compared to Hispanic and non-Hispanic white women.

There have been surprisingly few studies conducted that examine categorizations of behaviors as violence and attitudes relating to the appropriateness of various responses to intimate partner violence. One small study comparing the attitudes of Latin American and Asian male and female immigrants in the United States and United States-born men and women found that Asians were more likely to indicate that men could justifiably hit their wives, while those originating from

Latin America were more likely to label both the batterer and the victim as suffering from mental illness (Gabler, Stern, and Miserando, 1998).

ASSESSING PARTNER VIOLENCE

A number of different scales have been developed to assess the existence, frequency, and extent of abuse (Dutton, 1995). These include the Conflict Tactics Scale (Straus, 1979), the Severity of Violence Against Women Scale (Marshall, 1992), and the Psychological Maltreatment of Women Inventory (Tolman, 1989).

The Conflict Tactics Scale seeks to understand how each member of a couple attempts to resolve conflict that may arise within the relationship. The scale encompasses a spectrum of behaviors, ranging from calm discussion to threats, to mess serious violence, to severe violence, such as using a knife or gun. The scale has been criticized as ignoring the context, motivation, and meaning of the violent behavior (Dutton, 1995; Renzetti, 1999) and as failing to consider the frequency with which an event occurs (Dutton and Golant, 1995). Additionally, a man and a woman may obtain the same score on the scale, but the score fails to consider differences in their physical size that may be relevant to an understanding of the situation (Dutton, 1995).

Marshall's (1992) scale examines the frequency, ranging from never to many times, of 46 different behaviors, each reflecting a level of physical violence. A corollary scale, titled Severity of Violence Against Men, is available to assess the extent and frequency of violence against men. Unlike Straus' scale, Marshall's scale does not reflect a range of response that includes nonviolent approaches, such as discussion.

Tolman's (1989) scale assesses the frequency of certain actions on a spectrum ranging from not applicable to very frequently. Unlike either the Straus or Marshall scales, the Tolman inventory focuses on emotional and verbal abuse and the use of dominance and isolation to effectuate that abuse. The 58 items include such behaviors as insulting the partner in front of others, name calling, demanding obedience, interfering in other relationships, threatening harm, threatening abandonment or removal of the children, and threatening involuntary institutionalization.

2

THEORIES OF CAUSATION

He locked me in: his love—a prison.
His words and looks—padlocks.
I became blind and mute,
could no longer tell
a curtain from a river;
ashen grass, dead hair invaded me,
dead nails grew on my fingers,
a bluish skin covered my eyes.
I could no longer tell
a bracelet from a muzzle,
a waggon from a cello,
I was speechless—couldn't even answer
the call of the pomegranate seed,
or that kind of invitation of frogs in the sunset,
I wasn't even able to say 'hello',
—I lost a lot of friends...

                                        (Cassian, 1988b:14)

However it is defined or effectuated, the causes of intimate partner violence remain obscure. Numerous theories have been offered to explain its origin. Many of these theories are briefly reviewed below; the literature is too vast to permit more than a brief summary of each. Some of these theories operate at the societal level, while others apply at the level of the individual or the couple. Some theories are more likely to address the issue of why one partner beats another, whereas others focus on the question of why women who are beaten stay with the partners who beat them. The applicability and relevance of a specific theory of causation to domestic violence must be examined within the context of the specific culture and its definition of male and female roles and behaviors. Individual factors may also be relevant to the occurrence of domestic violence.

SOCIETAL LEVEL THEORIES

Culture of Violence Theory

Wolfgang and Ferracuti (1967) have theorized that in large, pluralistic societies, some subcultures develop norms that permit the use of physical force or violence to a greater degree than does the dominant culture. Levinson and Malone (1980) have used this theory to postulate that family violence will occur more frequently in violent societies than in peaceful ones. Bowker (1984: 135) has postulated that there exists a direct relationship between the extent to which a male is integrated into the male subculture and the violence in the home:

> [T]he myriad peer-relationships that support the patriarchal dominance of the family and the use of violence to enforce it may constitute a subculture of violence. The more fully a husband is immersed in this subculture, the more likely he is to batter his wife.

Numerous studies have been conducted to examine the effects of the portrayal of violence in the mass media on individuals' proclivity to commit violence or to act aggressively. Some such studies have indicated that an association may exist (Andison, 1977; Eron, Huesmann, Lefkowitz, and Walder, 1972; Huesmann and Eron, 1986). However, many of the studies have been laboratory-based and, accordingly, have been criticized as legitimating the very behavior that they were designed to observe, thereby encouraging its occurrence (Tedeschi and Felson, 1994). Additionally, many violent offenders are versatile with respect to the types of crimes that they commit (violent and nonviolent), thereby challenging the assumption that it is their exposure to media violence that predisposes them to engage in violent behavior (Felson, 1996).

Various writers have argued that the portrayal of violent acts against women, such as rape and sadomasochism, in the context of pornography encourages men to view women as sex objects desirous of such treatment (see Dworkin, 1981; Linz and Malamuth, 1993; MacKinnon, 1984). However, research has failed to demonstrate an association between pornography and violence against women (Felson, 1996); in fact, rapists have reported less exposure to pornography than have nonrapists (see Linz and Malamuth, 1993). For additional discussion of research relating to pornography, see the discussion of feminist theory, below.

Support for the culture of violence theory, however, derives from the observation that bizarre violent events that are seen on television may be imitated by viewers who have not otherwise engaged in such violent behaviors ("copycat" crimes)(Felson, 1996). Bandura (1983) has suggested that television informs viewers of both the negative and the positive consequences of violent behavior. When the violence is either unpunished or justified, the viewer may be less concerned with the potential negative consequences of such behavior. Felson (1996) has asserted that, in general, the messages conveyed by television about violence are unclear; violence is often justified as self-defense or as a necessary means to accomplish a predetermined end.

Ecological Theory

The ecological theory attempts to link violence in the family with the broader social environment. Bersani and Chen (1988: 76) explained:

> A person's environment can be understood as a series of settings,

each nested within the next broader level, from the microenvironment of the family to the macroenvironment of the society.

Belsky (1980) outlined an ecological framework for the understanding of child abuse and neglect. That four-level framework, with some modifications, may be equally relevant to an understanding of intimate partner violence:
1. the macrosystem--the culture
2. exosystem--the formal and informal social networks in which the family participates; and
3. microsystem--the family setting in which violence occurs; and
4. ontogentic-- the family history of the parents [partners].
The prediction of risk from assault requires an assessment of the abuser's profile utilizing factors from all four levels. For instance, an assessment of the potential for an assault by a man against his wife would include an examination of the man's attitudes and beliefs regarding the relations between men and women generally and the acceptability of violence (macrosystem); the extent of the man's isolation and stress (exosystem); the extent and nature of the couple's communication and conflict (microsystem); and the extent of the man's verbal skills, his ability to express affect, his ability to empathize, and his assumption of responsibility for his actions and habits (ontogentic level)(Dutton, 1995).

Evolutionary Theory

Evolutionary theory, originally advanced by anthropologists (Rohner, 1975; Narroll, 1970; Lenski and Lenski, 1970; Barry et al., 1967) to explain child abuse, may be equally relevant to intimate partner violence. Evolutionary theory posits that, as societies have changed from the relatively simple to the more structurally and economically complex, families have become smaller and nuclear in form and social relations have, paradoxically, become both more structured and more ambiguous. In less complex societies, caretakers of children are more likely to emphasize independence and self-reliance and, in comparison to caretakers in more complex societies, are less likely to rely on physical punishment to secure obedience. Obedience, it has been argued, is valued in societies which maintain a hierarchically organized social structure and in which a large amount of activity occurs in the context of formal social encounters outside of the home. It can be hypothesized, then, that if such high value is placed on obedience, obedience may be demanded of children and intimate partners alike. Where such obedience is not forthcoming, violence may be used as a means to secure it.

Levinson's (1989) examination of the link between social change and wife beating may lend some support to this theory. He notes, for instance, that following the shift in the Macedonia, Bosnia, Serbia, Croatia, and Littoral regions of the former Yugoslavia from an extended family household model to a money economy in 1900, women's status increased, men's status decreased, and wife beating became more common.

However, Morley's (1994) study of domestic violence in Papua New Guinea appears to refute the evolutionary theory. Morley specifically failed to find a link between modernization or urbanization and an increase in the prevalence of wife beating. She did find, however, that a husband's right to control his wife through violence was no longer greeted with unconditional acceptance. In contrast, men's perceived need to control their wives may have increased due to women's increasing autonomy.

Tracy and Crawford (1992) have argued that several species close to Homo sapiens on the phylogenetic scale have engaged in wife-abuse-like behavior. Such behavior may have served to guard the female mate from other males, thereby ensuring the male partner's sexual dominance and, possibly, reproductive advantage. In this context, wife beating is a "natural tendency" (Tracy and Crawford, 1992).

Wilson and Daly (1993) have advanced an evolutionary psychological perspective. They have hypothesized that sexual proprietariness is a psychological adaptation of the human male, much as various animals lay claim to their territory. This proprietariness, they argue, is reflected in double standards of adultery, whereby a married woman commits adultery by having sex with other than her husband, but a married man faces no such charge; in legal actions that permit monetary recovery for loss of consortium; in man's violent response to a woman's desertion of the relationship and his consequent loss of control over her reproductive capacity; and in the coercive, nonviolent control of women by men through economic inequity, forced marriages, practices such as foot binding, and the requirement of chaperones for women in some cultures. They further assert that men's jealousy, and related violence, is directly tied to a woman's reproductive value, the social sanctions against men's use of violence against their partners, and the female partners' resistance to male coercive control. Buss and Shackelford (1997) have characterized aggression as an adaptive mechanism developed to defeat intrasexual rivals, deter long-term mates from sexual infidelity, and to deter potential rivals from future aggression.

Thornhill and Palmer (2000) have advanced a thesis somewhat similar to that of Wilson and Daly, arguing that

> [r]aping an unwilling pair-bonded mate [intimate partner] may be a male tactic of sperm competition. A woman's sexual unreceptivity may suggest to her partner that she is having consensual intercourse with another male. Because men associate sexual unwillingness and resistance in their long-term mates with infidelity, sexual unwillingness may lead to sexual jealousy, and sometimes to rape as a sperm-competition tactic. (Thornhill and Palmer, 2000: 77)

They support their thesis by noting that rape of a long-term intimate is more likely to occur during or immediately following the severance of the relationship and that there is an association between men's battering of their wives and sexual jealousy and between wife battering and marital rape. They further assert that female resistance to rape may reflect

> an evolved mechanism for evaluation of the rapist's "genetic quality" in order to secure genes that will promote the mating

> success of their sons. Pre-mating resistance on the part of a female
> may indirectly assess male heritable quality by testing the would-
> be rapist's strength, endurance, and vigor. If females' resistance
> results in their mating with males adept at overcoming it, the sons
> of rapists will be similarly adept, having inherited the genes of
> their fathers. (Thornhill and Palmer, 20000: 83)

This theory, however, fails to explain why women who already have a "pair-bonded [male] mate" would have to evaluate their genetic quality; presumably, such an evaluation occurred prior to the pair-bonding. Additionally, if this theory of testing heritable quality through resistance of intercourse were true, one would expect that women impregnated during a rape would be no more likely than non-raped women to terminate the pregnancy through voluntary abortion. However, this writer has been unable to locate any empirical studies supporting this conclusion.

Finally, the evolutionary theory of wife-beating clearly has as one of its basic premises the heritability of at least a predisposition to resort to violence in specified situations. Rape is conceived of as an act of sex. This perspective is in striking contrast to that of feminist theorists, who assert that partner violence constitutes a form of domination and social control of men over women and that, accordingly, rape is an act of violence and not of sex.

Feminist Theory

There are numerous variants of feminist theory relating to intimate partner violence. Bograd (1990) has identified four elements common to all of these: (1) as the dominant class, men have differential access to material and symbolic resources and women are devalued as secondary and inferior; (2) intimate partner abuse is a predictable and common dimension of normal family life; (3) women's experiences are often defined as inferior because male domination influences all aspects of life; and (4) the feminist perspective is dedicated to advocacy for women.

Patriarchy Theory

Dobash and Dobash (1979) have identified three tenets basic to patriarchy theory: (1) wife assault is a systematic form of domination and social control of women by men; (2) assault is committed by men who believe that patriarchy is their right; and (3) the use of violence to maintain male dominance is acceptable to society. The postulated role of sexism in intimate partner violence is clear: "The use of physical violence against women in their position as wives is not the only means by which they are controlled and oppressed but it is one of the most brutal and explicit expressions of patriarchal domination" (Dobash and Dobash, 1979: ix). Patriarchal theory addresses intimate partner violence on a societal level and seeks to explain why men beat women (Dobash and Dobash, 1979).

A recent occurrence in Romania lends anecdotal support to the patriarchy theory. There, the Romanian edition of *Playboy* published an article entitled, "How to Beat Your Wife Without Leaving Prints." The article provided explicit instructions on the choice of instruments (police baton, pot stick, or washing machine driving belt) and how to hold the woman to facilitate the beating and thwart escape. The author, who remained unidentified, advised that any screams of pain would be bogus and that the wife would want to be beaten again. The article closed by wishing the reader a harmonious marriage. The significance of this incident is rooted not only in its occurrence, but also in its context. Romania has only recently begun to collect data on the incidence and prevalence of intimate partner violence, but it is believed to be widespread (USAID, 1999). Men have traditionally been granted significant freedoms not permitted to women; adultery and alcoholism have been tolerated since before World War II in exchange for the economic support of the family, and male superiority has been presumed (Gilberg, 1979). During Ceaucescu's regime spanning the years 1965 through 1989, women engaging in sexual relations without the benefit of marriage to the sexual partner were prosecuted as prostitutes; the men were not subject to sanction (David and Baban, 1996). In response to the significant outcry from women's groups, the Romanian editor of *Playboy* dismissed the article—and the women's marches launched in protest—as a "joke" (Personal communication, Randal Thompson, USAID, May 2000). Politicians seeking women's endorsement for the fall 2000 elections dismissed their concerns with the claim that women can stand to be beaten because they are strong and, consequently, do not need additional legal protections; that is why women who are beaten can still muster sufficient energy to kill their assaultive spouses.

Pornography has been postulated to be a factor in violence against women, although no clear link has been established. The Attorney General's Commission on Pornography (1986; see Lynn, 1986) defined pornography as "material predominantly sexually specific and intended for the use of sexual arousal." Pornography is of two types: (1) erotica, which focuses on nudity and explicit, consensual sex and (2) pornography, which features sexually explicit material containing violence, as well as nonviolent material that depicts domination and humiliation. Pornography has consistently portrayed women as enjoying such abuse (Cramer, McFarlane, Parker, Soeken, Silva, and Reel, 1998). The role of pornography, as such, in contributing to violent acts against women, such as marital rape, has been controversial. Social learning theorists assert that individuals learn such behavior from seeing such behavior (Bandura, 1977). Proponents of the catharsis theory argue that pornography actually serves as an outlet for those viewing it, thereby reducing the level of aggression (Reifler, Howard, Lipton, Lipzin, and Widmann, 1971). A recent study of 198 abused women found that almost 41% of their abusers used pornographic material (Cramer, McFarlane, Parker, Soeken, Silva, and Reel, 1998), although such an association does not constitute causality.

MacKinnon (1997) has described attitudes towards the rape of women to exemplify women's oppression and domination. Women's sexuality is a commodity "to be stolen, sold, bought, bartered, or exchanged by others" (MacKinnon, 197: 43). Once women have had sex, it is lost as theirs, thereby explaining men's apparent belief that a woman who has had sex has lost nothing if she is subsequently raped. Consent may be inferred in situations in which the woman and the man know each other or have been intimate in the past. The trauma resulting from victimization by a current or former intimate is often minimized by men, although women often feel more traumatized when a rape is committed by a known or trusted individual (MacKinnon, 1997). And, when a woman fails to demonstrate that she did not give consent, it is socially and legally as if she was not injured at all:

> The crime of rape is defined and adjudicated from the male standpoint, presuming that forced sex is sex and that consent to a man is freely given by a woman...Doctrinally, this means that the man's perceptions of the woman's desires determine whether she is deemed violated...[A]lthough the rape law oscillates between subjective tests and objective standards invoking social reasonableness, it uniformly presumes a single underlying reality, rather than a reality split by divergent meanings inequality produces...[W]omen are violated every day by men who have no idea of the meaning of their acts to the women. To them it is sex. Therefore, to the law it is sex. That becomes the single reality of what happened. When a rape prosecution is lost because a woman fails to prove that she did not consent, she is not considered to have been injured at all. It is as if a robbery victim, finding himself unable to prove that he was not engaged in philanthropy, is told he still has his money. Hermeneutically unpacked, the law assumes that, because the rapist did not perceive that the woman did not want him, she was not violated. Sex itself cannot be an injury. Women have sex every day....
>
> Men's pervasive belief that women fabricate rape charges after consenting to sex makes sense in this light. To them, accusations are false because, to them, the facts describe sex. To interpret such events as rape distorts their experience. Since they seldom consider that their experience of the real is anything other than reality, they can only explain the woman's version as maliciously invented. (MacKinnon, 1997: 50-51)

Cuklanz (2000: 5) concluded from her examination of prime time television programs from 1976 through 1990 that "the primary function of rape on prime time episodic television...was to provide material for the demonstration of ideal masculinity in terms that worked to contain feminist arguments." She found that many of the shows utilized a formulaic approach to the presentation of rape: a woman is brutally raped by an unseen, depraved rapist; the victim is portrayed as helpless and emotionally and physically devastated by the violent episode; the male detective/main character provides the victim with all the support that she could need; the protagonist triumphs over the "bad guy" (rapist) with the capture, imprisonment, and/or death of the rapist, thereby avenging the original crime. A "real rape" evoked sympathy because of its unpredictability and the woman's physical bruises evidencing that a rape, and not consensual intercourse, had, indeed, occurred.

Wrangham and Peterson (1996) have argued that patriarchy theory is supported by numerous practices in a variety of cultures, including the veiling and sequestering of women in a number of Muslim countries; by the once-traditional practice of binding women's feet in China; by the practice of *sati* in India; by the practice of infibulation in many countries in Africa; by the widespread practice of wife beating; and by the excessive mortality rate among young girls as compared to boys of the same age in numerous countries, such as Pakistan (Holloway, 1994). Rigakos (1995) suggests that his findings from a recent study of the practices of 13 police officers and 8 justice officials in Delta, Canada lend support to patriarchy theory. He found that (1) police officers felt that judges awarded restraining orders too easily; (2) police rationalized their inaction when protective orders were issued and violated by noting the many bureaucratic and technical impediments to obtaining a conviction; and (3) police often blamed the beaten woman for the violent incident and sympathized with the male partner's account and/or perceived the woman as a liar.

Patriarchy theory has been criticized on a number of grounds, including (1) its erroneous assumption that there is a direct linear relationship between the status of females in societies and the rates of wife assault (Campbell, 1992); (2) its failure to recognize that, even in patriarchal societies, it is a minority of men who assault their partners or who believe that such conduct is acceptable (Stark and McEvoy, 1970); and (3) its failure to recognize that there is no linear association between power and violence within the context of a dyadic relationship (Coleman and Straus, 1985). Additionally, the theory is challenged by a number of studies that have indicated that the use of violence by males and by females in marriage is approximately equal Straus, 1980; Straus, Gelles, and Steinmetz, 1980).

Feminist theory in general has been challenged as heterosexist and inadequate to explain battering that occurs within same-sex couples (Letellier, 1994). Explanations for same-sex battering have attributed the violence to differentials in power that mimic the traditional male and female relationship roles (Martin, 1967). These perceptions remain unchanged, despite evidence indicating that many lesbians and gay men reject such traditional roles in their own relationships (Peplau, 1991).

General Systems Theory

Straus (1978) developed the general systems theory to explain how family violence results from a positive, complex feedback system. That system, which operates at the individual, family, and societal levels, includes such factors and processes as the level of conflict inherent in the family, high levels of violence in society, family socialization to violence, cultural norms legitimizing violence, the sexist organization of society, and the multitudinous reasons for the battered person's toleration of the violence.

The high level of conflict in the family may be due to such things as impinging activities, intensity of involvement, age and sex differences in interests, and involuntary membership. A high level of violence in the larger society is reflected in rates of murder, assault, police violence, rape, war, and other forms of violence. Family members may be socialized to violence by observing violence between parents, being punished physically, seeing sibling violence being tolerated, and being taught pro-violence attitudes. Violence may then become integrated into an individual's personality and cultural norms may legitimize violence between family members. This system may be reinforced through the sexist organization of society and its family system reflected in restricted job opportunities for women, lower pay for women performing the same work, the delegation of child care responsibilities primarily to women, the presumption that the husband is the head of the household, the identification of masculinity with violence, and the socialization of women for subordinate roles. A woman may decide to tolerate the beatings because she is economically dependent on her male partner, she doubts her own abilities to provide, the male partner essentially controls the home, she lacks police protection, and she hopes that her partner will change and/or is experiencing guilt over what she did to deserve the beatings. The stigma of divorce, the belief that family members may hit each other in anger or to discipline another, and norms maintaining family privacy erect additional barriers to the woman contemplating leaving a violent intimate relationship.

Social Disorganization Theory

Social disorganization, social control, and social isolation theories are seen as complementary. Taken together, these theories hypothesize that the weaker the social bond, the higher the rate of assault on female intimate partners (Straus, 1994).

THE INDIVIDUAL/COUPLE LEVEL

Biopsychosocial Perspective

The biopsychosocial perspective is an attempt to integrate into one model the various biological, social, and psychological factors that have been found to impact on domestic violence (McHenry et al., 1995). Biological factors to be considered in the etiology of intimate partner violence include testosterone levels in the assaultive male partners (Booth and Dabbs, 1993) and levels of alcohol (Martin, 1992; Pernanen, 1991). Social factors include the level of social stress (Gelles, 1989), the quality of the marital relationship (Rounsaville, 1978a), the extent of social support available (Gelles, 1994; Steinmetz, 1987), and available income (Pan et al., 1994; Gelles, 1983). Psychological styles have been implicated as a factor in the commission of antisocial behavior (O'Leary, 1993). (Each of these domains is discussed in greater detail below.) One physician explained this formulation as follows:

> The boundaries between health and disease, between well and sick, are far from clear and never will be clear, for they are diffused by cultural, social, and psychological considerations....By evaluating all of the factors contributing to both illness and patienthood, rather than giving a primacy to biological factors alone, a biopsychosocial model would make it possible to explain why some individuals experience as "illness" conditions that others would regard merely as "problems of living," be they emotional

reactions to life circumstances or somatic symptoms. (Engel, 1977:
132-133)

Most recently, this theory has been referred to as the biopsychosocial systems
model, in order to emphasize the interactive nature of the biological, psychological,
and social influences which impact on the conceptualization of health and illness.

Biological Factors

Various biological factors have been found to be associated with increased
aggression, although no causal relationship has been established. Dabbs and Morris
(1990) found in their study of 4,000 male military veterans in the United States that
individuals with higher testosterone levels often reported having had difficulties
with parents, teachers, and classmates; having been assaultive towards other adults;
having used substances such as marijuana and other illicit drugs while in the
military; and having had a greater number of sexual partners. Booth and Dabbs
(1993) found in their study of former servicemen that the level of testosterone was
associated with the quality of the marital relationship; levels of testosterone, for
instance, were positively associated with hitting or throwing things at their female
partners.
    Alcohol has also been associated with levels of aggression, but a causal
relationship has not been demonstrated. Kantor and Straus (1987) found that
alcohol is associated with between 25% and 85% of instances of domestic violence.
Two explanations for the apparent association have dominated the literature. The
first posits a pharmacological pathway, whereby the alcohol acts as a catalyst for
physiological changes that essentially serve to disinhibit the individual (McHenry,
Julian, and Gavazzi, 1995). The second theory hypothesizes that behavior
associated with alcohol derives from the beliefs found in the cultural milieu in
which alcohol is ingested, e.g. cultural beliefs may permit drinkers to be absolved of
responsibility for behaviors committed while drunk (MacAndrew and Edgerton,
1969). High levels of testosterone have been associated with alcohol abuse in men
(Dabbs and Morris, 1990).

Social Factors

Violence within an intimate relationship has been found to be associated with high
social stress (Gelles, 1987) and, in particular, negative life events that threaten the
status of the traditional male role (Gelles, 1989; Steinmetz, 1987). Both Gelles
(1974) and Rounsaville (1978) have noted that relationship violence often follows a
sudden transition in the level of intimacy within the relationship. Lower income has
also been associated with partner violence. It has been hypothesized that
individuals in lower income groups must confront more negative life events as
compared to those of a higher economic status, and yet have fewer resources to
mediate the impact of these events (Gelles, 1993; Milner and Chilamkurti, 1991).
Individuals of higher economic status may have been socialized to resolve disputes

through mediation and consequently rely the use of verbal skills to resolve disputes occurring in the context of a relationship (Steinmetz, 1978).

Psychological Factors

Antisocial disorders have been found to be associated with levels of physical violence (O'Leary, 1993). Hostility as a personality characteristic has been found to be related to domestic violence, although it is unclear whether this operates directly or whether it serves as a response to stress induced by negative life events, family income, and relationship quality (McHenry, Julian, and Gavazzi, 1995). Individuals in abusive relationships have also been found to approach others from an egocentric, need-gratifying perspective, compared to a perspective of greater mutuality seen in nonabusive relationships (Cogan and Porcerelli, 1996). Shaming experiences as a child have also been linked to adults' commission of physical abuse against their intimate partners (Dutton, van Ginkel, and Starzomski, 1995).

Exchange Theory

Gelles (1983: 157) succinctly summarized the basic premise of exchange theory: "People hit and abuse other family members because they can." People's actions are essentially based on a cost-benefit analysis; they will use violence to obtain their goal as long as the benefit outweighs the cost. Nuclear family living arrangements, which tend to isolate the family, may render violence relatively cost-free to the perpetrator. This theory is somewhat challenged by the findings of Eisikovits and colleagues (1993) who noted in their study of 120 Israeli couples that the social supports of men who battered and women who were battered were as many in number and as adequate as those available to men who did not batter and women who were not battered. However, it is supported by ethnographic findings in a number of societies. As one example, Lambeck (1992) found that the people of Mayotte consider spousal abuse wrong. Violence in the context of a spousal relationship is considered inappropriate and the battering husband is subject to social censure. The cost of battering is simply too great and, consequently, it rarely occurs.

Investment Theory

Rusbult (1980, 1983) defined commitment to a relationship as a function of anticipated relationship satisfaction, the negative function of the attractiveness of perceived alternatives, and a positive function of the amount that has already been invested in a relationship. Rusbult posits that one's willingness to stay in a relationship increases as the balance of rewards over costs from staying in that relationship exceeds the balance of the rewards over the costs involved in alternative relationships.

   Rusbult (1983, 1980) hypothesized that there are two types of investments: intrinsic and extrinsic. Intrinsic investments include the amount of time already invested in the relationship, the level of self-disclosure, and the amount of time spent together. Extrinsic investments include such things as the development of mutual friends and family networks, shared possessions, and shared activities.

Resource Theory

Resource theory posits that the decision making power within a given family derives from the value of the resources that each person brings to the relationship (Blood and Wolfe, 1960). Such resources include money, property, prestige, and contacts, *i.e.* both material and organizational. Goode (1971) has argued that the extent to which a partner is likely to use violence to maintain control is related to the extent of his or her control of resources outside of the family, *i.e.* the more external control that one has, the less likely he or she will be use to use violence as a means of control.

Social Learning Theory

Social learning theory posits that family violence arises due to a constellation of contextual and situational factors (O'Leary, 1988). Key contextual factors include individual characteristics, couple characteristics, and societal characteristics, such as stress, violence in the family, and an aggressive personality. Situational factors, such as substance abuse or financial difficulties, will lead to violence in the presence of the above-mentioned contextual factors. Social learning theory has been used to explain the intergenerational transmission of child abuse (Ballard et al., 1980; Egeland et al., 1988; Davis and Leitenberg, 1987; Kaufman and Zigler, 1987).

Social learning theory is supported by numerous individual examples, such as the following.

> Craig doesn't remember now why he did it. He only knows that he hit Patsy with the cane, the cane he had just bought...He stood over her in a bedroom of her mother's house in the Bronx, raised the cane over his head and let it come down on her arms and hands (Straus, Gelles, and Steinmertz, 1980: 97).

Craig acknowledged during his treatment:

> I was a product of seeing my mother being beaten up. I was also beaten up, whipped with a belt. I thought once that maybe my mother died to get out of that relationship with my father. I mean, I know she died of cancer, but...That's the ironic part: I remember wanting to dial the police when they were arguing to protect her, and yet it's funny how I did the same things as my father (Straus, Gelles, and Steinmertz, 1980: 98).

Theory of Marital Power

Cromwell and Olson (1975) hypothesized that power falls into three realms: power bases, power processes, and power outcomes. Power bases consist of the assets and resources that provide the basis for one partner's domination over the other. These bases can include not only knowledge, skill, personal assets, and connections, but also the cultural definition of which partner has the authority within the relationship. Power processes refers to the interactional techniques that an individual employs to gain control, such as negotiation, assertiveness, and problem-solving. Power outcome refers to who actually makes the decision. According to this theory, those partners who lack power will be more likely to physically abuse their partners.

Serra (1993: 24), noting that the use of violence possesses a different meaning when acted out by a man (power) than by a woman (powerlessness), has extended the power base to include the moral choice to use or not to use violence:

> There is no moral code or reason for a "norm" forbidding woman's violence toward a man. Therefore, while *a man's nonaggression* toward a woman expresses *a norm inscribed in our morals and in our culture, a woman's nonviolence toward a man appears to be a form of nonpower*, a consequence of the biological fact that she is unable to overcome him. A man's *nonviolence* toward a woman takes on a sense of his "not wanting to"-- *a moral choice.* A man who does not react to a woman's blows by beating her shows respect for the other sex, while a woman who--having been hit by a man--does not react by attacking him, gives only an impression of powerlessness. Hence, neither violence, nor nonviolence, are reciprocal. (Italics in original.)

There is some empirical evidence to support the theory of marital power. Ganley and Harris (1978) have noted in their study of batterers that many suffer from communication difficulties. Bograd (1988) found that many battering husbands commonly indicate that they resorted to violence because there was no other way to address the situation that confronted them. Babcock and colleagues (1993) found in their study of 95 couples that violence was used by battering husbands as a compensatory behavior to make up for their relative lack of power in the marriage. Perilla, Bakeman, and Norris (1994) found in their study of 60 immigrant Latinas that the more a woman contributed to her family income, the more likely she was to suffer abuse. This appears to lend credence to the hypothesis that a perceived loss of power by a partner may be related to the use of physical violence.

Although the theory of marital power has not been invoked explicitly to explain same-sex partner violence, its emphasis on the context and meaning of violence is relevant. It has been estimated that approximately 71% of heterosexual battered women use violence against their assaultive partners at least once (Saunders, 1988). Such violence is often for the purpose of self-defense. Letellier (1994) has observed that it is not unlikely that battered gay and bisexual men who, as men, have been socialized to resort to violence more than women, would use violence at least as often in response to violence directed against them. As Renzetti (1992:107-108) has noted, "there are important differences between initiating violence, using violence in self-defense, and retaliating against a violent partner."

Traumatic Bonding Theory

Dutton and Painter (1993, 1981) have developed traumatic bonding theory to explain why beaten women remain with the men who beat them. They have identified two features which they argue are common to all such relationships: the existence of a power imbalance within the relationship, so that the battered partner perceives him or herself as dominated by the other, and the intermittent nature of the abuse. They hypothesize that over time, the power imbalance magnifies and as it does, the dominant person develops an inflated sense of his or her own power, while the subjugated partner feels more negative about him- or herself and gradually, as a result, becomes increasingly dependent on the dominator. Because the abuse occurs on an intermittent basis, and those interim periods are often characterized by positive behaviors such as attention and declarations of love and remorse, patterns of behavior result that are difficult to extinguish (Rounsaville, 1978b).

This loyalty between the batterer and the battered victim has been analogized to the Stockholm syndrome (Dutton and Golant, 1995). This loyalty results from the victim's identification with the aggressor as a means of fending off danger in a situation in which the victim is essentially powerless. This situation was observed during the Holocaust, with the emulation of Nazis by concentration camp inmates in an attempt to prevent or control severe, unpredictable punishment (Bettelheim, 1943). Herman (1997: 81) has described this process:

> As the victim is isolated, she becomes increasingly dependent on the perpetrator, not only for survival and basic bodily needs but also for information and even for emotional sustenance. The more frightened she is, the more she is tempted to cling to the one relationship that is permitted: the relationship with the perpetrator. In the absence of any other human connection, she will try to find the humanity in her captor. Inevitably, in the absence of any other point of view, the victim will come to see the world through the eyes of the perpetrator....
>
> The repeated experience of terror and reprieve, especially within the isolated context of a love relationship, may result in a feeling of intense, almost worshipful dependence upon an all-powerful, godlike authority. The victim may live in terror of his wrath, but she may also view him as the source of strength, guidance, and life itself. The relationship may take on an extraordinary quality of specialness. Some battered women speak of entering a kind of exclusive, almost delusional world, embracing the grandiose belief system of their mates and *voluntarily* suppressing their own doubts as proof of loyalty and submission. (Herman, 1992: 92)

Graham and Rawlings (1998: 124) have enumerated the symptoms that a woman who has developed Stockholm syndrome in connection with partner battering might experience:

- The victim and abuser are bidirectionally bonded.
- The victim is intensely grateful for small kindness shown to her by the abuser.
- The victim denies the abuser's violence against her, or rationalizes that violence.
- The victim denies her own anger at her abuser.
- The victim is hypervigilant to the abuser's needs and seeks to keep the abuser happy. To do this, the victim tries to "get inside the abuser's head."
- The victim sees the world from the abuser's perspective; she may not have her own perspective.
- In accordance with the indicator above, the victim sees outside authorities trying to win her release (for example, police, parents) as "bad guys" and the abuser as a "good guy." She sees the abuser as protecting her.
- The victim finds it difficult to leave the abuser even after her release has been won.
- The victim fears the abuser will come back to get her even after the abuser is dead, in prison, and so on.
- The victim shows signs of Post-Traumatic Stress Disorder.

3

HOW WOMEN AND MEN DEFINE EXPERIENCES OF VIOLENCE AND ITS CAUSES

> The power of naming is at least two-fold, naming defines the quality and value of that which is named—and it also denies reality and value to that which is never named, never uttered. That which has no name, that for which we have no words or concepts, is rendered mute and invisible; powerless to inform or transform our consciousness of our experience, our understanding, our vision, powerless to claim its own existence (Du Bois, 1983: 198).

To inquire of an individual whether he or she has been battered or abused, presumes that the individual posing the question shares the same definition of these terms as the individual being asked (cf. Kelly, 1990). How the question is asked and answered relates directly to our estimates of the incidence and prevalence of intimate partner violence, and to the development of strategies that can potentially abate the violence. Yet, few studies have embarked on this line of inquiry.

This chapter presents summaries of two different studies undertaken in an attempt to understand how women perceive partner violence, what they believe its causes to be, and what they feel are efficacious interventions. The various theories of causation that are explored in chapter 2 are reflected in the responses discussed here. The findings of these studies, although by no means definitive, both elucidate aspects of partner violence that have rarely been examined and raise significant issues requiring further study.

INTIMATE PARTNER VIOLENCE: PUERTO RICANS AND NON-HISPANIC WHITES, CUYAHOGA COUNTY

Background

Puerto Ricans and "Anglos" in Cuyahoga County

The term "Anglo" is used here to refer to non-Hispanic whites, who are classified as such based on self-identification. In Cuyahoga County, in northeast Ohio, non-Hispanic whites account for almost 73 percent of the county's population. Despite the seemingly homogeneous nature of this classification, non-Hispanic whites are remarkably diverse, claiming heritages from a variety of Eastern European countries, western Europe, and North America.

Puerto Rican migration to the mainland U.S. occurred in three phases. The first, duringthe period 1900 to 1945, saw the majority of newcomwers settling in and around New York City (Rodriguez, 1994). The first truly massive immigration

37

from Puerto Rico to the mainland did not occur until after World War II, despite the fact that Puerto Ricans are citizens by birth and can freely enter the United States (Lamberty and Coll, 1994). This second phase, from 1946 to 1964, was known as "the great migration." During this period, already-established Puerto Rican communities grew in size and settlements were begun in areas outside of the New York area (Rodriguez, 1994). To a large extent, this migration was driven by economic concerns and employment opportunities (Rodriguez, 1994). The third period of migration, from 1965 through to the present day, is known as the period of "revolving door migration," due to the fluctuating pattern of net migration (Rodriguez, 1994). Over one-third of all Puerto Ricans now reside on the mainland, where they have been at the lowest level of the socioeconomic ladder among Hispanics (Lamberty and Coll, 1994). In Cuyahoga County, individuals self-identifying as Hispanics account for approximately 2 percent of the county's population; of those, 67 percent are Puerto Rican (U.S. Census, 1990).

Compared to the Anglo population, Cuyahoga County's Puerto Rican population has had less education and has lower incomes. Of the 716,138 Anglos in the county who are over the age of 25, only 22 percent have not received either a high school diploma or equivalency; among Puerto Ricans over the age of 25, almost 45 percent have not completed high school. Of those for whom poverty status could be determined, 7.5% of non-Hispanic white households were found to have an income in 1989 below the poverty level, as compared with 31.6 percent of all Hispanics, including Puerto Ricans.

Male and Female Gender Roles

Male-Female Roles in U.S. Society. The preceding chapters and chapter 3, below, provide a more detailed discussion of the widespread nature of woman abuse and the historical abuse of women in the United States. That history reflects, in part, the traditional division of roles ascribed to men and women. It is believed that such sex-role stereotyping that occurs throughout U.S. society actually promotes violence against women (Hutchings, 1994). Men are believed to be stronger and physically dominant, while women are seen as more passive and nurturing of both their children and their partners. This depiction of women's roles is reinforced through media advertising and through pornography (Hutchings, 1994). Culturally sanctioned beliefs about the rights and privileges due to husbands have been used to justify the use of violence to control wives. Batterers may excuse their violent behavior by asserting that their wives acted "unwifely" (Adams, 1988; Dobash and Dobash, 1979; Ptacek, 1988).

Socialization into team sports has also been identified as a detrimental factor, in that it encourages deference to authority through the establishment of a hierarchy and emphasizes winning above all else, regardless of the detrimental effect on the individual (Thorne-Finch, 1994). One must "win at all costs." Language derived from sports has even been appropriated and used to refer to intimate relations with women: "Did you make it all the way to home?" "Did you score" (Thorne-Finch, 1994: 44).

Machismo and Marianismo. It has been hypothesized that various features of Hispanic culture may support wife abuse, even more so than the "dominant" U.S. culture. Kantor and colleagues (1994: 209) have asserted, for instance, that

> Hispanic family characteristics such as the presence of male dominance are consistent with typical predictors of wife abuse. Authoritarian role structures ascribing dominance to the husband and demanding absolute obedience by the wife are said to persist at least as an ideology of ...Puerto Rican cultures....

Latino families in general have been characterized as strongly patriarchal, with strict cultural norms and strong church influences (Castro de Alvarez, 1990). The patriarchal nature of the family has been said to influence or control every facet of a woman's life, including her dress, activities, interpersonal relationships, courtship, marriage, and childbearing. In addition, it tolerates or encourages multiple sexual relationships for men, while negatively sanctioning women for the same behavior (Castro de Alvarez, 1990).

This emphasis on patriarchy and maleness, and the concomitant devaluation of females and femaleness, is reflected in various expressions and behaviors. Puerto Rican men who produce only daughters are known as *chancleteros*, men who produce only slippers, an object of minimal value (Alvarez, 1977). *Machismo* has been used to refer to maleness or virility, and males' superiority over females and the deference that is naturally due to them as a consequence. *Machismo* is said to be evidenced by sexual freedom, physical dominance over women, alcohol consumption, the control of female behavior and sexuality (Burgos and Diaz-Perez, 1986; Christensen, 1979; de la Vega, 1990; DeYoung and Zigler, 1994; Giraldo, 1972; Mosher, 1991; Pearlman, 1984), callousness towards women, verbal abuse of women, and demands for menial services (Stevens, 1973).

Machismo represents more than a stereotypical set of negatively valued behaviors, however (Bach-y-Rita, 1982). It encompasses men's roles as providers and protectors of their families, responsible for upholding family honor and maintaining the integrity of the family unit (Gutmann, 1996; Obeso and Bordatto, 1979; Panitz, McConchie, Sauber, and Fonseca, 1983; Scott, Shifman, Orr, Owen, and Fawcett, 1989). Consequently, *machismo* prohibits a showing of weakness, potentially precluding help seeking or health seeking attempts (Quesada, 1976). The complexities of *machismo* have been explained as follows:

1. Machismo underpins the continuous evaluation of men, and rests on the discrete categorization of women.
2. Machismo has men as its reference group: it is in the eyes of other men that a man's manhood is confirmed, but it is through women that it is reflected and enacted. Thus men are socially and emotionally vulnerable to other men, through the behavior and moral evaluation of women.
3. The very articulation of machismo not only points to the precariousness of being a man but also underscores the

ambiguity of being a woman, showing how women's sexuality
is an ambivalent source of virtue (Melhuus, 1996: 241).

However, despite the positive traits associated with *machismo*, a recent study of
Latinos' perceptions of it found that only 15% of the 39 respondents had positive
associations with the characteristics, such as assertiveness, responsibility, and
selflessness, possession of a general code of ethics, sincerity, and respect (Mirande,
1997). Negative associations were much more common and included a sense of
exaggerated masculinity, male dominance, authoritarianism, violence, aggression,
self-centeredness, and egotism (Mirande, 1997).

Machismo is believed to be valued and displayed across all socioeconomic
strata (Giraldo, 1972). The behavioral expression of machismo, though, has been
shown to vary by region, ethnic group, social class, age cohort, and time period
(Andrade, 1992; DeYoung and Zigler, 1994; Gutmann, 1994; Thompson, 1991). A
recent study of cultural practices of young Hispanic adults found that expressions of
machismo varied across levels of acculturation (Mikawa, Morones, Gomez, Case,
Olsen, and Gonzalez Huss, 1992). Consequently, generalizations regarding the
nature and expression of *machismo* should be made with great caution. Care must
be taken to distinguish *machismo* from "cool pose," also known as "coolin'" or
"chillin'." This concept, which refers to racial resistance or a specific social posture
towards social inequities, may converge with concepts of *machismo* and masculinity
in male gender roles among U.S. urban Latino youth (De La Cancela, 1993).

Marianismo represents the female counterpart to *machismo* (Giraldo, 1972) and
underscores the duality inherent in the concept of *machismo*. *Marianismo* derives
from the Virgin Mary; women are considered men's spiritual superiors and,
consequently, can endure the suffering that is inflicted on them by men (Stevens,
1979). Accordingly, Puerto Rican women are expected to accept and adapt to their
husbands' behavior (Comas-Diaz, 1988). It is not uncommon for Latina women to
internalize this expectation to nurture and maintain family unity and connections,
even in the face of abuse and severe unhappiness (Vasquez, 1994). Gil and
Vasquez (1996:8) have enumerated "the ten commandments of *marianismo*:"

1. Do not forget a woman's place.
2. Do not forsake tradition.
3. Do not be single, self-supporting, or independent-minded.
4. Do not put your own needs first.
5. Do not wish for more in life than being a housewife.
6. Do not forget that sex is for having babies—not for pleasure.
7. Do not be unhappy with your man or criticize him for
   infidelity, gambling, verbal and physical abuse, alcohol or
   drug abuse.
8. Do not ask for help.
9. Do not discuss personal problems outside the home.
10. Do not change those things which make you unhappy that you
    can realistically change.

Marianismo emphasizes the central role of motherhood. The Puerto Rican
mother is expected to be morally superior, spiritually strong, and self-sacrificing for

her children (Christensen, 1975). In contrast, the concept of *hembrismo* encompasses "doing what is needed" for the benefit of the family, rather than accepting a self-sacrificing role (Steiner, 1974). Christensen (1975) has argued that, faced with a conflict in role expectations, the Puerto Rican woman will choose her role as a mother above all else.

Women who fulfill these expectations of a "good" woman are to be protected by the *macho* male. Those who are "bad," such as those who have sex outside of marriage, are labeled as "bad" (*mujer mala*) or "whore" (*puta* or *putita*) and are "fair game" to be seduced by *macho* males (Stolen, 1991). In essence, women are the "moral custodians of male behavior" (Vance, 1989: 4), although they are clearly unable to control men's behavior.

Traditional values such as *respeto*, respect towards older males, *humilidad*, humility, and *familismo*, the promotion of loyalty to and from the family, have been thought to limit Puerto Rican females' autonomy and freedom of expression (Comas-Diaz, 1988; Jenkins and Cofresi, 1998). Additionally, this sharp demarcation of partner roles is believed to impact on the socialization of the couple as a couple and their participation in activities together (rarely) (Mertz, 1973).

In this context, gender role, sex, and violence may become intimately entwined. A recent ethnography of low-income, predominantly second-generation, mainland Puerto Rican adolescents found that both males and females condoned the use of physical violence as a punishment for those females who were perceived to be sluts, i.e., those whose sexual behavior was perceived to be similar to that of males (Asencio, 1999). Females could have intercourse without becoming sluts only if they were truly in love. Accordingly, females who left relationships "too early" or had not sacrificed sufficiently to preserve the relationship were suspected of having engaged in sex out of desire and not love. As a result, young women often stayed in abusive relationships in order to protect their reputations. In addition, some males believed that a female could not leave a relationship until the male said that she could. If the female left the relationship and was with a new male partner, she was potentially subject to physical violence from her former partner because she was perceived as a slut (Asensio, 1999). Bourgois (1996) documented in his ethnography of Puerto Rican crack dealers in East Harlem the use of violence by Puerto Rican men against women, including sexual conquest and gang rape, as one mechanism for the men's re-empowerment in situations in which the woman was economically superior to the man or unresponsive to his sexual demands. These behaviors were also used by men in attempts to gain acceptance from other males in the community.

Help seeking in such situations may be problematic. First, language may constitute a barrier to obtaining assistance (West, Kantor, and Jasinski, 1998). Second, resources that are obtained, such as reliance on a spiritist, may prove ineffectual. Harwood (1987) related an incident involving a husband and wife who had not been having sexual relations for some time. The husband was involved with another woman in Puerto Rico. In retribution, the wife in New York had an affair with one of his friends. When the husband returned to New York and his wife continued to refuse his sexual advances, he threatened her with a knife. On another occasion, he attempted to force sexual relations upon her. The wife subsequently utilized the services of a spiritist in an attempt to identify from her spirit guides a spell that would make her husband leave.

Study Methods

A total of 26 Puerto Ricans, 10 men and 16 women, and 19 U.S.-born non-Hispanic whites, 9 men and 10 women, participated in this pilot study. Individuals were recruited through organization-based network sampling at clinics, social service organizations, churches, and civic groups. One of the Puerto Rican women (6.2% was recruited through a residential drug and alcohol treatment program, 3 (18.8%) were recruited through a social service agency dedicated to the provisions of various types of services to families, 2 (12.5%) were recruited through an agency dedicated to the provision of various types of services to Hispanic families in Cuyahoga County, and the remaining 10 (62.5%) came through various Catholic, Seventh Day Adventist, and Pentecostal churches. Of the 10 non-Hispanic white women participating, 6 (60%) were recruited through various churches, 2 (20%) responded to information about the study that was distributed to agencies serving battered women, and 2 (20%) were recruited through information distributed about the study at hospitals and clinics. The majority of the Puerto Rican men (60%) were recruited through various churches, 3 (30%) were recruited through hospitals and clinics, and 1 (10%) was recruited through a drug and alcohol treatment program. Almost half (44.4%) of the non-Hispanic white male participants came to the study through recruitment efforts at churches, 2 (22.2%) heard of the study through intervention programs for batterers, and 3 (33.3%) responded to information posted at local colleges and universities. Because participants were volunteers, no claims can be made regarding their representativeness. Recruitment materials indicated that participants were not required to have had any experience with intimate partner violence in order to participate.

In addition to basic demographic information, participants were asked about their perceptions of intimate partner violence. This was accomplished through the use of vignettes and a series of questions based on the vignettes and on respondents' initial reactions to the vignettes.

Vignettes have been described as "carefully constructed description[s] of a particular situation under investigation" (Lanza and Carifio, 1992), "short stories about hypothetical characters in specified circumstances, to whose situation the interviewee is invited to respond" (Finch, 1987), and "stories which contain precise references to what are thought to be the most important factors in the decisionmaking processes of respondents (Alexander and Becker, 1978). Vignettes may be presented in writing or through computer animation, or through video or audio presentation (Lanza and Carifio, 1992). Vignettes have been utilized as a research methodology to examine such diverse issues as the stigmatization of homelessness (Phelan, Link, Moore, and Stueve, 1997), caregivers' sensitivity to conflict (Rahman, 1996), psychologists' attitudes towards people with AIDS (Fliszar and Clopton, 1995), physicians' acceptance of behavioral treatments and pharmacotherapy for behavioral disturbances in adults, public attitudes towards tenants of mental health residences (Aubry, Tefft, and Currie, 1995), and attributions of blame in situation involving rape (Bell, Kuriloff, and Lottes, 1994). Vignettes have been particularly useful as a strategy in child abuse research (Giovanni and Becerra, 1979), elder abuse research (Ikels, 1990; Gioglio and

Blakemore, 1982; Pratt, Koval and Lloyd, 1983), and research relating to rape (Bourque, 1989).

Vignettes offer various advantages as a research technique, in comparison with either written questionnaires and closed questions in an interview or survey format. First, vignettes permit the investigator to introduce for consideration by the interviewee the elements that are believed to be important in decisionmaking, and to vary the levels of those instruments. Because the responses are open-ended, they are not confined to a predetermined range, as would be the case with a closed-question format. Reliance on vignettes permits an assessment of individuals' perceptions of intimate partner violence, regardless of their prior (in)experience with such an event. Further, because the responses pertain to a hypothetical cast of characters, the respondent may feel less threatened in discussing his or her own circumstances and may be more candid than he or she would be otherwise. The literacy level of the participant does not affect the responses where the vignettes are presented orally.

This study relied on 10 series of vignettes, indicated below, which were constructed around marital status, battering and rape, and the sex of the person effectuating the behavior and the person being acted upon.

Series 1: Husband-wife; husband is violent
Series 2: Husband-wife; wife is violent
Series 3: Husband-wife; violence bi-directional
Series 4: Male-female, unmarried; male violent
Series 5: Male-female, unmarried; female violent
Series 6: Male-female, unmarried; violence bi-directional
Series 7: Female-female; violence unidirectional
Series 8: Female-female; violence bi-directional
Series 9: Male-male; violence unidirectional
Series 10: Male-male; violence bi-directional

The variation in the sexes of the batterer and the battered is premised on previous observations that the meaning of violent behavior depends on the sex of both the perceived aggressor and the perceived victim (Serra, 1993).

The construction of the vignettes around marital status, battering, and rape (in those vignettes in which a man was violent), reflects research findings pertaining to the reactions of victims of nonsexual battering, marital rape, and nonmarital rape. First, victims of marital rape have been found to be more likely to seek help from relatives, social service agencies, and police than are women who are battered, but not raped, by their marital partners (Frieze, 1980). Rape versus nonsexual battering thus becomes relevant to the study participants' responses regarding what should be done by the victim or another individual in the context of a specific vignette. Several researchers have suggested that because many women are financially and emotionally dependent on their husbands, they cannot define their husbands as rapists and continue to live with them. Consequently, they may define the incident as battering but not rape, or not battering at all (Finkelhor and Yllo, 1980; Russell, 1975). Previous research has also demonstrated that the "forcible rape of a former spouse" is nor perceived as a particularly serious offense (Rossi, Waite, Bose, and Berk, 1974), but that it may be more serious than the rape of a current spouse because the more intimate the victim, the less serious the assault is perceived to be (Finkelhor and Yllo, 1983).

Table 1 provides a sample of the vignettes in Series 1. As demonstrated within this series, each vignette within a series reflects a different act, e.g., throwing something versus hitting, and a different consequence, e.g. the individual is hurt or not hurt. Because some of the participants were unable to read or had limited reading ability, and in order to standardize interviews, the vignettes were read to each participant. When they were read, the names of the actors in each vignette were varied in order to be congruent with the ethnicity of the individual being interviewed and in order to assess more accurately individuals' perceptions of violence within their own communities. Each participant was asked to indicate what he or she believed provoked the incident in the vignette, how he or she believed the assaulted individual could respond, what the assaulted individual's response should be, and how anyone else could and should respond to the portrayed incident.

Table 1. Vignettes, Series 1: Husband-Wife; Husband Is Violent

Leonardo and Carmelita [Leonard/Carol] are married. He yells at her loudly.

Manuel and Lupita {Manny/Linda] are married. Manny throws something at her. She is not hurt.

Manuel and Susanna [Manuel and Susan] are married. He hits her. She is not injured.

Joanna and Luis [Joanne and Louis] are married. He hits her. She develops a dark bruise where he hit her.

German and Monica [Joe and Monica] are married. He tries to stab her with a knife. She is not injured.

Alma and Roberto [Amy and Robert] are married. He stabs her with a knife, causing a bleeding wound.

Javier and Isabella [James/Isabel] are married. He forces her to have sex even though she doesn't want to. She is not hurt.

Esperanza and Jose [Hope and Joseph] are married. He forces her to have sex even though she doesn't want to. She is hurt physically.

Results

The results presented here are qualitative in nature, with the exception of the demographic characteristics of the participants (Table 2) and their responses to questions relating to whether they had ever seen another individual hurt, ever been hurt by someone themselves, or ever hurt others themselves (Table 3).

Table 2. Demographic Characteristics By Ethnicity

Characteristic	Puerto Ricans	Anglos	p-value
Sex			
Male	10	9	.56
Female	16	10	
Marital status			
Married or living with partner	11	7	.72
Single, widowed, divorced	15	12	
Age			
<40	13	13	.22
>=40	13	6	
Education			
<=12 years	19	4	.001
>12 years	7	15	
Religion			
Roman Catholic	5	5	.83
Evangelist	1	0	
Pentecostal	2	0	
Lutheran	3	7	
Methodist	1	3	
Christian, unspecified	14	4	
Employment			
Unemployed	10	4	.90
Service industry	4	6	
Clerical	4	2	
Health, allied health	1	1	
Professional	2	3	
Construction, manual labor	4	3	
Missing	1	0	
Earnings			
High (>=$30,001/year)	6	10	.06
Mid ($10,001-$30,000)	12	5	
Low (<=$10,000/year)	2	1	
Missing	2	1	

Table 3. Experience with Violence by Ethnicity

Characteristic	Puerto Ricans	Anglos	p-value
Ever seen others hurt physically			
Yes	25	19	1.00
No	1	0	
Ever been hurt by someone physically			
Yes	16	14	.34
No	9	4	
Missing	1	1	
Ever hurt others physically			
Yes	9	9	.26
No	14	8	
Missing	3	2	

Vignettes—What Caused the Situation

Numerous explanations were offered as to the causes of the conflicts presented. These can be classified into the following broad categories: (1) arguments over finances, (2) use of drugs or alcohol, (3) infidelity or jealousy, (4) the inherent nature of men, e.g. their hormones, (5) the individual's failure to conform to traditional role expectations and/or exertion of power and control, and (6) mental illness on the part of the violent partner. Men appeared more likely to attribute the cause of the violence to financial difficulties, while Puerto Ricans, in general, were more likely to ascribe it to a breach of tradition. Characteristic responses are presented below for each such cause.

Finances. One Puerto Rican woman with an eighth grade education explained why a husband and wife were arguing:

> It is economic, economic, because he doesn't want to work and they have three children. The smallest one is one year old, the other is four, and the other is eight and he doesn't work so she must get welfare and exist with this money and she has no peace and they fight because she doesn't want to give him the money for beer and that's what happens.

A Puerto Rican man, age 30, explained why an unmarried man and woman tried to stab each other:

Um, they just got into a big argument and started fighting and grabbed knives and stabbed each other. About bills or something, maybe he didn't want to pay the bills or something and they just got into a big argument and started fighting and stuff. Yeah, it happens in my house. My girlfriend's father, he'll go out and get drunk and then when he comes home, she, her mom, be arguing with him because he don't have no money and they get into a big ass fight.

One of the non-Hispanic men, age 30 with a graduate school education, observed:

I wouldn't say it's the major cause, but I would tend to say it tends to be the biggest reasons, financial reasons tend to get people to argue. Cause finances are the way of supporting themselves, it causes tensions, and if the person's using, usually if the person's going to use drugs or do something wrong like using drugs or drinking alcohol, they're taking it out of the family finances to support that mostly so it's going to cause tension with the other party cause it's taking food out of their mouths or it's money that could be spent on other things besides drugs or alcohol.

The emphasis by some respondents on economic difficulties as a causal factor in partner violence is consistent with the biopsychosocial perspective. As described in chapter 2, this theory postulates that individuals with lower incomes confront more negative life events, but have fewer skills and resources that can be utilized to mediate these stressors. Although there were no statistically significant differences between the Puerto Rican and the Anglo respondents with respect to income level (see Table 2), a higher proportion of Puerto Ricans as compared to Anglos explained domestic violence as resulting from financial strain (26.9% compared to 15.8%). This may reflect Puerto Ricans' relatively low socioeconomic status as a group, both nationally and in Cuyahoga County.

Alcohol and Drug Use. The theme of alcohol and drug use was notably common across sex and ethnicity in the context of all vignettes, irrespective of the level of conflict, the sex of the partners, or the marital status of the partners in the vignette. This explanation is, again, consistent with the biopsychosocial model. It is unclear from these explanations, however, whether respondents believed that the violent behavior resulted from the pharmacological effects of the drugs/alcohol or whether the drugs/alcohol are thought to merely provide an excuse for the violent behavior. One Puerto Rican woman in her 40's explained why a husband and wife tried to stab each other:

They're both drug users. Possibly they could be drug users, maybe one had more dope than the other. I mean, I've seen it done. Could be one or the other has affairs on the side. Or they could just be drunk. See to me I pertain a lot of things to drugs and alcohol because I've seen so much violence with alcohol and

drugs. I never really seen an argument or fight that didn't have to
do with alcohol and drugs.

A 37-year old non-Hispanic woman with a high school education related to her own
experience a vignette in which a woman stabbed the husband :

> Um, we had a maintenance worker here and his girlfriend did it
> twice to him. I don't know what they argued about, but she
> stabbed him twice, once when he was sleeping on her sofa and he
> went back with her and then like a month later she stabbed him
> again while he was in bed, and I thought, oh, my God, and he
> didn't prosecute her the first time and the second time the state
> took her and prosecuted her because that, you know, is violence.
> No, I know he was, uh, it could have been something with drugs
> cause I know he did drugs and I know she did drugs, so I figure
> that had to be it, that had to be it, something with drugs, but I don't
> know what.

A Puerto Rican man, age 36 with some high school education, explained how drugs
and alcohol affect a person:

> Because when you got problems at home or work...you try to drown
> yourself in alcohol and on drugs and think that's okay but when you wake
> up they're still there but at that point you don't care....

Infidelity or Jealousy. The theme of jealousy and infidelity as an explanation
for violence between intimate partners was common across groups. Despite the
apparent emphasis within at least some Hispanic cultures on men's sexual prowess
and the concomitant emphasis on a woman's value as rooted in her viginity and
fidelity, there was little difference between the Puerto Rican and Anglo
respondents' attribution of the violence to infidelity (50.0% versus 47.7%,
respectively).

A 37-year old non-Hispanic woman who grew up in Appalachia drew on her
own experience with her sister and brother-in-law and their arguments about
infidelity to explain how it came to pass in a vignette that a woman hit her husband,
leaving a dark bruise:

> He [my husband] only physically abused me really bad once and
> that was the time I hit him back, but most of the time it's just
> slapping, which hurts. It hurts my feelings more so than anything,
> but as far as really punching me or anything like that, never, except
> one time he tried to choke me....My sister was married to the same
> man for 19 years and he accused her of cheating on him and she
> hadn't and he accused her every time you turned around but that's
> because he cheated on her a lot and he kind of, you know, and men
> have this problem of they can't forgive, they truly can't, it's harder
> for a man to forgive in a situation than a woman. He kept telling

her she was cheating on him and she kept telling him she wasn't, so finally she did because he accused her so much. She said, "I'm being accused so much I might as well." So she slept with someone and so what happens is stupid of her. She found out that her husband was sleeping with her best friend and so he was accusing her of the guy and she was accusing him of the woman and then when she admitted it to him he lost it and I wasn't down there. He beat her so bad, he beat her so bad and I didn't know for almost one week and I talk to her almost every day. I did not know how bad he beat her until I saw the pictures. I mean he beat her black and blue from the top of her head to the bottom of her feet and he took the bed that they had slept in and he burned it so everybody would think she was a real slut, you know.

A 51-year old non-Hispanic man explained why a man in the vignette had thrown something at his female intimate:

She may have seen him talking to another girl or something, he may have seen her talking to another guy, jealousy ensues. Well, she probably saw him drinking at a bar with some lady. Okay, in her mind she put two and two together that they were, that he was cheating on her and she probably bottled up at home...and her kept going back and forth and you know, all of a sudden, he grabbed an ashtray and threw it at her.

These explanations of partner violence are consistent with both patriarchy theory and evolutionary theory. Patriarchy theory posits that, on a systemic level, violence is condoned as a means by which to control women. Violence, then, should not be an unexpected response to a man's lack of control, such as when he perceives that his partner has been unfaithful. Evolutionary theory posits that in complex societies, a high value is placed on obedience to the caretaker. A lack of obedience, such as that displayed through infidelity, provides a sufficient basis to utilize violence as a punishment. Analogous to this perspective, the evolutionary psychological model views sexual proprietariness as a psychological adaptation of the human male, i.e. laying claim to his territory. The battering of an unfaithful mate, then, represents an attempt to gain control over territory without directly confronting the threat (another male), which may be superior in strength. The evolutionary model of partner violence is similarly implicated in respondents' explanations that focuses on male hormones and evolution, discussed in the next section.

Male Hormones and Evolution. Approximately one-fifth of the non-Hispanic respondents and one-third of the Puerto Rican respondents attributed intimate violence to "male hormones," man's nature, or the evolutionary process. Interestingly, more women (30.8%) than men (26.3%) identified male violence as somehow being biologically inherent. The following, from a 45-year old non-Hispanic male, is representative of this perspective.

There's 2 to 3 women for every man. He's got choices. But that's very down the line. Man has never been monogamous. Women have been and that is part of our biological make-up and part of the social make-up. A man, the more pants he can get into, the happier he is. The only difference between the animals and us [is that] there's almost the same amount of males as there is females in human race while in all other animals, in males, there's less males than there is females. So that's why we don't go out there, but there isn't as many females to choose as to fight over in the animal kingdom and that, I think, has been inbred in us for probably over 4 million years, our ...human ancestors all the way up to now. We are animals and anybody that says we're not is a fool. We are animals. We can use our intellect, but we are animals. And Mother Nature still has control over us, no matter what. I think there was probably less violence when we used our instinct more than when we start using our intellect. Because [in] most of the animal kingdoms, the male does not really get violent towards the female....I think the worst animal on this planet is us. We're the only ones who kill each other.

Violation of Traditional Role, Power and Control. "Traditional role" refers here to references made by interviewees with respect to the function and expectations of men and women in heterosexual relationships and the functions and roles of the partners in a same-sex relationship. Responses to vignettes that attributed partner violence to violation of such roles consistently reflect issues at the juncture of sex and ethnicity, as exemplified by the following representative comments. One Puerto Rican woman, for instance, explained why a man threw something at his wife in a vignette:

He had a bad day at work, his dinner wasn't ready. She's a mother, she has kids, maybe her day didn't go well. So dinner wasn't prompt. A lot of Latinos, they pick up things and throw. That is true about the Latinos. You know, the Latinos, they are very jealous. See, a lot of Latino men like to have their wives, they like to beat them, impregnate them, have kids, and have them sit in the house.

A Puerto Rican man explained why the husband in a vignette injured his wife:

Maybe cause they like to come home and have dinner on the table and dinner's not. Now I've seen that a lot, they expect the wife to be [at home] when they get home and their dinner is served, especially the Spanish people. I been noticing that a lot, that they expect the wife to cater to them, you know, instead of a 50-50 thing, you know, one day, take turns or something.

Another Puerto Rican man explained why the vignette character forced the female to have sex against her will:

> He has a great desire to live with her, but she doesn't want to accept him, so he treats her badly, physically or sexually. Because she has religious customs and comes from good culture or a good family and she doesn't want a condition like that. She wants to have a home (*hogar*) to marry and be happy. I think that he, no, he comes from a lower (*baja*) family and he is accustomed and his parents are also living in a condition like that and so he wants a life like that. In this situation, she must explain to him point by point that she wants to have an engagement with him, pure, that she wants to have a good feeling in the house (*buena alma de casa*) and wants to be happy.

One married non-Hispanic male respondent explained the reasons underlying the violence between a man and a woman:

> Male is predominantly dominant, okay, he is the majority of the time the main breadwinner and he expects certain things. Like if a woman's home all day, he expects his dinner to be done. He expects his children to be raised like they're supposed to be, where he puts certain responsibilities on the woman and he does whatever the man's job is. There's like a division and it can get out of hand where either one or the other doesn't do the job that their social upbringing brings in my social upbringing. Cause the whole society is leaning towards matriarch [sic] and female domination and this is a big problem in today's relationships. It started with the war when women during the war were working in the factories to make money. Then, after the war the guys came home, the women still wanted to work because they had money, they had power, they're not going to listen to the husband anymore. The divorce rate went sky high because everybody wants everything....They forget what's their relationship, what's their duty in the relationship....The American white male is being stomped on. He's guilty of everything, of every social problem that exists. He created everything that's here today, all the good things we have and part of the bad things we have and it's very easy for someone to step in when the job is already done. And that causes a lot of problems today where it comes to violence.

One Puerto Rican woman explained partner violence by describing the differences between men and women and men's perceptions of women:

> For we women, we more quickly admit that something is bad or wrong, to see it, to understand it, it is easier for us, we have more opportunities, more compassion. You know what, the man, the machismo is like they feel that they are very macho, that they don't

have to lower themselves to anyone, that they are the chief, that
what they say is what goes, that they are strong even though they
are dead in the back, they are not going to show anything....It
could be that when he came home and she had her sister there with
her and the food wasn't ready and the house was dirty and he is an
egotistical man and he like it, you know, that when he arrives
home she is there for him and that she is very attentive to him and
this bothered him and he yelled at her that she is lazy (*baga*), that
she is useful for nothing, that look at the house, how dirty it is, that
the food isn't made, that if he leaves, nobody will want her because
she is good for nothing, not even in bed. You know what these
things do to somebody.

A much larger proportion of the Puerto Rican respondents (57.7%) attributed the
violence in the vignettes to role violation as compared to the Anglo respondents
(21.1%). On a broader, societal level, this greater reliance on role violation as an
explanation may reflect a relatively greater cultural investment in patriarchy. At the
dyadic level, however, role violation as an explanation may reflect a perceived
imbalance of power within the relationship and a consequent attempt by the male
partner to reassert his dominance. For instance, if according to cultural definition,
the male partner has the authority within the relationship but the female violates that
authority by failing to fulfill an expectation, violence provides a means by which to
restore the original balance of power. In this context, the male violent response
appears to constitute both an implicit acknowledgement of vulnerability and a
concomitant attempt to refute or negate the perceived loss of power.

Mental Illness. Mental illness also emerged from the responses to the vignettes
as a factor underlying partner violence. Significantly, the mental illness was
attributed to the partner displaying the violent behavior. This should be contrasted
with the responses of women in Romania to similar vignettes, described below, in
which the respondents attributed the mental illness to the individual who suffered
the violence. One Puerto Rican woman explained, for instance, why a woman
might stab her husband:

Okay, the possibility is that she could be ill, mentally restless and
needs medication. There were other situations in her life before
when she lost, a person tries to stab another, that wants to kill
another being, a lover, it is because she has lost, she has lost her
normal sound mind (*sus cabales mentales bien normales*) because
one human being defends another....When she has lost her mental
sense, she doesn't know what she is doing, she doesn't know what
has happened, it could be that she was abused physically, she could
have a chemical imbalance.

WOMEN'S PERCEPTIONS OF PARTNER VIOLENCE, ROMANIA

Background

Very little is known regarding the incidence or prevalence of intimate partner violence in Romania. The country is only now beginning to collect such data. For the period 1997 through 1998, a total of 544 cases of intimate partner violence committed against women were reported; 34 of these incidents resulted in the woman's death (USAID, 1999).

Several aspects of the Romanian context are particularly relevant to an understanding of both the occurrence of intimate partner abuse and women's responses to such treatment. These include, in particular, the legacy imprinted on Romanian society by Nicolae Ceaucescu prior to his downfall, a heritage of patriarchy dating back to before World War II, and an extraordinarily depressed economy.

The Ceaucescu Legacy

The rule of Nicolae Ceaucescu spanned a period of 23 years, from his 1965 assumption of the presidency, to his violent overthrow in December 1989. His regime was characterized by a level of fear that is almost inexplicable in its depth and pervasiveness. Ceaucescu's almost absolute control was fostered and maintained the arbitrary and often violent actions of the Romanian State Security Police (*Securitate*) (Treptoe, 1996) and the widespread surveillance of Romania's populace to suppress all internal dissent (Cockerham, 1999; Stokes, 1993). This surveillance was often effectuated through the coerced recruitment of family members and neighbors as informants for the benefit of the State. As a consequence, an atmosphere of extreme distrust even now surrounds most personal and social relationships, rendering cooperation between individuals difficult, at best (Hord, David, Donnay, and Wolf, 1991).

The ability of individuals to forge cooperative alliances was reduced even further through Ceaucescu's abolition of non-governmental organizations (Hord et al., 1991), resulting in the eradication of Romanian civil society. As a result, little technical expertise currently exists to develop and maintain such organizations that, in countries such as the United States and those of Western Europe, would be critical sources of support to individuals and communities. Ceaucescu's persecution of the clergy and the *Securitate*'s enlistment of both clergy and church-going individuals as informants eliminated the church as a source of solace or refuge from crisis.

A Heritage of Patriarchy

Prior to World War II, Romania was predominantly rural and was characterized by traditional patriarchal values and moral standards (Gilberg, 1979). These standards portrayed the ideal woman as subordinate, submissive, nurturing, and devoted to her family. A woman's virtue was judged in relation to her sexual passivity, thereby proscribing her enjoyment of sex. Men, however, were permitted significantly greater freedom; adultery and alcoholism were tolerated in exchange for the economic support of the family. Male superiority was presumed (Gilberg, 1979).

Following World War II, the government and communist party adopted these attitudes, first by eliminating sexuality as a topic of public discourse and, later, by attempting to control sexual relations. Unmarried couples were prohibited from sharing a hotel room. Early morning police checks of hotel rooms could result in a woman's conviction for prostitution, with no repercussions to the man involved (Harsanyi, 1993).

Education during Ceaucescu's regime reinforced and extended these standards. Women were taught to believe that sex outside of marriage, which was by definition without procreation as its objective, was both immoral and a cause of insanity. The ideal woman was one who sacrificed her individuality for the sake of the community and obeyed her father, her husband, and the State. Although women were touted as men's economic equals, social conditions mandated and sanctioned their dependence (David and Baban, 1996).

Women's limited ability to control their own lives was further curtailed by Ceaucescu's decree limiting the availability of abortion to women who (1) were over the age of 40, (2) had 4 or more children, (3) were endangered by the pregnancy, (4) suffered from a severe disease that could be transmitted or that could cause severe congenital malformations or (5) were pregnant as the result of rape or incest (Ceaucescu, 1966). Ceaucescu's 1985 modifications to this decree further restricted women's control by increasing the age at which abortion would be permitted from 40 to 45 and by prohibiting abortion to women who had fewer than 5 living children under the age of 18 (Ceaucescu, 1985). Ceaucescu declared "the fetus [to be] the socialist property of the whole society. Giving birth is a patriotic duty. Those who refuse to have children are deserters, escaping the law of natural continuity" (Ceaucescu, 1986: 217-218).

Concurrent with the implementation of the 1966 decree, the government instituted numerous pronatalist policies that further restricted women's freedoms. The included the award of tax incentives and monetary sums to couples who had children, the imposition of disincentives on childless couples and unmarried adults, the lengthening of the divorce process, and the cessation of the importation of contraceptives (David and Wright, 1971). This latter action was modified in 1985 to formally ban all forms of contraception (Hord et al, 1991). Women and their physicians were closely monitored for compliance with these restrictions through the imposition of monthly birth quotas on factory physicians and employees, the conduct by the Securitate of investigations of alleged abortions, the posting of agents in all maternity wards and obstetrical-gynecological clinics, and the imposition of prison terms on physicians who violated the abortion restrictions (David, 1990a,b,c). In essence, Ceaucescu's marriage between demographic concerns and nationalist policies turned women's bodies into instruments to be used in the service of the State (Kligman, 1992).

Current Romanian law continues to reflect the secondary status traditionally afforded to women. For instance, the imposition of any punishment for an act of violence against a spouse or partner acting in the capacity of a spouse is dependent upon the severity of the resulting injuries. Injury resulting in anything less than death or loss of an organ or body part, or in hospitalization for less than 60 days, is unlikely to be criminally penalized (Codul Penal art. 180, 181, 182).

The Romanian Economy

Romania is currently experiencing severe problems as a result of Ceaucescu's economic policies. Romania's population at the conclusion of Ceaucescu's regime was characterized as one "whose standard of living had been depressed to hitherto unseen levels" (Treptow, 1996: 567). This decline in economic status has been attributed to the hyper-centralization of the economy, severe resource misallocation, widespread shortages of consumer products and raw materials, and a demoralized labor force (Treptow, 1996). The gross domestic product (GDP) decreased by 13% in 1991 and by an additional 16% in 1992. Agricultural production declined by 14% from 1989 to 1990, while industrial production decreased by 22% from 1989 to 1991 and an additional 21.8% in 1992 (Europa Publications Limited, 1992, 1993). Health expenditures declined from 2.9% of the GDP in 1990 to 2.5% in 1996 (Cockerham, 1996). Inflation had reached 62% by the end of 1994, while exchange rates depreciated by 24.7% during the period from April 1994 through August 1995 (Treptow, 1996). As of 1995, over one-half of Romania's 23.5 million residents lived below the official poverty line of $160.00 per month (Cockerham, 1996).

Against this backdrop, we conducted this preliminary study to assess the incidence and prevalence of abuse against female partners, and to examine women's perceptions of such incidents.

Methods

The data for this study were collected between May 1998 and May 1999. Participants were recruited through family planning clinics and nongovernmental organizations providing educational, vocational, supportive, and referral services to women and their minor children. We conducted the study in two different regions of Romania: Bucharest and Iasi. Bucharest is the capital of Romania and the largest urban area. Consequently, it receives a disproportionate share of the nation's financial and human resources. Iasi, located in the northeastern region of Moldova, is the second largest urban area in Romania. Compared to Bucharest, it is reputed to be significantly poorer, ethnically more homogenous, and politically and socially more conservative. The areas of Bucharest and Moldova recently reported the highest numbers of partner assaults against women among all regions in Romania providing such statistics (USAID, 1999).

A total of 83 women volunteered to participate. Interviews were conducted in Romanian, with two-person teams consisting of a U.S. social worker or social work student and a Romanian physician or psychologist. All of the Romanian professionals conducting these interviews were fluent in both English and Romanian. In deference to the women's reluctance to have the interviews recorded on tape, a third person, fluent in both Romanian and English, joined each interview team as a note-taker. This individual recorded the interview as close to verbatim as possible.

The interview instrument consisted of three components: basic demographic questions, questions relating to the participant's experience with violence in general and with violence against themselves and effectuated by themselves against others, and questions relating to a series of vignettes. The interview instrument was translated from English to Romanian and then back-translated from Romanian to English to assure accuracy of translation.

The vignette portion of the interview consisted of 12 vignettes depicting varying interactions between the husband and the wife. These vignettes constituted Series 1 in the study above and are contained in Table 1, above. Study participants were presented with three randomly selected vignettes for examination. Each participant was asked to explain what might have caused the event to happen and what could and should be done and by whom. Interviewers were instructed to avoid using the words "violence" or "abuse" so as not to direct the interviewees' responses to the questions posed.

Results

Demographic Characteristics

The women interviewed ranged in age from 20 to 65; more than half (57.8%) were under the age of 30. Almost all (96.4%) reported that they were of Romanian ethnicity, while 2 women self-identified as Hungarian (2.4%) and 1 (1.2%) as Roma. Almost all (98.8%) were of the Orthodox faith. Slightly over half (59.0%) had completed high school; 10 (12%) had more than a college education. Slightly over half (57.8%) of the women were either married or living with an intimate partner at the time of the interview, 16.8% were separated or divorced, and the remainder (25.4%) were either never married or widowed. The women reported having from 1 to 7 children, with an average of 2.8 minor children. Only 14% of the women reported being unemployed. Household income ranged from the equivalent of $14.00 per month to more than $139.00 per month; approximately one-half (52.4%) of the women reported that their monthly household income was under $139.00.

Experience with Violence

The women's experience with violence was extensive. A total of 84.3% of the women reported ever having seen one person physically hurt another. Approximately one-quarter (26.5%) of the respondents reported that the violence they had seen was between intimate partners, while an additional quarter (25.3%) reported that the violence they had seen occurred between other family members, such as a parent and a child. Sixty-four of the 70 women who reported having seen violence (91.4%) characterized the physical "hurt" that they had seen as moderate to severe in nature; 7 of the 70 women (10.0%) reported that the violence had been so severe that it had necessitated immediate medical attention. Fifty-four (65.1%) of the women indicated that they had been a victim of physical violence at some point during their lives, while almost one-third (31.3%) reported that the violence was committed by their husband or an intimate male partner. Twelve of the women (14.4%) indicated that they had been the victim of violence during the previous year; 9 of these 12 women (75.0%) attributed the violence to their intimate partner.

The women also reported instances during which they had physically hurt another individual. Twenty-six of the women (31.3%) indicated that they had hurt another individual physically at some point during their lives; 23 of the 26 (88.5%) reported that the violence had been moderate. Of the 26 women reporting that they had physically hurt another individual, 4 (15.4%) indicated that their acts had been directed against an intimate partner, while 15 (57.7%) had committed acts of violence against a child. A total of 10 women (12.0%) reported that they had physically hurt another individual during the previous 12 months.

Responses to Vignettes: What Caused the Situation

The most common reasons cited as having caused the situations portrayed in the vignettes were similar to those proffered by women in Cuyahoga County: the male's level of stress resulting from a bad economic or employment situation, the male partner's use of alcohol, the male's jealousy, and the woman's failure to fulfill her responsibilities. Mental illness was also mentioned as a cause.

Economic Difficulties. Many women explained that the economic situation caused significant stress, resulting in violence. One woman, responding to the vignette in which the husband threw an object at his wife, explained, "Income is a problem. They must understand that their money must not rule." Another woman explained why a vignette husband hit his wife, leaving a bruise:

> Maybe he's upset because he has little money. You can't afford a
> normal life. The first problem is the money.

Alcohol. One woman explained the role of alcohol in bringing about the vignette situation in which the husband forced his wife to have sex, resulting in her injury. The vignette characters became interwoven with an account of her own situation:

> I didn't want to have sex. He beat me. He ripped off the clothes,
> and beat her, hit her. I ran to the children's room. He came in and
> became calm. Again, he was drunk, he wanted to quarrel. I didn't

give him any attention. He should ask can we make love...When I
saw my husband with a knife or drunk, I ran away.

Jealousy.   Jealousy was a common explanation for male violence against
intimates.   The respondents believed that jealousy could be triggered by even
minute variations in the woman's routine.   In one representative response, one
woman explained how the wife's delay at the supermarket led to her husband
stabbing her:

> Maybe because of her schedule, she took too long in the
> supermarket. She could be late and he could be suspicious and
> jealous...She must consider whether the next time she will be
> killed or maimed. She must consider whether she has enough
> courage to stay in the house with him.

Woman's Failure to Fulfill Responsibilities/Power. In response to a vignette in
which the husband slapped his wife, one woman told her own story:

> My husband slapped me. If I told him to do something, he was
> upset. I was working very hard, 10 to 12 hours a day. I was also
> with the children, so I asked him to help me. Now I don't trust
> anybody. If a man wants to be the leader of the family, then he
> must take care of them...He didn't hit me often, but when he hit
> me, I never called for a doctor or the police.... The last time we
> argued about money and he beat me and I went to the police and
> filed a statement but the policemen considered that I am crazy
> because I am melancholic [depressed]. I gave up my accusation
> [withdrew my complaint]. At the court they promised me that my
> husband will be forced to leave the house but now they don't do
> anything, so tell me, I am right or no when I say that there is no
> justice here.

A number of women commented on men's need for control or respect.   In a
representative comment, one woman described her own husband:

> He does not want to show me his good parts. He is afraid he won't
> be respected. He prefers to be a tough guy with me and to show
> affection to me. I have a bad opinion about this. I've told him
> there will always be problems if this is so between us. But he
> remains the same guy, a little too tough. He confuses me,
> sometimes he's sentimental, sometimes tough.

Another offered the following observation about the differences between men and
women:

All men are violent. The men are born violent. They have no patience, no feelings. Looking at history, what does patriarchy mean? It means violence, not with words. Women are sentimental, understanding; they search for solutions.

In contrast with the vignette response in the Cuyahoga County study above, in which many respondents attributed the battering to the assaultive partner's *perception* of the "wrongness" of the partner's behavior, many of the women in the Romania study attributed the men's violence to the *inherent "wrongness"* of the women's actions. For instance, one respondent explained in a representative response why the vignette husband threw something at his wife:

She said something wrong. Maybe she didn't cook, maybe she did a wrong thing. She showed disrespect regarding his friends or parents.

When asked if this was only the husband's perception that the wife had done something wrong, the respondent indicated that, in fact, the husband would not have had to throw something if the wife had acted appropriately. Similarly, a number of women perceived a male partner's use of force to obtain sex as a legitimate response to what they perceived as a wife's frigidity in not wanting to have sex with her husband. Many of the women interviewed indicated that it is a wife's duty to provide sex to her husband upon demand.

Mental Illness. Mental illness was offered as an explanation for the violence most often when the violence was perceived as quite severe. For instance, one woman explained, in response to the vignette in which the husband stabbed his wife, causing a bleeding wound, that "The devil took his mind," meaning that he was mentally ill.

DISCUSSION

The commonality of specific themes across both studies—economic difficulties, drugs and alcohol, jealousy and infidelity, failure of the women to fulfill responsibilities, mental illness—may reflect a commonality across women's experiences in relationships, irrespective of culture, religion, or political structure. The notable emphasis of the Romanian respondents on the inherent wrongness of the woman's failure to perform an act as expected, rather than the male character's attribution of "wrongness" to the failure to act, may be reflective of the relatively more entrenched level of patriarchy in Romanian society and generally lower level of tolerance for deviation from expected norms.

Among the Romanian respondents, 15 of the 54 women who had ever been the victim of violence (27.8%) indicated that they had committed violence against their children. This finding is consistent with the strong association noted between frequent child abuse and severe marital violence (Stark and Flitcraft, 1996; Straus, 1983). These data are also consistent with the social learning theory of violence, in that women who suffered violence as children later, as adults, inflicted violence on their own children.

The relatively high lifetime prevalence of violence reportedly experienced by women and men in the Cuyahoga County study (66.7%) and by women in the Romanian study (65.1%) must provoke an examination of violence, and partner violence in particular, in a broader context: Is violence to be considered deviant behavior in some way, thereby necessitating not only an individual-level response to it, but a formal, societal-level condemnation of it as well? This issue is explored in chapter 4.

4

VIOLENCE AS DEVIANCE? THE SOCIETAL RESPONSE

Nothing is perhaps so wasted in our culture as the energies of its women.

(Heilbrun, 1990)

INTIMATE PARTNER VIOLENCE AS DEVIANT BEHAVIOR

One approach to an examination of the societal response to intimate partner violence is to view it within the framework of deviance: does our society consider domestic abuse "normal," or is it to be considered "deviant," warranting a response as such? This approach requires first an exploration of what constitutes deviance.

What Is Deviance?

Perceptions of deviance vary widely. For instance, a 1965 (U.S.) study of public perceptions of deviance revealed wide diversity in what and who people classify as deviant: homosexuals (49% of responses), drug addicts (47%), alcoholics (46%), prostitutes (27%), murderers (22%), lesbians (13%), the mentally ill (12%), perverts (12%), communists (10%), and atheists (10%), to name a few (Simmons, 1965).

Various approaches have been offered in an attempt to better understand the nature of deviance. Thomas (1982) has identified three basic paradigms: social facts, social constructionist, and Marxian perspectives. The social facts perspective views persons as acted upon, separates theory and practice, emphasizes the primacy of "facts," and is essentially ahistorical. This paradigm encompasses biosociological theories of deviance, anomie theory, and conflict theory. (The theories of deviance are discussed in greater detail below.)

The social constructionist paradigm also views individuals as acted upon, maintains a distinction between fact and value, and emphasizes the primacy of the subject of knowledge. This paradigm encompasses labeling theory, existential sociology, and ethnomethodology. Research tends to search for the social meanings of deviance and an understanding of the social processes that gave rise to deviant behavior (Thomas, 1982).

Marxian perspectives focus on class relations. Deviance is seen as a reflection of the social arrangements of capitalism, and facts and values are inseparable. Theories classified as within the scope of Marxian perspectives include Marxian theory, critical criminology, and radical political economy. Theorists maintain that an understanding of deviance will ultimately yield greater understanding of larger social issues, such as the maintenance of class domination in society.

In contrast, Orcutt (1983) has suggested that deviance can be viewed two ways: (1) as behavior that violates social norms or (2) as behaviors that are defined as deviant by the social audiences viewing them. The former definition is termed the "normative" perspective, while the latter is termed "relativistic." Orcutt's classification will be followed here to examine the nature of deviance in greater depth.

The Normative Approach

The normative view of deviance is premised on the observation that rules or expectations for behavior, *i.e.* norms, are shared by members of a group or society (Orcutt, 1983). Although Edgerton (1985) premises his discussion of deviance on rule violation, the concept of the norm is closely related. Edgerton (1985: 24), for instance, has defined a rule as "a shared understanding of how people ought to behave and what should be done if someone acts in a way that conflicts with that understanding." Edgerton (1985: 24) further explains that

> rules may differ in the extent to which they are known, recognized, accepted as just or proper, and uniformly applied to members of the society. Rules may also vary in the severity of the sanctions that may be incurred by their violations as well as in their consistency of enforcement. They may vary in the degree to which they are internalized, in the mode of their transmission, and in the amount and kind of conformity they receive...[S]ome rules are relatively explicit while others are implicit, and some clear while others are ambiguous. Some rules contradict others, while others stand for the most part unchallenged.

A "norm" has been variously defined as

> a rule or a standard that governs our conduct in the social situations in which we participate. It is a societal expectation. It is a standard to which we are expected to conform whether we actually do so or not (Bierstedt, 1963: 222).

> legitimate socially shared guidelines to the accepted and expected patterns of conduct (Birenbaum and Sagarin, 1976: 11).

> shared convictions about the patterns of behavior that are appropriate or inappropriate for the members of a group; what group members agree they can, should, might, must, cannot,

should not, ought not, or must not do in any given situation (DeFleur et al., 1977: 620).

a rule which, over a period of time, proves binding on the overt behavior of each individual in an aggregate of two or more individuals. It is marked by the following characteristics: (1) Being a rule, it has a content known to at least one member of the social aggregate. (2) Being a binding rule, it regulates the behavior of any given individual in the social aggregate by virtue of (a) his having internalized the rule; (b) external sanctions in support of the rule applied to him by one or more other individuals in the social aggregate; (c) external sanctions in support of the rule applied to him by an authority outside the social aggregate; or any combination of these circumstances (Dohrenwend, 1959: 470)

[existing] when there are (1) agreements, or consensus, about the behaviors group members should or should not enact and (2) social processes to produce adherence to these agreements (Thibaut and Kelly, 1959: 239).

a rule, standard, or pattern for action... Social norms are rules for conduct. The norms are the standards by reference to which behavior is judged and approved or disapproved. A norm in this sense is not a statistical average of actual behavior but rather a cultural (shared) definition of desirable behavior (Williams, 1968: 204).

Several elements emerge from these definitions that permit us to better define what is meant by deviance: (1) consensus, both as to what constitutes a rule and a violation of that rule and (2) agreed upon consequences in response to that violation. A review of several definitions of deviance supports this conclusion:

Deviant behavior is conduct that is subject to social control (Black, 1976: 9).

[D]eviance constitutes only those deviations from norms which are in a disapproved direction and of sufficient degree to exceed the tolerance limits of a social group such that the deviation elicits, or is likely to elicit if detected, a negative sanction (Clinard and Meier, 1979: 14).

[Deviance is] any form of opposition to established rules, standards, or practices of elites; deviance may be a political label, a popular stereotype, or a form of sanctioned behavior. In conflict theory, deviance is political opposition to coercive control (Davis, 1975: 227).

Deviance is the name of the conflict game in which individuals or loosely organized small groups with little power are strongly feared by a well-organized, sizable minority or majority who have a large amount of power (Denisoff and McCaghy, 1973: 26).

Deviance is…the violation of a norm that somebody believes is important (Feldman, 1978: 5).

[D]eviant behavior refers to conduct that departs significantly from the norms set for people in their social statuses (Merton, 1966: 805). [W]e may define deviant behavior in terms of public consensus. We may define it as *any behavior considered deviant by public consensus that may range from the maximum to the minimum* (Thio, 1978: 23).

However, these definitions leave numerous questions unresolved: Whose consensus? Whose opinion is to be considered in "calculating" consensus and what weight is it to be given in that "calculation"? How many/what proportion of a group must agree for there to be consensus? Does the absence of a consequence to an act or behavior validate that behavior as a norm? What kind of reaction must occur for an act to be defined as or considered deviant? If norms change over time, does "deviance" also change? If so, what drives these changes? And yet additional issues are raised by the definitions of deviance. Deviance, according to some of these definitions, is linked to power (those who define deviance) or its absence (those who are defined as "deviant"). What constitutes deviance is linked to social status. And deviance may exist at the far end of a spectrum of tolerance. However, if classification of a behavior as deviant is linked to social status and power, then can the same behavior be classifiable as "not deviant" based on context and/or observer? If there exists a spectrum of tolerance with respect to individuals' acts or behaviors, is there also a spectrum of tolerance relating to the consequences that can be meted out in response to an act that is termed deviant?

LeVine (1982) has argued that deviance may result not only from norm or rule violation, but also from norm exaggeration. He posits that a cultural environment may induce individuals to behave in a manner that exaggerates "normal" and culturally distinctive behavior. He argues, for instance, that the relatively high rate of suicide among the Japanese may, in fact, be an exaggeration of the cultural value of self-sacrifice.

The degree to which individuals conform to a norm may vary. LeVine (1982), for instance, developed the idea of the J-curve. At the lower (left) side of the curve is a small percentage of individuals who regularly violate the norm. The center portion of the curve represents the percentage of individuals who have infrequently violated the norm and, for the most part, have conformed to it. The right side of the curve reflects the largest proportion of the population, those who have consistently acted in conformity with the norm.

Edgerton (1985) explored situations in which rule violations are not deemed to be acts of deviance. He noted, for instance, that some rules have exceptions. Others are only loosely enforced, while still others are enforced with surprising rigidity. Edgerton contrasts, as an example, the early Confucianist approach to rule violation with that of the later legalists. The early Confucianists stressed the flexibility of rules and the need for exceptions, whereas the legalists rejected the exceptions and instituted universal laws, applicable to all, regardless of status.

How is it that some rule violations will provoke a consequence while others are not enforced? How is it that some rules have exceptions? To some extent, this depends on the nature of the rule, as indicated, and on the status of the violator. However, the consequences may also turn on the account of the violation that is proffered by the violator (Edgerton, 1976). That account, or explanation, can exacerbate the violator's situation, excuse it, or justify it (Edgerton, 1976; Scott and Lyman, 1968). The process of account giving and consequence "is usually more akin to a negotiation than to a mechanical or impartial effort to support propriety or administer justice" (Edgerton, 1976: 30).

If we are to consider intimate partner violence as deviance within the paradigm of the norm, we must examine, then, whether there are rules against such behavior, whether there is a shared expectation regarding the non-commission of such behavior, and whether there are external sanctions for the violation of this norm. We must also consider whether, if a rule exists that prohibits intimate partner violence, situations also exist in which a violation of this norm will not be considered to be acts of deviance. The chapters focusing on the responses of the medical and legal systems to intimate partner violence are particularly instructive in assessing whether intimate partner violence is considered to be deviant in the context of the normative approach.

The "Social Audience" Approach

The "social audience" approach defines deviance quite differently, with an emphasis on those viewing the behavior rather than on a violation of a norm:

> Basically the ultimate measure of whether or not an act is deviant depends on how others who are socially significant in power and influence define the act....One could commit any act, but it is not deviant in its social consequences if no elements of society react to it (Bell, 1971:11).

> [A]cts and actors violating the norms of society will be termed "rule-breaking behavior" and "rule breakers," while the terms "deviant behavior" and "deviant" will be reserved for acts and actors labeled as deviant by a social audience (Cullen and Cullen, 1978: 8).

> Deviance is not a property *inherent* in certain forms of behavior; it is a property *conferred upon* these forms by the audience which directly or indirectly witness them (Erikson, 1962: 308).

Ben-Yehuda (1990:36) has argued that "who interprets whose behavior, why, where, and when is very crucial...." He offers two specific examples, those of Joan of Arc and of the Nobel Laureate chemist Louis Pauling. Joan of Arc, convicted of being a heretical deviant and executed in 1431, was later canonized by Pope Benedict XV. Pauling, supported by thousands of scientists from all over the world, lobbied the United Nations in the late 1950s to end nuclear weapons testing. His efforts led to an interrogation by the U.S. Senate and he was prohibited from attending various international scientific meetings. In 1962, he was awarded the Nobel Prize for his efforts in promoting peace (Ben-Yehuda, 1990).

However, the "social audience" definition is also unable to address all issues satisfactorily. Kitsuse's (1962: 253) definition of deviance underscores some of the difficulties with this approach:

> Forms of behavior per se do not differentiate deviants from non-deviants; it is the responses of the conventional and conforming members of the society who identify and interpret behavior as deviant which sociologically transform persons into deviants.

It is unclear, however, what kind of response, both in nature and degree, is either necessary or sufficient to merit classification of a particular behavior as deviant. It is also unclear what kind of acts, both in nature and degree, are necessary or sufficient to provoke a necessary and sufficient response. If there is no response to certain acts, such as murder and torture, can it be said that these acts are not "deviant?" The same could be asked of intimate partner violence: if there is no response, from either the victim or from the larger society, or if the responses that are evoked are minimal, can it be said that such violence is not deviant? But, if these acts are inherently "deviant," regardless of audience response, can it really be said then that classification as "deviant" rests entirely on definition by the audience, without reference to a norm?

Definitions of Deviance Compared

These varying approaches appear to have implications at the individual and societal levels. If, for instance, a "deviant" is anyone who has ever violated a norm, then it would appear that almost all adults are somehow deviant. (Does deviance then become the norm?) If one relies upon the social audience's evaluation of the behavior, then any individual who is labeled as deviant, regardless of the form, *e.g.,* mental illness, drug use, etc., is, in fact, deviant.

The social audience approach appears to take a more relativistic approach than does the normative view. For instance, pursuant to the normative approach a colonial-period wife who defied her husband, who then had her placed in the pillary for public display, would be considered deviant. The social audience approach, however, permits varied responses to the wife's and the husband's behavior (Suchar, 1978). A slave suffering from drapetomania, *i.e.* running away from his white master, could be considered deviant based on a normative view, as framed by those in power, but could be seen as not deviant based on a social audience perspective, *e.g.,* if the "audience" consists of abolitionists (Conrad and Schneider, 1980).

Neither of these basic approaches takes a synchronic view of deviance. Ben-Yehuda (1985) has argued that deviance can be understood only in the context of larger social process and change and stability. Various other researchers have suggested that deviance must be examined in a dynamic historical and political perspective (Terry and Steffensmeier, 1988; Scull, 1984; Piven, 1981). A brief history of the treatment of partner violence in the United States is presented below, in order to provide a more synchronic perspective.

A Synchronic View of Intimate Partner Violence

The Puritans

Pleck's (1987) extensive study of domestic violence indicates that family violence was not accepted within the Puritan community of colonial times. A man who beat his wife was characterized as one who "shames his profession of Christianity, [who] breaks the Divine law, [who] dishonours God and himself, too" (Wadsworth, 1712: 25, quoted in Pleck, 1987: 18). A woman who beat her husband was a "shame to the profession of Christianity; she dishonours God and provokes the glorious God, tramples his Authority under her feet; she not only affronts her Husband, but also God her Maker, Lawgiver and Judge" (Wadsworth, 1712: 36, quoted in Pleck, 1987: 18). Neighborly surveillance helped to maintain at least the appearance of domestic tranquility, particularly when threatened with potential accusations of witchcraft in response to a failure to conform. Transgressions were punishable by public confession in church and a promise to reform (Pleck, 1987).

The enactment of the Massachusetts *Body of Liberties* served to prohibit wife-beating; a later amendment prohibited husband-beating as well. However, the Puritans prioritized the preservation of the family above the physical protection of beating victims and, consequently, infrequently granted divorce and often promoted reconciliation (Pleck, 1987).

Gradually, however, the intimate bonds between church, family, and state were eroded due to the increasing heterogeneity of the community resulting from immigration of diverse nationalities from the Old World, the increased pressure from the Crown to conform to English law, and the failure of many young Puritans to gain full church membership (Pleck, 1987).

Post-Civil War to the Early 1900's

Examination of divorce complaints filed in Los Angeles in the post-Civil War period indicates that many were premised on what we would now call marital rape: the forcing of a wife to engage in intercourse by her husband (May, 1975). Nineteenth century rape laws did not specify whether a husband could be prosecuted for the rape of his wife; such exemptions were not established until the twentieth century (Pleck, 1987). Attempts in Massachusetts in the 1870s to enact statutes that would protect women from the abuse of their husbands by permitting divorce and awarding custody and support payments to the wife met with defeat. However, legislation permitting wife-beating husbands to be punished at the whipping-post was enacted in Maryland in 1882, Delaware in 1901, and Oregon in 1905 (Pleck, 1987). Although such measures were proposed in other states, they were never adopted. Underlying the support for such legislation was the belief that the abusive husband would be deterred from beating his wife by the threat of the severe pain that would be engendered by the whipping (Pleck, 1987). Opponents of the punishment argued that the state was needlessly inflicting pain and degrading the men, while others asserted that wife beating resulted from uncontrolled passion and, accordingly, such men were immune to rehabilitative efforts. Surprisingly, Theodore Roosevelt addressed the issue of wife-beating in his 1904 annual message to Congress:

> The wifebeater...is inadequately punished by imprisonment; for imprisonment may often mean nothing to him, while it may cause hunger and want to the wife and children who have been the victim of his brutality. Probably some form of corporal punishment would be the most adequate way of meeting this crime (in Israel, 1977: 2116).

World War I and Beyond

Courts of domestic relations first came into being in Buffalo in 1910, as an extension of the juvenile court (Pleck, 1987). Many of these judges believed that cases involving domestic violence were not truly criminal cases and that those appearing before the courts were not hardened criminals. A complaint from the wife of physical abuse was the most frequent impetus for the appearance of a couple before such courts. The official judicial position was one of reconciliation, due in large part to the women's inability to provide for herself and her children economically. The court procedures were devised so as to discourage separation and divorce: interviews with the women bringing such complaints, inspections of the women's housekeeping, and encouragement by the caseworker to return to her home. Apart from divorce or reconciliation, the only existing alternative within the legal system was a separation and the provision by the husband to the wife of support payments (Pleck, 1987).

The 1920s and 1930s saw a decline among caseworkers of a moralistic approach to partner violence, and the existence of an increasingly therapeutic approach. Concomitantly, Freud's theories greatly influenced other analysts who focused on the psychology of women. Deutsch (1930), for instance, argued that women are innately more masochistic than men; that a young girl is at first furious at her father for the presumed loss of her penis, where there exists only a clitoris; and, ultimately, that the girl's sadistic fantasies resulting from her rage at the loss of her penis are ultimately turned inward to combine pain and sexual pleasure. Horney (1935), however, contested this explanation, asserting instead that masochism was abnormal in women and that, when it existed, it was manifested by low self-esteem, submission, and the use of helplessness and weakness to manipulate men. Ultimately, it was Deutsch's view that most impacted psychiatry. Women's complaints of abuse were transformed into unconscious encouragement of their husbands' brutality, and the women's own unconscious dependencies and sexual tensions (Pleck, 1987). During this same period, American popular culture as expressed and seen through Hollywood equated male domination through the use of force with love, and female submission with fulfillment.

Renzetti (1999) has argued that the notion of deviance is once again being applied to the victim of battering, in addition to or instead of the assaultive partner. In support of this premise, she notes that women who fight back against their attackers are increasingly being ordered by the courts to attend batterers' treatment programs under mandatory arrest policies and that judges often order mutual restraining orders against the assailant and the victim. Renzetti (1999: 48) has explained how victims themselves come to be viewed as the deviant party:

> A worthy victim is innocent of wrongdoing. The notion of "wrongdoing" here rests on certain assumptions about femininity—in particular, *respectable* femininity. A woman may deviate from the standards of respectable femininity in at least two ways. One is by not behaving as a lady should—for example, drinking or using drugs, dressing "seductively," having an extramarital affair....[A] woman who has been abused may be deemed a worthy victim, but when she uses violence against her intimate partner, she is no longer innocent. Her "unladylike" behavior discloses her culpability in her own victimization.
>
> A second, not unrelated way in which a woman can violate social standards of femininity is by being too much like a man. Women who engage in behavior stereotyped as masculine are deemed abnormal and certainly ineligible for worthy victim status.

Felder and Victor (1996: 21) have similarly argued that society continues to view the victim as the deviant actor, asking "Why didn't she just leave?" Instead, responses to the violence should consist of queries that more appropriately focus on the behavior of the batterer and potentially concrete solutions to abate the violence:

> "How can that man get away with that?"
> "Where were the police?"
> "Was he arrested?"
> "Was he thrown out of his house?"
> "Will he stand trial and be convicted and serve a stiff jail sentence?"
> "Will the victim get police protection, financial aid, medical care, legal advice, child support?"
> "How will that woman and her children survive, financially and emotionally?" (Felder and Victor, 1996: 21)

This extremely brief foray into the social history of partner violence demonstrates that our response to it has not been consistent across time or place. Responses to domestic violence have assumed various forms, as do responses to what is perceived as deviance. This characterizes, as well, our contemporary views of domestic violence, its causes, and its remedies.

Theories of Causation

A number of the theories as to what causes deviance are not dissimilar from those that have been formulated to explain intimate partner violence. Edgerton (1976) has grouped theories of deviance causation into five categories: (1) social strain; (2) subcultural conflict; (3) psychological defense or commitment; (4) biological defect; and (5) human nature. This classification scheme is followed below, with references to contrasting classification schemes. These theories are compared to those discussed above that have been formulated specifically to explain partner violence.

Strain Theory

Strain theory (Merton, 1968, 1964, 1959, 1938) is premised on the assumption that man is highly moral and both respects and internalizes the rules of society. Consequently, deviant behavior is unlikely under normal circumstances. However, individuals will engage in deviant behavior if a major disjunction exists between their goals and the legitimate means by which they can be achieved ("strain"). Strain can also be characterized as an imbalance between ability and responsibility (McGrath, 1970). This theory of deviance provided the impetus for the "opportunities" programs and policies in the United States during the 1960s (Rosenfeld, 1989; Short, 1975).

Merton (1938) postulated that people will experience anomie when their ability is inferior to the responsibility of role performance that is required to achieve socially emphasized goals. Anomie also implies confusion, disorientation, and relationships that are meaningless and/or insubstantial (Durkheim, 1951). Anomic individuals, then, seek predictable social order and security, a state in which their abilities are consonant with the demands that are placed upon them.

Alienation has been considered as the opposite end of the continuum of social experience from anomie (Coser, 1969). Mitchell (1984: 332) defined alienation as "a kind of disjuncture between goals and means," which can lead to forms of deviance, e.g., actively seeking out instability to address the sense of alienation.

Both anomie (Merton, 1938) and alienation (Mitchell, 1984), then, can lead to deviance. Anomic and alienated individuals may utilize any of four means of adaptation to strain: innovation, ritualism, retreatism, and rebellion.

Ritualism may take the form of either a reduction of aspirations to conform to available opportunities or an intentional restriction of abilities due to the lack of meaningful challenges. Mitchell (1984) illustrates the former with the example of a husband and a wife who accept their current unhappy marriage and abandon all hopes for a creative experience.

Innovation refers to the acceptance of creative self-expression as a goal and the concomitant rejection of conventional approaches to achieve that goal. A dissatisfied husband, for instance, may choose to have an extramarital affair (Roy, 1974), while a frustrated homemaker may engage in shoplifting (Cameron, 1964). Physical aggression and abuse within the home may also constitute an attempt to effect a meaningful impact within the context of one's primary role (McKinley,

1964). However, innovation may also represent the relatively unexplored "positive" side of deviance. Douglas (1977), for instance, argued that "creative deviance" warrants further examination:

> Deviance is the only mutation that is generally destructive of society, but it is also the only major source of creative adaptations of rules to new life situations.

Retreatism represents a rejection of the possibility of creative self-expression within the context of primary roles (Mitchell, 1984). Rebellion involves a complete restructuring of one's perceptions, such as through the adoption of a different religion (Mitchell, 1984).

At least some empirical evidence appears to support strain theory. Young (1989) found in his study of 113 undergraduate students that alienation as measured by Dean's Alienation Scale was associated with self-reported criminal deviance in men, such as property crimes, violence, the use and sale of illicit substances, and drinking while intoxicated. No such relationship was noted among the female study participants.

Conflict Theory

Subcultural Conflict. Subcultural conflict theory, also known as the theory of differential association (Sutherland and Cressey, 1960), posits that individuals behave in a manner that is consistent with the expectations of their reference group, but these expectations may differ from and conflict with the expectations of the dominant society. As a consequence, that dominant culture defines the subgroup behavior as deviant. (To an extent, then, subcultural conflict theory dovetails with social audience theory in that what is considered deviant flows from its labeling as such by others.) Sutherland (1956: 20) provided an example of this dichotomy:

> This lack of homogeneity is illustrated in extreme form in the criminal tribes of India. Two cultures are in sharp conflict there. One is the tribal culture which prescribes certain types of assault on persons outside the tribe, in some cases with religious compulsions. The other is the legal culture as stated by the Indian and provincial governments and made applicable to the criminal tribes....When members of the tribe commit crimes, they act in accordance with one code and in opposition to the other. According to my theory, the same principle or process exists in all criminal behavior, although the conflict may not be widely organized or sharply defined as in the Indian tribe.

Not surprisingly, this theory has been used to explain juvenile delinquency by relating a youth's actions to those of the members of his or here reference groups (Edgerton, 1976).

Kornhauser (1978) has criticized this theory, arguing that it assumes that (1) socialization is always successful; (2) individuals are incapable of violating the social norms of the group to which they belong; (3) everyone completely internalizes social norms and conforms to them; and (4) belief in the norms of a group is sufficient to ensure compliance with these norms. Kornhauser concludes that because individuals must conform to the norms of their referent group, individuals cannot be classified as deviant. Rather, subgroups or subcultures are deviant. This theory of deviance is analogous to the culture of violence theory used to explain the genesis of intimate partner violence (see above).

Marxist Conflict Theory. Although not discussed by Edgerton, the Marxist approach to deviance represents one form of conflict theory. Marxist conflict theory holds that deviance results from an unjust structure of economic institutions which, in turn, impact on a society's social and political institutions. The structure of the society in general, then, is "criminogenic" (Beirne and Quinney, 1982; Greenberg, 1981).

Psychological Defense or Commitment

Sociopath/psychopath. Edgerton (1976) has included four theories of deviance within the larger category of psychological defense theory: psychopathology and sociopathology, social learning theory, reaction formation, and labeling. The psychopath/sociopath lacks a concern for morality and his/her fellow individuals. Consequently, such individuals can commit heinous crimes without regret or remorse. Such persons can be constrained only through fear of externally imposed punishment.

Social Learning Theory. Although Edgerton (1976) has classified social learning theory as a type of psychological defense, it should be noted that other researchers consider social learning theory and subculture theory to be interrelated (Akers, 1996; Orcutt, 1983). Although there are numerous permutations of social learning theory, its basic premises include the following: (1) criminal behavior is learned in much the same way as any other behavior; (2) criminal behaviors result from perceived reinforcement from a person's environment; and (3) primary groups are the major source of reinforcement (Burgess and Akers, 1966). The social learning theory of deviant behavior is akin to the social earning theory of family violence.

Reaction Formation. Reaction formation refers to a rejection of something perceived as unacceptable or dangerous to the self through the adoption of apparently oppositional behaviors and attitudes (Edgerton, 1976). Although Edgerton has placed this theory within the psychological defense framework, Orcutt (1983) views it instead as a component of subcultural conflict theory. Cohen (1955), in fact, relied upon Merton's strain theory and Sutherland's subcultural theory as the basis for his explanation of youth's participation in destructive and malicious activities.

Cohen (1955) hypothesized that "working class" youth aspire to achieve success as it is defined by middle class standards. However, they become frustrated at their inability to meet middle class expectations, e.g., in school, and develop a sense of personal inadequacy as a result. In response to this adjustment crisis, the youths formulate a collective response: delinquent subculture, through which they establish new norms. These new norms define various behaviors as appropriate precisely because they are in opposition to those of the dominant culture. Consequently, behaviors such as aggressiveness and vandalism are rewarded.

Cloward and Olin (1960) also extended the work of Sutherland, Merton, and Cohen as it relates to subcultural conflict theory. (It is discussed here because it flows directly from the work of Cohen which, using Edgerton's schema, falls within the category of psychological defense.) Cloward and Olin (1960) theorized that opportunities to engage in illegitimate activities, like legitimate activities, vary between and within economic strata. Consequently, differing social conditions give rise to different expressions of delinquency. Lower class adolescents tend to form in communities in which illegitimate opportunity is open. Conflict subcultures are more likely to form in lower class areas where adult crime is not highly organized and illegitimate opportunity is closed to adolescents. Retreatist subcultures, which are organized around drug use, represent lower class youths' double failure due to the unavailability of both legitimate and illegitimate opportunities.

Sykes and Matza (1957) have questioned Cohen's portrayal of delinquent youth as contracultural. They assert, instead, that delinquent youth do not conform to values and norms that are in direct opposition to the dominant culture. Rather, they temporarily loosen their commitment to dominant culture's values and share rationalizations to justify a particular action, e.g., they are not stealing a care but "borrowing" it, which permits a denial of the victim and implies that no one is hurt by the action.

Labeling. Edgerton's (1976) fourth category of psychological defense/commitment is that of labeling, also known as social audience theory (Orcutt, 1983), the interactionist theory of deviance (Becker, 1973), and an offshoot of symbolic interactionism (Blumer, 1969; Mead 1934). Erikson (1962: 308) has explained:

> Deviance is not a property inherent in certain forms of behavior; it is a property conferred upon these forms by the audiences which directly or indirectly witness them. Sociologically, then, the critical variable in the study of deviance is the social audience.

Lemert (1951) has explained how this dynamic comes about. He notes that norms vary across time and place. He asserts that members of society become aware of norms only after they have been violated. Such deviation can be measured objectively:

> [T]he sum total of deviation in a given situation will consist of the variance of the actions from the prescribed social norms multiplied by the number of persons who engage in such actions (Lemert, 1951: 51).

The societal response to this deviation corresponds to the degree and visibility of the deviation. In some cases, the response is extreme in proportion to the actual breach. Lemert (1951: 56) explains such "spurious" reactions as the result of "rivalry or conflict of groups...as they aspire to power or struggle to maintain their position."

Lemert distinguished between primary deviation, which refers to instances of norm violation in which individuals do not view themselves as deviant, and secondary deviation. Secondary deviance arises from the societal response to primary deviance:

> When a person begins to employ his deviant behavior or a role based upon it as a means of defense, attack. or adjustment to the... problems created by the consequent societal reaction to him, his deviation is secondary (Lemert, 1951: 76).

Becker (1963) expanded on Lemert's theory by identifying distinct aspects of the social audience's role: (1) the formulation of rules; (2) the application of these rules; and (3) the labeling of particular individuals as outsiders or deviants. The process through which individuals are so labeled often depends more on who is doing the labeling and who is being labeled than on the nature of the behavior involved. Consequently, behavior cannot be labeled as deviant until after the response has occurred. Becker (1963: 9) explained:

> Social groups create deviance by making the rules whose infraction constitutes deviance, and by applying those rules to particular people and labeling them as "outsiders." From this point of view, deviance is not a quality of the act the person commits, but rather a consequence of the application by others of rules and sanctions to an offender. The deviant is one to whom that label has successfully been applied; deviant behavior is that people so label.

Kitsuse (1962) posited that audiences create deviance through a three-stage process: (1) interpretation of behavior as deviant; (2) definition of individuals who engage in that behavior as deviant; and (3) response to the individual(s) in a manner considered appropriate to the specific type of deviance. An individual is not considered deviant until the third stage, when he or she is subject to the verbal or physical repercussions of the behavior.

Lauderdale and colleagues (1984) explored the relationship between external threat and deviance, in an attempt to better understand when and why behavior and individuals are labeled as deviant. Their research revealed that (1) the level of threat is directly related to the extent of rejection and negative definition of a group member; (2) high-status actors are more involved in the rejection of the "deviant"; and (3) the level of group solidarity is related to the extent of rejection and negative definition, e.g., a severely threatened group appears to regain solidarity following the designation of an individual as deviant.

Reese and Katovich (1989) have examined the role of temporality in audience perception of deviance. Specifically, whether an act will be labeled as deviant is directly tied to its timing, frequency, duration, tempo, rhythm of occurrence, sequencing within the context of other acts, and chronicity. Whether a person is labeled "alcoholic," for instance, depends on the frequency, timing, sequencing, and chronicity of his or her drinking. Absence from school can constitute truancy only if it occurs during certain time intervals, i.e., weekdays when school is in session.

Raybeck (1991) has posited that (1) deviance is a matter of degree and (2) labeling occurs less frequently in simple than in complex societies. Raybeck distinguishes between soft deviance which, although inconsistent with cultural and social norms, does not threaten the social order and hard deviance, which does endanger the social order. (Note the reliance on rule/norm violations, despite the overriding emphasis on labeling.)

Raybeck further argues that labeling serves to increase the predictability of social life. Labeling in simple societies, he further argues, does little to increase the already predictable social life. Additionally, because labeling individuals serves to exclude them from various activities or statuses, labeling would have a severe impact on relationships in small-scale societies.

Raybeck (1991) supports his position with the results of various ethnographic studies. He notes that although the !Kung engage in mild labeling through the use of nicknames, they are greatly concerned with group acceptance. Consequently, they attempt to conform to group rules as much as possible. The Kalantanese of Malaysia, a peasant society, although generally unconcerned about behaviors that violate state and national laws, are extremely concerned with behaviors that represent a threat to the community's welfare. Raybeck (1991) further relies on Hollos' (1976) description of changes within a Norwegian mountain farming community as evidence for his view. Prior to industrialization, strong consensus about norms and values existed in the village. Following industrialization and increased complexity, one faction of the community advocated for the imposition of formal sanctions and engaged in labeling to a greater degree than in the past.

Savishinsky (1991) has expanded labeling situations to encompass situations in which the audience deliberately provokes the deviant behavior in the actor, e.g., the provocation of German employers by Bahamian workers into a public rage that they themselves would not display. Savishinsky asserts that such staged situations are characterized by (1) informal and essentially nonpunitive responses; (2) both pleasure and disapproval on the part of the audience; and (3) a lack of awareness on the part of the actors as to the meanings attributed to their behavior by the audience. Sagarin and Kelly (1982) have similarly relied on labeling theory to explain staged situations that are deliberately created and manipulated by an "agent provocateur, " i.e. a government agent placed within an organization or movement who encourages, suggests, and supports activities that, while seemingly beneficial to the movement, will ultimately discredit it and its members.

Various researchers have argued that the media is directly responsible for encouraging audience interpretation of behavior as deviant and for provoking a negative response or sanction. Erikson and colleagues (1987) posit that journalists serve as information brokers who reproduce knowledge about what they consider to be newsworthy. Such "newsworthiness" often encompasses crime and crime control and the nature and acceptability of the account preferred by the actor(s). For many individuals featured in the news, '[d]eviance constitutes their very "news value"....' (Gitlin, 1980: 152). McLeod (1995) has demonstrated empirically with his use of media reports of social protests how subtle differences in media portrayal of events and accounts can affect audience perceptions of the protesters and the police response.

Labeling theory has been applied not only to criminal behavior, but also to mental illness (Scheff, 1974, 1966; Szasz, 1961, 1960; Goffman, 1961), physical disability (Scott, 1969; Freidson, 1966), mental retardation (Mercer, 1973), and victimless crimes, such as addiction (Schur, 1965). It has provided a foundation for attribution theory, which posits that audience reactions, i.e. perception of deviance, is directly dependent on audience perceptions of the situation and the cause of the actor's behavior (Hawkins and Tiedeman, 1975; Prus, 1975). It has also been extended to encompass self-labeling processes, by which individuals internalize both social norms and negative societal attitudes regarding norm violation (Kaplan, Jasinski, and Bailey, 1986; Thoits, 1985).

Labeling theory may be critical to an understanding of how and why responses to intimate partner violence have changed over time, as indicated by the brief historical overview presented at the beginning of this chapter. It is not the behavior itself that has changed. Rather, it may be the level of visibility of such behavior and its consequences that, in addition to context, are chiefly responsible for the variations in societal response and the response of help-providers. (See chapters 5 and 6, respectively, for a discussion of the health and legal systems' responses to partner violence.)

Biological Defect

Edgerton (1976) include in this category explanations of deviance that are premised on biological causes, such as genetics (Rosenthal, 1970), improper nutrition (Birch and Gussow, 1970), and birth trauma (Windle, 1969). To this list can be added mental deficiency (Goring, 1913), feeblemindedness (Goddard, 1912), physical stigmata (Lombroso, 1911), and chromosomal abnormalities (Jacobs, Brunton, and Melville, 1965). Biology has been linked to "deviances" such as homosexuality, aggression, and mental illness (Edgerton, 1976). This theory is analogous in some respects to the evolutionary theory of partner violence, described earlier, which posits that intimate partner violence may be attributable to an evolved genetic mechanism.

Human Nature

Edgerton's (1976) final explanation of deviance posits that human beings are equally disposed to deviance and to conformity. This theory is generally referred to as "social control theory" (Hirschi, 1969). Social control theory is based on the assumption that it is conformity, rather than deviance, that is problematic. People will commit deviant acts, given an opportunity, if those acts will provide them with immediate benefit(s), regardless of the long-term consequences (Hirschi and Gottfredson, 1994). Individuals refrain from deviancy because they are bonded to conventionality. That bond consists of four elements: commitment, attachment, involvement, and beliefs.

Commitment refers to an individual's investments in conventional activities that could be placed in jeopardy through delinquent conduct. Attachment refers to the emotional ties that have been established with conventional others, such as parents. Involvement concerns the time and energy that have been invested in conventional activities. The fourth and final element of beliefs refers to the legitimacy that one attributes to conventional moral prohibitions against deviant acts. Clearly, then, one of social control theory's underlying assumptions is the existence of a single set of beliefs in society, which constitute the conventional moral order (Hirschi, 1969). Additionally, control theory assumes the existence of two types of control mechanisms: external mechanisms such as community and inner mechanisms such as conscience (Ben-Yehuda, 1990).

There is some empirical evidence to support Hirschi's theory. McGee and Newcomb (1992), for instance, found in their longitudinal study of adolescence and adulthood that social conformity was moderately to strongly negatively correlated with drug use and criminal behavior (stealing, confrontational acts such as physical fights, and property damage.)

There are parallels between Edgerton's theory of human nature and Gelles' exchange theory of partner violence. Each assumes that specified acts will be committed if the opportunity to do so is present and if those acts result in an immediate benefit. Gelles postulated that the isolation of the nuclear family from a broader context would result in the reduction of costs associated with battering behavior, thereby facilitating its occurrence. Similarly, the social control theory of deviance posits that a reduction or elimination of external mechanisms to compel or promote conformity will encourage the commission of deviant behavior.

Responses to Deviance

An examination of responses to deviance necessarily requires an examination of both the response of the "deviant" actor and of those witnessing the deviance. These responses can be compared to those of the health and legal systems, discussed in chapters 5 and 6, respectively, and those of the batterer, discussed in chapter 7.

Audience Response

Gove (1982) has delineated various classes of responses to deviance: social reaction, deterrence, prevention, incentives, treatment, amelioration, and self-curative. To these can be added acceptance (Bogdan and Taylor, 1987). The literature relating to each of these strategies is extensive and will only be touched upon briefly.

Social Reaction. This strategy of response advocates the redefinition of a situation so that the behavior initially viewed as a problem is no longer viewed as such. This type of response is exemplified by the rejection of forcible intercourse within marriage as rape; the failure to define the behavior as a criminal act or problem essentially negates its existence and the need to address it at all.

Deterrence. Punishment is one of the most common strategies for dealing with deviant behavior. The use of a deterrence approach is premised on operant theory, which posits that individuals perform an act when the rewards of that act exceed the costs (Gove, 1982). Operant theory suggests, then, that punishment, as in the criminal justice system, must be systematically and rapidly applied. Neither, however, occurs, due to a variety of reasons, including overburdening of the courts and plea bargaining (Gove, 1982). The failure of criminal punishment of partner violence to effectuate long-term behavioral change of the batterer is addressed in chapter 6.

Prevention. This strategy focuses on the identification of what is perceived to be the weak link in a complex causal process and the manipulation of that link in order to prevent the potentially developing deviance. This strategy encompasses a broad range of interventions, including legislation, such as gun control measures (Gove, 1982), increased religious participation (Bainbridge, 1989; Tittle and Welch, 1983), education (Gove, 1982), and the provision of employment opportunities (Covington, 1986). This approach to the prevention of deviance is analogous to attempts to prevent occurrences of partner violence through the development of punitive legislation and the establishment of mandatory counseling programs for batterers. These measures are discussed in chapter 7.

Incentives. Gove (1982) notes that the use of incentives to reward nondeviant behavior, thereby encouraging nondeviant behavior while simultaneously discouraging deviant behavior, is rarely utilized. Possible examples might include school incentive programs to encourage reading or attendance and employee incentive programs to encourage attendance and discourage absences. It is more difficult to conceive of systemic incentivex as a reward for not beating one's partner.

Treatment. Treatment is one of the most common responses to deviance and often occurs in response to deviance forms that have become medicalized, such as gambling (Rosecrance, 1985) and exhibitionism (Marshall, Ecles, and Barbaree, 1991). The form of the treatment necessarily depends on the form of deviance or malady. The Kamba, for instance, often combine drugs and magical treatment in their attempts to cure psychosis, whereas the Hehe generally rely on drugs (Edgerton, 1966). In the United States, we have used a variety of means to treat mental illness, including hydrotherapy (Farmer, 1994), lobotomy, medications, and institutionalization (Chesler, 1989). "Treatment" of the battering and the battered partners is discussed in chapters 7 and 8.

Self-Curative. Gove (1982) indicates that some forms of deviance are believed to be self-curative, e.g., an individual will "grow out of it." As an example, this author has been informed by various physicians in Laos and Thailand that homosexuality is normal through adolescence, and that individuals are expected to "grow out of it" by the time they reach their late teens. The behavior is seen as deviant only after mid- to late adolescence when the "self-cure" has not taken root.

Similar beliefs exist in the domain of intimate partner violence, whereby it is believed that battering behavior may be less frequent and/or less severe among older couples because the individuals may have grown too old, less energetic, and more accustomed to each other to continue in this pattern of behavior. This belief, however, is contradicted by the frequency of abuse between elder partners and the observation that such abuse may be partner abuse grown old (Matlaw and Spence, 1994).

Acceptance. Bogdan and Taylor (1987:35) define acceptance as a

> [relationship]...between a person with a deviant attribute and another person, which is of long duration and characterized by closeness and affection and in which the deviant attribute does not have a stigmatizing, or morally discrediting, character. Accepting relationships are not based on a denial of difference, but rather on the absence of impugning the different person's moral character because of the variation.

Such relationships are generally founded on feelings of family, a sense of religious obligation or commitment, humanitarian orientation, and feelings of friendship. Accepting relationships are often characterized by formation in stages over a period of time; increasing levels of trust and comfort as the relationship develops; shared contempt between the "deviant" and the nondeviant for "outsiders" who manifest their discomfort; de-emphasis of the differences and emphasis on the positive aspects of the relationship; and empathy from the nondeviant individual with the discrimination and/or rejection experienced by the "deviant."

Acceptance in the context of intimate partner violence is discussed in detail in chapter 8. However, there are several parallels between acceptance of deviance and acceptance of partner violence. First, in each circumstance, acceptance may be premised on feelings of commitment or obligation. Second, the relationship between the deviant and the nondeviant, the batterer and the battered, is often characterized by feelings of trust and a shared contempt for "outsiders." In the case of partner violence and violence in general, these latter characteristics are reminiscent of the Stockholm syndrome, discussed previously.

Response of the "Deviant" Actor

Responses of the "deviant" may include the proffering of an account, secondary deviance, and/or attempts to cover deviance.

The Account. Scott and Lyman (1968:46) have defined an "account" as "a linguistic device employed whenever an action is subjected to valuative inquiry." They elaborate:

> By an account, then, we mean a statement made by a social actor to explain unanticipated or untoward behavior--whether that behavior is his own or that of others, and whether the proximate cause for that statement arises from the actor himself or from someone else. An account is not called for when people engage in routine, common-sense behavior in a cultural environment that recognizes that behavior as such.

Scott and Lyman (1968) distinguish between accounts that are excuses and those that constitute justifications. Excuses will mitigate or relieve the actor from his or her responsibility. Excuses include appeals to accidents, to defeasibility, to biological drives, and to scapegoating. Justifications will not only neutralize an act or its consequences, but will also assert the positive value of the act. Justifications include denial of injury, denial of the victim, condemnation of the condemners, and appeal to loyalties. Whether any account will be honored will depend on the character of the social circle in which it is utilized and the expectancies of the audience receiving the account.

The response of the audience may well depend on the nature of the account that is offered. For instance, where the audience response is likely to be one of deterrence, i.e., punishment, the account given to explain a criminal act may determine (a) whether there will, in fact, be any punishment and (b) the extent of that punishment, if imposed.

Secondary Deviance. Secondary deviance arises from the societal response to primary deviance, which refers to instances of norm violation in which individual do not view themselves as deviant:

> When a person begins to employ his deviant behavior or a role based upon it as a means of defense, attack or adjustment to the... problems created by the consequent societal reaction to him, his deviation is secondary (Lemert, 1951: 76).

Covering. Covering refers to attempts to hide the deviance from others, in an attempt to "blend" with the nondeviant (French, Wilke, Mayfield, and Woolley, 1985). Covering attempts may include the use of a wig to hide baldness due to chemotherapy or elaborate routines to "cover" one's mental retardation. Goffman (1963) documented, for instance, one blind man's attempts to hide his blindness from a date. Throughout numerous dates and several movies, this gentleman held the hand of his date, so that she unwittingly led him where he needed to go, giving her the perception that he was a sighted person. Edgerton (1973) documented in detail the efforts of formerly institutionalized mentally retarded adults to "pass" by lying about where they were from to avoid discovery of the prior institutionalization; by marrying to appear normal and to emphasize their status as a free person; by acquiring "memorabilia" so as to have a history; by finding excuses to explain their lack of a car; and by devising mechanisms to simplify others' responses, such as asking whether it is 9:00 yet (responses: almost, no, just after) rather than asking the exact time (responses: 8:40, 20 minutes to 9, etc.).

The mechanism of covering is reminiscent of the "Dr. Jekyll/Mr. Hyde" descriptions of batterers that was noted previously, whereby a male batterer may appear to function well in superficial relationships, so that the battering behavior is hidden from others. However, the concept of covering also suggests that the victim of the battering views him- or herself as the deviant actor in that the victim often covers his or her bruises and hides the true cause of the injury from others, permitting the intimate relationship to "pass" as one that is at least tolerable, if not ideal.

5

RESPONSES OF THE HELPING PROFESSIONS

To maintain justice and preserve [human beings] from harm means first of all to prevent harm being done to them. For those to whom harm has been done, it means to efface the material consequences by putting them in a place where the wound, if not to deep, may be cured naturally by a spell of well-being. But for those in whom the wound is a laceration of the soul it means further, and above all, to offer them good in its purest form to assuage their thirst.

(Weil, 1977: 335)

THE HEALTH CARE PROFESSIONS

The response of the health care professions has taken a number of forms including (1) programs to increase health care worker awareness of domestic violence, (2) the development of screening protocols to assess whether an individual has been a victim of domestic violence, (3) the development of screening protocols to identify batterers, (4) the development of procedures for the examination of patients believed to have been the victims of domestic violence, (5) the formation of community consortia for the provision of health care to victims of domestic violence, and (6) consideration of ethical issues related to the diagnosis and treatment of domestic violence. Each of these responses is discussed below.

Increasing Health Care Worker Awareness

Health care providers have often been found to be the least helpful of all professionals in assisting individuals who have been battered. This is not infrequently due to the providers' inability to recognize the problem. It has been found, for instance, that emergency room staff identify battering in only 5 to 10 percent of the total cases that are ultimately found to involve women who have been battered (Reynolds, 1993). However, battered women may account for anywhere from 22 to 35 percent of all women who seek emergency department treatment (Flitcraft, Hadley, Hendricks-Matthews, McLeer, and Warshaw, 1992). Researchers have found that 40 percent of all injuries of women presenting at emergency departments may result from abusive relationships (Kurz and Stark, 1988) and 25 percent of all emergency department visits by women may be prompted by incidents of battering (Stark, Flitcraft, and Frazier, 1979).

In explaining why medical personnel have been unable to identify battering, Felder and Victor relate an exchange between a resident and a woman who presented with ear pain:

> A resident, who couldn't figure out his physical findings, once asked me to see a woman who had pain and redness under her right ear. I came into the room, introduced myself, looked at the patient, and asked if someone had hit her. When she answered in the affirmative, I asked her who. She hesitated only a moment before telling me that her boyfriend hit her and when I asked why she hadn't told the resident, her response was that he hadn't asked (Felder and Victor, 1996: 75-76, quoting Carol Warshaw).

This failure to ask the patient about the cause of her injuries may have the unintended effect of exacerbating the patient's isolation. Similarly, Warshaw described an incident in which a battered woman presented at a hospital for treatment. The nurse recorded that the woman was "hit on upper lip, teeth loose and with dislocation. Happened last night" (Warshaw, 1989: 512). The nurse recorded a diagnosis of "blunt trauma face." Warshaw (1989: 512) commented:

> The nurse's note does not mention who hit her, what her relationship to this person was, what the circumstances of the attack were, or why she waited five hours to seek medical help.

Yet, these items may be critical in developing a discharge plan that will actually assist and support the patient.

Although the Surgeon General of the United States recommended in 1992 that physicians increase their awareness of domestic violence (Novello, Rosenberg, Saltzmann, and Shosky, 1992), recent studies continue to underscore deficiencies in health care worker awareness. Chambliss and colleagues (1995) found in their survey of all residents in obstetrics and gynecology that the majority were unable to recognize at least one of 10 common clinical scenarios suggestive of battering. The majority also appeared to seriously underestimate the prevalence of battering in the patient population. Chambliss and colleagues concluded that medical education is failing to prepare residents to address relatively common situations that they would encounter in practice. Saunders and Kinney (1993) similarly concluded from their evaluation of residents and faculty that more extensive training of medical personnel is required to adequately detect and document the abuse. Accordingly, medical personnel have been urged to

> observe for patterns of injury (bruising, lacerations, sprains or swellings) in any pregnant woman. Consider if the explanation or the injury is logical. For instance, bumping into a door would likely produce a bump on the forehead or bruising on the extremity, but not a full black eye or swelling of the jaw (Helton and Snodgrass, 1987: 146).

The Council on Scientific Affairs of the American Medical Association (1992: 3189) recommended that:

> training on interviewing techniques, risk assessment, safety planning, and procedures for linking to resources be incorporated into undergraduate, graduate, and continuing medical education programs.

The resulting increased awareness is critical to the primary, secondary, and tertiary prevention of partner violence.

However, such training must focus not only on the recognition of physical signs of battering and an assessment of safety with referral to appropriate resources, but also on the health care providers' own responses to situations involving victims of battering. For instance, some staff may believe that the victim of battering is responsible for her own situation (Stark, Flitcraft, and Frazier, 1979) and use this is as basis to maintain distance from the victim and refrain from questioning him or her about the circumstances surrounding the injuries (Tilden, 1989). Staff may believe that direct questioning about the cause of the injuries constitutes prying (Tilden, 1989) and, consequently, is intrusive and inappropriate (Kurz and Stark, 1988; Warshaw, 1989). Prior experience with battered women who have subsequently returned to their batterers may have convinced staff that efforts to intervene are futile (McFarlane, 1989). Physicians may also believe that their responsibility stops with the treatment of the physical illness or injury. However, their duties go much further:

> The aim of medicine is to address not only the bodily assault that disease or an injury inflicts but also the psychological, social, even spiritual dimensions of this assault. To heal is to make whole or sound, to help a person reconvene the powers of the self and return, as far as possible, to his [or her] conception of a normal life (Thomasma and Pellegrino, 1988: 10).

Because extrication from an abusive relationship may involve a long and complex process, physicians cannot easily effectuate a "cure," i.e. the departure of the woman from the relationship. And, by "taking control" to expedite a departure, the physician may inadvertently replicate the sense of coercion that a battered woman experiences with her abusive partner (Sugg and Inui, 1992; Warshaw, 1989; Worcester, 1995).

Various provider characteristics and behaviors have been identified as promoting communication from a battered patient about her situation: acknowledgment that the problem was real, initiation of the discussion by the provider, expressions of concern, and continuity of care from the same individual provider (Rodriguez, Bauer, Flores-Ortiz, and Szkupinski-Quiroga, 1998). Conversely, several characteristics and behaviors of the provider have been found to discourage communication: an apparent discomfort on the part of the provider in discussing abuse, the failure of the provider to address the issue directly, an emphasis by the provider on issues pertaining only to physiological problems to the exclusion of psychological and social issues, the absence of a longstanding relationship with the same individual provider (Rodriguez, Bauer, Flores-Ortiz, and Szkupinski-Quiroga, 1998), and callousness of the provider towards the victim's situation (Websdale, 1998).   And, training alone will be insufficient absent institutional support of appropriate responses to partner violence.

> Thus, addressing this issue requires some fundamental changes in the nature of most medical training and in the culture of medical institutions.   Creating practice environments and policies that model nonabusive ways of interacting, that support clinicians' efforts to address complex issues with skill and compassion, and that reimburse the more labor-intensive tasks of listening and advocating   for   change,   are   important   components   of institutionalizing   effective   responses   to   domestic   violence (Warshaw, 1996: 90).

Intervention by a health care worker may be rendered more difficult, even with adequate training and institutional support, in situations in which the physician provides care both to the injured individual and to her assaultive partner. Additionally, a woman who is battered may be particularly reluctant to disclose the source of her injuries to her physician if her intimate partner is a patient of the same physician (Alpert, 1995). However, members of an expert panel and a consulting group consisting of individuals with backgrounds in medicine, law enforcement, social work, nursing, psychology, and law, as well as previously abused women and abusive men, concluded that in such situations

> It is not a conflict of interest for the physician to deal with abuse of the female partner when both partners are patients. Both patients have a right to autonomy, confidentiality, honesty, and quality care.   Patients should be dealt with independently, thereby facilitating assessment of the magnitude and severity of the victim's injuries. Physicians should not discuss the possibility of domestic abuse with the male partner without the prior consent of the abused female partner.   Joint counseling is generally inadvisable and should be attempted only when the violence has ended, provided both partners give independent consent and the physician has adequate training and skills to deal with the situation without escalating the violence. If the physician feels unable to deal effectively with either patient because of the dual relationship, referral to another qualified physician is preferred (Ferris, Norton, Dunn, Gort, Degani, 1997: 851).

The provision of joint or marital counseling to the couple by their common physician while violence remains ongoing is inadvisable because joint counseling is premised on the assumption that both parties in the counseling enjoy an equal relationship, a premise which is untrue in the context of partner violence (Ferris, Norton, Dunn, Gort, and Degani, 1997).

Medical Protocols for the Identification and Treatment of Victims

Screening Protocols

Large numbers of health care providers have recently developed screening protocols to detect intimate partner violence among its victims. These initiatives have often been a response to heightened awareness of both the seriousness and prevalence of intimate partner violence (Quillian, 1996), the passage of legal mandates requiring the development of such protocols (Freeman, 1995; Mixon, 1995; Bell, Jenkins, Kpo, and Rhodes, 1994), and/or the requirements of the Joint Commission for the Accreditation of Healthcare Organizations that hospital emergency departments implement written policies and procedures for the identification, assessment, treatment, evaluation, and referral of victims of abuse (Joint Commission on Accreditation of Healthcare Organizations, 1992). The heightened awareness of the problem has prompted the initiation of routine screening of female patients:

> Domestic violence and its medical and psychiatric sequelae are sufficiently prevalent to justify 'routine screening' of all women patients in emergency, surgical, primary care, pediatric, prenatal, and mental health settings (Flitcraft, Hadley, Hendricks-Matthews, McLeer, and Warshaw, 1992: 8).

It is beyond the scope of this chapter to examine in detail the various screening protocols that have been developed. Numerous mechanisms have, however, been developed, including multi-level screening procedures based on prior history of abuse and presentation with injuries (Quillian, 1996), a two-question assessment tool (McFarlane, Greenberg, Weltge, and Watson, 1995), a single-item assessment tool (Freund, Bak, and Blackhall, 1996), a five-question screening instrument (Norton, Peipert, Zierler, Lima, and Hume, 1995), and a three-question screening tool focusing on past violence and perceived personal safety (Feldhaus et al., 1997). A two-question screening protocol has been found to have a sensitivity of 71 percent and a specificity of almost 85 percent in the detection of partner violence: (1) Has anyone at home hit you or tried to injure you in an way, and (2) Do you ever feel unsafe at home? (Feldhaus, Koziol-McLain, Armsbury, Norton, Lowenstein, and Abbott, 1997) The extent to which any of these tools can detect partner violence among either non-English speakers or specific immigrant groups with differing values remains unclear and uninvestigated.

Screening for partner violence has also been recommended as a component of pediatric assessments (Duffy, McGrath, Becker, and Linakis, 1999; Groves, 1994). The pediatric visit represents an opportune occasion for such an assessment. Even though women may avoid the medical care system with respect to their own needs, often due to fear of discovery or fear of their abusive partner, they will nevertheless seek care for their children's ills (Barkan and Gary, 1996). For instance, it was found that of a sample of 157 mothers who sought treatment for their children at an urban pediatric emergency department, 52% had experienced adult physical abuse, 21% reported adult sexual abuse, and 10% had suffered violence during the previous year. Of those who had been abused, 67% had suffered the physical abuse by their intimate partner (Duffy, McGrath, Becker, and Linakis, 1999). Unfortunately, pediatric emergency department physicians often do not receive adequate training regarding intimate partner violence and are frequently employed in a setting which lacks a formal protocol for such screening (Barkan and Gary, 1996; Krugman and Wissow, 1998; Tanner, 1995; Wright, Wright, and Isaaac, 1997), although violence between a child's parents or caregivers may have serious implications for the child (see chapter 9).

The Physical Examination and Assessment

Examination procedures are relevant in situations where the clinician has reason to believe that physical violence against an intimate partner by the other has occurred.   In conducting such examinations, the health care worker must be cognizant of the role of the family and the community and of ethical issues that may arise.

Suspicion of battering should be raised in situations in which the woman presents with headache or nonspecific pain, sleep disorders, anxiety, dysphagia, or hyperventilation (Stark and Flitcraft, 1996).   Substance use may also indicate battering because the use of substances may represent an attempt to self-medicate. Various gynecological and reproductive problems, such as abdominal pain, self-induced or attempted abortions, multiple miscarriages, and dyspareunia, may also indicate abuse.

Most examination protocols recommend detailed documentation of the injuries, including a body chart (Mississippi State Medical Association, 1995; Sheridan and Taylor, 1993), a description of the event that produced them with photographs of the resulting injuries (Mississippi State Medical Association, 1995; Sheridan and Taylor, 1993), relevant laboratory tests (Mississippi State Medical Association, 1995), and an assessment for the risk of homicide (Sheridan and Taylor, 1993). Complete documentation may be critical to future legal proceedings.   The documentation of the violence should include the location, depth, character, and appearance of any wounds, using specific medical terms.   Photographs should be obtained if the patient consents (Eisenstat and Bancroft, 1999).   Some hospitals have developed detailed protocols for obtaining photographs and for maintaining these records to ensure that they will later be admissible in court, if needed.   In some instances, the physical examination and the provision of medical care may be difficult due to the intrusion of the assaultive partner (Stark and Flitcraft, 1996).

It is critical that the assessment for partner violence not be conducted in the presence of either the partner or a non-professional interpreter, such as a relative or a friend (Eisenstat and Bancroft, 1999).   If the health care provider discovers through the initial screening that the individual has been physically abused, he or she should then conduct a more complete assessment.   The assessment should address such issues as the nature of the abuse; the date, time, and circumstances of the incident; whether there were any previous assaults; and any resulting injuries (Eisenstat and Bancroft, 1999).

The following questions have been utilized in assessing partner violence.   The risk increases with each affirmative response.

a) Have weapons been used, or has there been a threat with weapons?
b) Is there access to or ownership of guns?
c) Have there been threats to kill?
d) Does the violence appear to be escalating or occurring more frequently?
e) Has there been destruction of property?
f) Has there been forced sex?
g) Has there been a threat to, injury of, or killing of a pet?
h) Is there a history of psychological problems?
i) Is there an obsessiveness to the partner? Does he manifest extreme jealousy?
j) Is there alcohol or drug abuse?
k) Has the marital situation changed recently? (Ferris, Norton, Dunn, Gort, and Degani, 197: 855).

It may be difficult for a health care provider to address partner violence in situations in which such violence is suspected and possibly escalating, but the battered partner is unable to acknowledge what is happening. Two suggestions have been proffered to address this situation. First, the provider can introduce the issue of partner violence to the woman and discuss a hypothetical safety plan if the injuries hypothetically were the result of partner violence. Second, the health care provider can furnish the woman with educational material relating to partner violence as part of a package of educational materials on various health topics (Ferris, Norton, Dunn, Gort, and Degani, 1997).

Discharge Planning for Battered Adults

A number of hospitals have developed therapeutic interventions for victims of partner violence. Some of these initiatives, such as those at Brigham and Women's Hospital in Boston and Harborview Hospital in Seattle, have utilized a social service trauma team that consisted of social workers (Stark and Flitcraft, 1996).

Discharge planning must consider the possibility that woman, once discharged, will face life-threatening violence. Suicide is also a risk, particularly where the woman is feeling depressed, anxious, or trapped and hopeless. Stark and Flitcraft (1996) have suggested that safety planning should consider the woman's priorities in relation to her available options and resources and should reinforce strategies that she is already utilizing to prevent or minimize the violence. An extended hospital stay may be warranted if the woman has no safe option upon discharge. A number of hospitals have established safe-rooms for this purpose, so that a woman presenting at the hospital who is found to have been the victim of physical violence and who has no immediate options for safety may stay overnight, while a social worker attempts to arrange other options.

Discharge planning also involves the development and establishment of hospital procedures that capitalize on the woman's available resources and will help to maintain her safety:

Assessment of patients' immediate resources is an inquiry common
to any crisis intervention process. In terms of battered women, this
means inquiring about family and friends, job or supervisory
support, finances, child care, assistance from school personnel, and
general safety in the home (Roberts and Roberts, 1990: 106).

Various strategies may be used to increase the woman's safety. If, for instance,
the victim of the battering moves to a shelter, her address should not be disclosed in
her medical record or to any family member or friend. A woman who has been
accompanied to the hospital by her assaultive partner should not be given her
medical chart to hold because her partner may read it. Rather, the information
should be kept in an alternative location where it is not readily accessible (Eisenstat
and Bancroft, 1999). Other components of a safety plan include

- telephone numbers for emergency assistance and for family,
  friends, police, hospitals, shelters, and help lines
- the location of nearby shelters
- information about educational services, along with their
  addresses and telephone numbers (include language and
  ethnic-specific services if necessary)
- information about legal rights (support and custody issues)
  and immigration rights
- recommendation to pack and hide a suitcase in case of an
  emergency
- information on how to plan an emergency escape route (Ferris,
  Norton, Dunn, Gort, and Degani, 1997).

The National Domestic Violence Hotline (1-800-799-SAFE) provides information
on community-based resources that may be needed.

Although mental health services may be recommended, and the battered patient
may be desirous of these services, care must be taken in assigning a diagnosis. In
order to receive such services, a diagnosis must be assigned. However, the
psychiatric diagnosis required for the receipt of mental health services may later be
used by the assaultive partner to "prove" that the woman is an unfit mother or that
she is "crazy," and therefore not fit to have custody of her children. Women may be
refused health insurance at a later date, based on the belief that they are at higher
risk for injury and death as a result of the battering (Kaiser, 1995). Women who
receive medical care through their husband's insurance may suffer additional harm
should the husband receive the insurance statements and discover that she is seeking
help (Warshaw, 1996).

Mandatory Reporting

As of March 1994, 45 states had laws in place that required, to varying extents, that
health care practitioners reports instances of domestic violence to the police
(Hyman, Schillinger, and Lo, 1995). Often, the reporting requirement was framed
in terms of the cause of a particular injury, such as that resulting from a knife or gun

wound or one suffered in connection with the commission of a crime. As of 1995, five states—California, Kentucky, New Mexico, New Hampshire, and Rhode Island—required that health care practitioners report any case to the police in which the physical injury of an adult resulted from abuse (Hyman, Schillinger, and Lo, 1995).

Numerous concerns related to such provisions have been raised. These include the possibility that the assaultive partner will blame the injured party for the report, despite his or her lack of decision making in this regard; the likelihood that the assaulted partner will suffer retaliation as a result of the report being made; the possibility that clinicians will equate reporting as the equivalent of providing adequate care, thereby depriving patients of care that they may need; and the possibility that battered individuals will refrain from disclosing the physical abuse to their health care providers because they fear that the providers will then report the occurrence, thereby unleashing a chain of events that they are unable to control and they may act to their own detriment (Hyman, Schillinger, and Lo, 1995; Rodriguez, Craig, Mooney, and Bauer, 1998). Research findings from a focus group-based study involving 51 women from diverse ethnic backgrounds have indicated that women may, indeed, refrain from disclosing the true cause of their injuries if they believe that they will be able to play no part in the decision of whether to report the incident to the police (Rodriguez, Craig, Mooney, and Bauer, 1998). Although many women desired police protection, many expressed distrust of the legal system. Additionally, women commented on the likelihood of retaliation following police intervention and the possibility that the family would ultimately be harmed through the loss of the male head of household, the loss of the male partner's income, or their own separation from their children. Despite the many voiced concerns, however, an ecological time-trend study of the effect of California's mandatory domestic violence reporting law found no increase in dispatches to medical facilities by the Los Angeles Sheriff's Department. Rather, an increase was noted following the murder of Nicole Simpson and Ronald Goldman (Sachs, Peek, Baraff, and Hasselblad, 1998).

Screening for Batterers

Generally, batterers are identified through victim reports, rather than self-identification. Chelmowski and Hamberger (1994) have suggested that health care workers use a "funneling technique" to determine whether a patient engaged in violent behavior. Accordingly, questions may initially focus on the patient's relationship with his or her intimate partner and become progressively more specific about techniques for handling anger within the couple. The extent to which such a technique would be successful with individuals whose cultures do not encourage the discussion of feelings or relationships is unclear. Although there is generally no legal duty to report past abuse, Chelmowski and Hamberger (1994) caution that there may be a duty to notify the partner if the threat of further intimate partner violence appears high.

Physicians, however, may be able to screen for partner violence as well. Psychopathology has been identified in 80 to 90 percent of court-referred and self-referred partner assaulters (Hart, Dutton, and Newlove, 1992; Saunders, 1992).

Certain disorders are associated with violent behavior: psychopathy, personality disorders, hallucinations, suicidal ideation, suicide attempts, substance abuse, schizophrenia, bipolar affective disorder, delusions, and impulse control disorders ((Ferris, Norton, Dunn, Gort, and Degani, 1997). A physician who diagnoses one of these disorders may, in the presence of other indicators, wish to address the issue of partner violence.

More recently, the routine screening of male patients for aggressive behavior toward their intimate partners has been recommended as a component of primary care (Oriel and Fleming, 1998). In one recently conducted study, it was found that of 375 men screened in three family medicine clinics, 32 men had committed acts of physical violence against their intimate partners during the preceding 12 months. Those who were most likely to report having been violent had increased alcohol consumption, depression, or had experienced abuse as children (Oriel and Fleming, 198).

Social Models, Social Services, and Community Consortia

Interagency domestic violence consortia have been proposed as a remedy to the often fragmented care and attention that domestic violence victims often receive (Langford, 1990). Interagency domestic violence consortia could potentially include services from and linkages between educational programs, shelters, and health care facilities. This enhanced cooperation could lead to the formualtion and adoption of standardized protocols and policies, the development of quality assurance standards, and the development and implementation of surveillance strategies (Langford, 1990).

The AWAKE program, based at Boston's Children's Hospital, is one example of a hospital-based program that functions in conjunction with non-health care provider entities (Felder and Victor, 1996). The project assumes that in situations in which a mother is suffering abuse from her partner, any children in the home who witness such violence must also be suffering. The program strives to protect both the mother and the children. The children are treated as the primary patients, but mothers are interviewed in an attempt to determine whether the children's injuries result directly from family violence. In situations where the child are suffering from violence, the woman is presented with two options: to cooperate with the police and the "system" in the prosecution of the abuser, or risk losing her children. In general, the program recommends that the children not be removed from their mothers. Instead, the program recommends that the male assaultive partner be held responsible for the violence because it was he who put the woman in the position of being unable to defend herself and of being unable to care for her children (Felder and Victor, 1996).

Womankind, originally developed as a nonprofit corporation, is a component of the Fairview Hospital System in Minnesota (Hadley, 1992). Womankind provides in-service training to the medical staff around such issues as the identification of victims of battering, the documentation of injuries, the existence of community resources, the provisions of domestic violence statutes, and the requirement for the issuance of temporary restraining orders. Additionally, the program provides information, education, and advocacy services to battered women.

Harborview Hospital in Seattle, Washington has developed and implemented a protocol for the detection and documentation of adult abuse that integrates both the medical and the legal systems (Klingbeil and Boyd, 1984). The protocol integrates social work, medical, and legal services and provides for photographs of the injuries, a description of the batterer, and an account of the circumstances leading up to the battering incident.

Innovative forms of partnering between the medical, legal, and business communities have been developed in an effort to increase the safety of those experiencing abuse. Verizon Wireless, for instance, has given away more than 15,000 cell phones to women experiencing partner violence. These cell phones are programmed to permit the user to contact "911" by pressing any of the buttons, thereby circumventing abusers' efforts to thwart the victims' attempts to reach help. Phones were distributed to community groups, shelters, police departments, and district attorneys' offices for distribution to victims (Goodman, 2000).

Ethical Issues

The Council on Ethical and Judicial Affairs of the American Medical Association (1992) has stated that (1) physicians should routinely inquire about domestic violence as a part of the medical history; (2) physicians may have a duty to familiarize themselves with diagnostic and treatment protocols for domestic violence; (3) physicians should prevent societal misconceptions about domestic violence from interfering with the diagnosis and management of abuse; (4) "[t]he medical profession must demonstrate a greater commitment to ending domestic violence and helping its victims; and (5) physicians must be better trained to diagnose domestic violence and to work cooperatively with available community resources. Consequently, the diagnosis and treatment of physical injuries is insufficient. Rather,

> the aim of medicine is to address not only the bodily assault that disease or an injury inflicts but also the psychological, social, even spiritual dimensions of this assault. To heal is to make whole or sound, to help a person reconvene the powers of the self and return, as far as possible, to his [or her] conception of a normal life (Pellegrino and Thomasma, 1988: 10).

THE RESPONSE OF THE VETERINARY PROFESSION

It has recently been recognized that violence against pets may signify the beginnings of family violence (Arkow, 1995). It has been estimated that veterinarians treat hundreds of thousands of abused pets each year (Landau, 1999). The American Veterinary Medical Association (AVMA) has recognized that veterinarians may have occaaion to observe cases of cruelty to animals, animal abuse, or animal neglect as defined by state law or local ordinances. When these observations occur, the AVMA considers it the responsibility of the veterinarian to report such cases to the appropriate authorities. Such disclosures may be necessary to protect the health and welfare of animals and people (American Veterinary Medical Association, 1997).

Despite this injunction, approximately 90% of all veterinarians in the United States are not mandated by law to report their suspicions of abuse (Landau, 1999). Additionally, most veterinary curricula do not have hospital policies for reporting suspected animal abuse and even fewer address the reporting of human abuse that is encountered by veterinary practitioners (Landau, 1999).

THE RESPONSE OF CLERGY

Clergy have not infrequently failed to address battering as a chronic problem and have minimized the lethality of domestic and sexual violence. Additionally, clergy have been criticized for responding to instances of domestic violence by redefining the batterer's criminal conduct as a psychological problem, failing to maintain the confidences of the battered victim, identifying with the male batterer, emphasizing forgiveness by the victim as a remedy, and stressing the "covenant" of marriage (Adams, 1993).

More recently, some clergy have advocated a deeper examination of the meaning of forgiveness. (Fortune, 1998: 50) has vigorously criticized the popular notion of forgiveness:

> The problem for Christians is that somehow the notion and practice of forgiveness has been romanticized and placed in a vacuum due in large part to the canonization of "forgive and forget" theology. If we ask most Christians today where to find "forgive and forget" in the Bible, none of them will know where it is, but they will swear that it is there somewhere. It is not....
> When the expectation of agency in response to harm done by one to another is passed to the one harmed and away from the one causing harm, then three things happen:
> 1. No one (including us as bystanders) ever has to deal with accountability for the offender. This is particularly advantageous for the nonrepentant offender.
> 2. The victims, whose priority is their own individual healing, can decide that they have the power to bring about this healing by their own agency in the "act" of forgiveness. This is a cruel hoax for the victim.
> 3. The bystanders...can stand by and do nothing, self-righteously assured that we have no lines in this play.

Rather, Fortune argues, forgiveness cannot occur in the absence of justice. Justice cannot occur in the absence of truth-telling, acknowledgement, compassion, protection of the vulnerable, accountability for the offender, restitution to the survivor, and vindacation for the survivor (Fortune, 1989).

McClure (1998) has encouraged members of the clergy to become educated about family violence and to avoid preaching "one-shot" sermons on the subject. He has urged the adoption of a nonviolent theology, "in which violence is clearly identified as evil and in which...neither the ways of God towards people nor the ways of God's people toward others are impolicitly or explicitly violent" (McClure, 1998: 113). This, he advises, will require a reassessment of various biblical doctrines. Procter-Smith has warned that

> Sermons which speak without nuance of the virtue of "submitting to the will of God," for example, or of the way in which "God sends us suffering to test our faith" may have critical or even fatal consequences when heard and believed by a woman who may be considering leaving an abusive husband (Procter-Smith, 1995: 432).

Rather, sermons should consider their audiences, which simultaneously consist of victims and survivors of violence, perpetrators of violence, and bystanders of violence (McClure, 1998). The liturgy and sermon should constitute a "holding environment" and "lament" for the victims and survivors, so that the sanctuary is recognized as a "safe place"; "an exercise in clarity" for the perpetrators, so that they can see the damage that they have inflicted and that it cannot be undone; and a challenge to the bystanders to "break ranks" with the perpetrators in order to eliminate even tacit endorsement of the battering behavior (McClure, 1998: 115-116). McClure (1998: 118) provides the following story, excerpted from a sermon, as an example of how the message can be conveyed in a way that the listeners are able to hear:

> A woman in Massachusetts wrote about her experience of being married to a man who battered her and stopped at nothing to control her and isolate her, including manipulating the children to report on her activities. One day in her prayers, this woman was focusing on a mental image of Christ on the cross. Suddenly, the image moved from being in front of her to being beside her. She understood this to mean that Christ was not going to rescue her like a hero. Instead, Christ was suffering alongside of her and wanted her to be healthful and happy. The decision to leave was up to her, and Christ would remain beside her either way. Because her invisible, inner spiritual world was all-encompassing, Christ would be with her wherever she was. Because her life with God was not confined to a place or time of day or marital status, but was her very world, she could leave her tormentor without leaving God.
>
> She did leave, one day when her husband was distracted in the back yard. It takes courage to leave someone who is likely to come after you in a brutal rage...And it takes boldness to speak the

good news of God's grace for battered women (M. McClure, 1994, quoted in J.S. McClure, 1998: 118).

6

THE LEGAL RESPONSE

[T]here were some terrible seeds on the plant…and these were the seeds of the baobab. The soil of the planet was infested with them. A baobab is something that you will never, never be able to get rid of if you attend to it too late. It spreads over the entire planet. It bores clear through with its roots. And if the planet is too small, and the baobabs are too many, they split it in pieces….

(de Saint-Exupery, 1971: 18)

THE CRIMINAL JUSTICE RESPONSE

Domestic violence calls constitute the single largest type of calls received by the police each year (National Clearinghouse for the Defense of Battered Women, 1990, cited in Browne, 1995). The criminal justice response comprises numerous elements, including the police, the prosecutor and the prosecutorial infrastructure, the judicial system, and the legislative response. Six goals have been identified as being of primary concern within this interrelated, interactive system: (1) the safety of the persons being battered, (2) the cessation of the violence, (3) the accountability of the perpetrators, (4) the divestiture of the perpetrators from those being battered, (5) the restoration of the persons being battered, and (6) the enhancement of agency in the lives of those being battered (Hart, 1997). These goals are discussed below in the context of the responses of the police, the legislatures, and the courts. In general, the criminal justice system within the United States has more recently attempted to respond to intimate partner violence through increased frequency of response by the police (Tolman and Weisz, 1995; Schmidt and Sherman, 1993; Hirschel and Hutchinson III, 1992; Polsby, 1992), the imposition of increasingly punitive legal sanctions as a deterrent, including arrest (Grasmick, Blackwell, Bursik Jr., and Mitchell, 1993; Jolin, 1983), and the notification of victims of their legal rights and the availability of supportive services (Hart, 1993). Change is also evident in the increasing willingness of some courts to admit evidence relating to the battered woman syndrome in connection with trials of women for criminal offenses against their batterers and the availability of remedies for abused immigrant women under United States immigration law.

The Police Response

The police response to domestic violence calls has varied considerably and has, unfortunately, often been inadequate: failure to respond to the calls, refusal to arrest the assailant, failure to file reports, and harassment of the victim of such violence. For instance, during a nine-month period of time, police in Cleveland received more than 15,000 calls relating to partner violence. They responded to 700 of these calls and made arrests in 460 (Attorney General of Ohio, 1989).

Pence (1983: 252) described the following scenario as an illustration of the inadequacy of the police response where officers are afforded "unschooled discretion:"

> Police officers are dispatched to a home at 10:30 p.m. on a Saturday night. The officers are met at the door by an angry woman who is bleeding from the nose. She is extremely agitated and is swearing at the police to get her husband out of the house. The woman explains that her husband hit her because she yelled at him from spending the grocery money. He admits to having hit her, but only after listening to her yell at him "for twenty solid minutes." Both the man and the woman see her behavior as, at least partially, having caused the assault... It does not appear that the woman is in immediate danger. The officers talk to both parties until they are calm and ask the man to leave the house for the evening. The man agrees to go to a friend's house. The officers have separated the parties and presumably prevented an escalation of the violence.

There is no indication, however, of what happens when the husband returns home the following day.

The well-known case of Jena Balistreri further illustrates the inadequacy of the police response (*Balistreri v. Pacifica Police Department*, 1990). The police officers responding to Balistreri's call, which followed a severe beating inflicted by her husband, did not offer her any medical assistance and refused to arrest her husband, although she had sustained injuries to her nose, mouth, eyes, teeth, and abdomen. The officers convinced her not to file a report. She obtained a restraining order against her former husband in an attempt to halt the continuing harassment. Her ex-husband violated the restraining order by making harassing phone calls and by driving his car into her garage. The police refused to investigate or arrest him, and denied the existence of the restraining order. Ultimately, Balistreri's ex-husband tossed a firebomb into her home, which caused severe fire damage. The police took 45 minutes to respond to the emergency call. Balistreri brought suit against the police department for their lack of responsiveness (*Balistreri v. Pacifica Police Department*, 1990).

Despite the apparent inattention to incidents of intimate partner violence, exemplified by the above situations described above, the police response may assume a number of alternative forms including arresting the batterer, providing mediation, providing transportation or other services and forcing the batterer to leave (Feldberg, 1985). This discussion focuses primarily on arrest and the provision of services to the victim of the assault.

Arrest

The increased frequency of arrest and the notification to victims of their rights are police practices of relatively recent origin. These changes reflect a change in attitude generally towards the role of the police in such situations. For instance, one commentator suggested in 1967 that arrest was an inappropriate response to intimate partner violence (Parnas, 1993). However, the same commentator observed 10 years later:

> Efforts at therapy can, and I suppose should, be included in the process but should not be given undue emphasis, for there is simply no evidence that we know how to diagnose much less treat, disputants' problems in a manner that will prevent repetition. Simply put, we must go on with what we know. And we know that we cannot ignore or condone acts or threats of imminent violence. We know that the police are best equipped to protect others and themselves. We know how to punish, whether by fine, incapacitation, other denials of full liberty, embarrassment, inconvenience, etc. And we know punishment is a clear statement of the personal responsibility of the offender and the condemnation and retribution of society. We also know that where punishment is to be imposed, the criminal process provides the best safeguards that such punishment is imposed on the appropriate person under the most adequate circumstances....Thus the criminal law, the police, the prosecutor and the courts should not only continue to respond to incidents of inter-spousal violence, but should emphasize the importance of the traditional response of arrest, prosecution and sanction as a sign of public disapprobation and protection.... (Parnas, 1977, cited in Parnas, 1993: 187-188).

The impetus to effectuate such changes came in 1984, with the occurrence of three events. First, Tracey Thurman successfully sued the city of Torrington, Connecticut and its police department, claiming that her right to equal protection had been violated. Thurman alleged that she had informed the police several times that her husband had threatened her life. On the night of a near-fatal attack, her estranged husband stabbed her 13 times while a police officer waited nearby for other officers to arrive. The court found that the police department failed to provide protection to women who claimed to be abused by their intimate partners and that they did not receive the same level of protection as individuals assaulted by strangers (Anon., 1985; *Thurman v. City of Torrington*, 1984). It thus became clear that municipalities could be financially liable for failure to protect victims of battering.

Other claims against police departments for failure to provide protection to battered women were premised on violations of the equal protection clause, arguing that individuals assaulted by intimates are treated differently than those who are assaulted by strangers (*Balistreri v. Pacifica Police Department*, 1988; *Bartalone v. County of Berrien*, 1986; *Sherrell v. City of Longview*, 1987; *Thurman v. City of*

Torrington, 1984; *Watson v. City of Kansas City*, 1988); on violations of due process in instances involving a special, although noncustodial relationship, between the police and the victim, such as where the police have knowledge of an attacker's threats and of a restraining order and yet fail to protect the victim (*Balistreri v. Pacific Police Department*, 1988); and on a theory of negligence under state tort law, where a special relationship exists between the victim and the police (*Sorichetti v. New York*, 1985). Whether there existed a "special relationship" between the police and the victim was to be determined based on an examination of various factors:

> (a) an assumption by the municipality, through promises or actions, of an affirmative duty to act on behalf of the party who was injured; (2) knowledge on the part of the municipality's agents that inaction could lead to harm; (3) some form of direct contact between the municipality's agents and the injured party; and (4) that party's justifiable reliance on the municipality's affirmative undertaking. (*Sawicki v. Village of Ottawa Hills*, 1988: 478.)

More recently, suits have been brought where the police failed to act in accordance with a state statute, such as a failure to act in accordance with a statutory provision that mandates the arrest of an individual who has violated the terms of a restraining order (Soble and Minnet, 1994). Many claims based on due process arguments ultimately proved unsuccessful (see *Balistreri v.Pacifica Police Department*, 1990; *Salas v. Carpenter*, 1992), following the United States Supreme Court's finding that the Due Process Clause prohibits the state from depriving individuals of life, liberty, or property without due process of law, but does not generally require that the state guarantee to its citizens protection of life, liberty, and property against invasion by other private actors (*DeShaney v. Winnebago County Department of Social Services*, 1989). However, police departments may have changed their policies because of the potential liability resulting from such lawsuits.

Second, the results of the Minneapolis Experiment were released, indicating that of three different intervention strategies designed to reduce or prevent misdemeanor spouse abuse—arrest, separation, or mediation—arrest was associated with the lowest recidivism rate among batterers (Sherman and Berk, 1984). Third, the United States Attorney's Task Force on Family Violence issued its final report, which contained a number of recommendations for reform. These included (1) the processing of all complaints of family violence as criminal offenses, (2) immediate response to violations of protective orders, (3) the maintenance of a current file of all protection orders valid in the relevant jurisdiction, and (4) the adoption of arrest as the preferred response (Attorney General's Task Force on Family Violence, 1984). Ironically, the 1985 book *Domestic Crisis Intervention for Law Enforcement Officers*, a book "written by a law enforcement officer for law enforcements officers" (Duncan, 1985: 14) advised that "[t]he great majority of domestic crises do not involve a criminal violation of the law," and that "for the most part the police are called upon to provide a social service," i.e. "to quell the incident and return the disputants to a level of behavior that is not disruptive" (Duncan, 1985: 18-19). Yet, the author acknowledged that domestic crises usually involve criminal actions, such as assault and battery; these were dismissed as "not very serious" (Duncan, 1985: 139).

The number of police departments with arrest policies has gradually increased since 1984. A telephone survey of police departments in 1984 revealed that only 10% maintained policies relating to arrest in situations involving domestic violence. That percentage increased to 31% by 1985 and to 46% by 1986 (Cohn and Sherman, 1986). As of 1995, 47 states and the District of Columbia authorized or mandated warrantless, probable cause arrests for crimes involving intimate partner violence (Bachman and Coker, 1995).

It has since become unclear, however, whether arrest actually serves as a deterrent to subsequent domestic violence. Tolman and Weisz (1995) reported similar findings similar to the Minneapolis Experiment from their study of arrest in DuPage County, Illinois. However, a reanalysis of the data from the Minneapolis Experiment which included only the findings attributed to officers who generated more than 10 cases and who had more closely followed the experimental protocol suggests that arrest did not have a statistically significant effect on the rate of recidivism, contrary to the original analysis (Gartin, 1995). Sherman and Smith (1992) found that arrest had no significant effect on recidivism, while Pate and Hamilton (1992) found in their study of Dade County, Florida that arrest significantly increased the likelihood of a subsequent assault in certain circumstances (see Berk, Campbell, Klap, and Western, 1992). Other studies have also failed to find an association between arrest and a decrease in the rates of recidivism (Hirschel and Hutchison III, 1992). Dunford (1992) found no difference in the rate of recidivism based on the type of intervention in his replication of the Minneapolis Experiment in Omaha. Syers and Edleson (1992) conducted a follow-up study to evaluate the effects of a community intervention project in Minneapolis. Assailants who were both arrested and received court-ordered treatment were the least likely to repeat violence during a twelve-month period. Those who were not arrested were the most likely to repeat violence, while those who were arrested but did not receive court-ordered treatment fell between these two groups. The researchers concluded that the most effective criminal justice response is one which combines arrest and   court-ordered treatment (Syers and Edleson, 1992).

Research has demonstrated that individuals' willingness to involve the police and the police response to incidents of domestic violence is not consistent across populations. Bachman and Coker (1995), utilizing data from the National Crime Victimization Survey, found that victims who suffer injury, whose attackers had never assaulted them before, and who are black are more likely to contact the police. In contrast, Berk and colleagues (1984) found that victims were more likely to call the police if the victims had been assaulted by the same individual previously. They also found that victims were more likely to notify the police if other family members were present and if the abuser was a boyfriend rather than a spouse. (See chapter 8, addressing responses of victims of partner violence, for additional detail.)

The likelihood that bystanders to an incident of intimate partner violence will notify the police is related to the presence of other witnesses, the severity of the injury, and the destruction of property (Berk, Berk, Newton, and Loseke, 1984).

Police have been found to be more likely to arrest the assailant in situations in which the victim suffered injury, the attacker had not previously assaulted the individual, the victim was married, the attack occurred between a black man and a black woman rather than a white man and woman (Bachman and Coker, 1995), the assailant was drunk (Berk, Fenstermaker, and Newton, 1988), or the violence occurred in the officer's presence (Chaney and Saltzstein, 1998). Response time has been found to be shorter in rural and suburban areas as compared with urban areas (Bachman and Coker, 1995).

Additional factors have been implicated in police decisions to arrest or not to arrest. Belknap (1995) found in a survey of 324 law enforcement officers in a Midwestern metropolitan area that almost three times as many officers preferred mediation to arrest in addressing situations of partner violence. Older officers were more likely to take victims' requests for arrest seriously. City-based officers, as compared with county-based officers, were more likely to think that the police should use formal action or arrest in response to such situations (Belknap and McCall, 1994). Breci (1987) found from his questionnaire-based study of officers' attitudes that police officers with a high school education or less were more likely to perceive mandatory arrest as a long-term solution. A proarrest departmental policy has also been found to be associated with officers' willingness to arrest the assailant (Feder, 1997; Lanza-Kaduce, Greenleaf, and Donahue, 1995). Use of a weapon (Fyfe, Klinger, and Flavin, 1997; Mignon and Holmes, 1995) and an attack on the responding officer (Fyfe, Klinger, and Flavin, 1997) also increase the likelihood of arrest.

Research findings relating the degree of injury to the decision to arrest the offender are conflicting. Some studies have reported that the seriousness of the injury appears to have no effect on the likelihood of arrest (Fyfe, Klinger, and Flavin, 1997), while others indicate that victim injury is related to officers' willingness to attribute blame to the alleged assailant and effectuate an arrest (Waaland and Keeley, 1985).

Officers have been found less likely to arrest an offender pursuant to provisions of criminal law where the assault is directed against a spouse, as compared to assaults against other family members (Bell, 1985) and less likely to arrest in situations involving partner assault than stranger assault (Buzawa, Austin, and Buzawa, 1995; Eigenberg, Scarborough, and Kappeler, 1996). Offenders are also less likely to be arrested if they leave the scene of the assault, regardless of the severity of the injuries inflicted, the level of violence used, or the victim's desire to have the assailant arrested (Feder, 1996). Recent reports have documented the propensity of a substantial minority of police officers to arrest the *victim* of domestic violence, particularly where the assailant and the assaulted continue to argue in front of the officer (Saunders, 1995).

It appears that significant dissonance may exist between victims' beliefs regarding an arrest or conviction of the assailant and the actual proceedings. Fleury and colleagues (1998) found from their interviews with 137 battered women who had spent at least one night in a shelter in a Midwestern city that victims were more likely to believe that an arrest had occurred than was indicated by the official records. The authors concluded that the victims' lives could be in danger, as they often made decisions based on their perceptions of the criminal justice system's response. There exists a similar dissonance between victims' desire for arrest of the assailant and actual arrest. A questionnaire-based study of women in four shelters in Florida found that although 36 of the 51 respondents had wanted their abusers to be arrested, the police actually arrested only 12, despite Florida's proarrest stance (Yegidis and Renzy, 1994).

The Provision of Services

Public expectations of the police's role in situation involving intimate partner violence have been found to vary. A telephone survey of randomly selected adults in Minnesota found that the majority of respondents favored police fulfilling a service role in such situations, but believed that police viewed themselves in an authoritarian role (Breci and Murphy, 1992). Women who had been abused in the past were more supportive of an authoritarian role for the police than were nonabused women. Stalans (1996) found in her study of 157 members of the Fulton County, Georgia jury pool that the police provision of informal advice was preferred over arrest. Arrest was more likely to be recommended by those with higher levels of education and in situations in which blame is attributed to the offender and the courts are perceived as being more effective. Stalans and Lurigio (1995) found in their vignette-based study conducted with members of the Fulton County, Georgia jury pool that preferences for counseling and jail varied by respondents' personal experience of victimization. For nonvictims, the preferences varied according to the intentionality and the history of violence that was depicted in the vignettes that were presented. More than half of the respondents indicated that court-ordered mediation was the preferred court disposition. Women favored the issuance of restraining orders by the courts more than men; the preference was particularly notable in situations in which there was a history of past abuse. Individuals who had experienced partner violence were more likely to favor court-issued restraining orders than were individuals who had no such personal history.

Bowker (1986) has noted that help-seeking via the police differs in three significant aspects from help-seeking through other resources. First, the police rarely offer suggestions; instead, their advice is prescriptive. Second, they deal directly with the abuser. Third, the activities of the police are public and, consequently, may have a greater deterrent effect on batterers than imprisonment. Bowker found in his study with battered women that police officers provided a real service in approximately one-half of the situations to which they were called.

Referral of the victim to social service organizations has been found more likely among officers with higher educational levels and among officers of the sheriffs department, as compared with urban area police (Belknap and McCall, 1994). Police are more likely to refer the victim to a shelter and to assign blame to the husband in situations in which the victim is visibly injured and/or the assailant suffers from hallucinations (Finn and Stalans, 1995).

Police effectiveness in addressing situations involving domestic violence can be potentially increased through the development and maintenance of partnerships with organizations providing services to battered women and/or batterers. A study of the effectiveness of the partnership developed between the Chicago police and a family service agency found that the rate of police referral of domestic violence calls to a social service partner varied across police districts. These differences were attributable, in part, to differing levels of enthusiasm among district commanders (Caputo, 1991). Interestingly, the Domestic Violence Reduction Unit (DVRU) of the Portland, Oregon police department, together with community representatives, adopted an approach to reducing intimate partner violence that was premised on the social learning approach at the individual level and patriarchy theory at the societal level. The DVRU had as its goals an increase in the number of prosecutions for misdemeanor domestic violence charges, regardless of the victim's willingness to cooperate, and an increase in victims' ability to negotiate the criminal justice system (Jolin and Moose, 1997).

Research has demonstrated that community-policing concepts can be utilized to increase the public's confidence in the police and the public's reporting of incidents of partner violence. The Domestic Violence Intervention Education Project (DVIEP) was conducted in public housing projects in three precincts in New York. One of two treatments was assigned to families reporting domestic violence incidents: public education, which included both oral presentations and the distribution of leaflets and posters at community and tenants' meetings, and home visits from a team consisting of a social worker and a police officer, who provided victims with information about their rights and advised assailants of the potential criminal consequences of their behavior. Although the interventions did not appear to reduce the level of violence, it appeared that they were associated with an increase in the reporting of events (Davis and Taylor, 1997).

Barriers to Police Involvement

Victims, batterers, and/or bystanders may be reluctant to call on the police for protection and/or assistance in resolving an incident of intimate partner violence for a multiplicity of reasons, relating to the specific circumstances surrounding the incident, past experiences with the police, and/or the anticipated response of the police. These reasons are reviewed briefly here. Chapter 7, which is devoted to a discussion of the responses of individuals who have been the object of partner violence, should be consulted for additional detail.

Abused immigrants may be particularly reticent to seek police intervention for domestic violence due to cultural norms (Ho, 1990), fear of being reported to the Immigration and Naturalization Service by their partner or the police, or fear of retaliation by their partner. Such fears are not unfounded. Immigration attorneys have frequently observed that an undocumented individual often comes to the attention of the INS as the result of a well-placed telephone call by his or her intimate partner (Loue and Faust, 1998).

The involvement of the police in episodes of partner violence is impeded not only by barriers which deter victims from availing themselves of police services, but also by systemic barriers and beliefs which handicap and frustrate police officers. Ellis (1987) explored two beliefs that appear to be related to officers' reluctance to respond to domestic violence calls: the belief that domestic disturbance calls are extremely dangerous and the acceptance of this belief, without questioning, throughout law enforcement literature. Ellis' review of the literature found that the figures most often presented with respect to the numbers of officers killed during such calls reflect the absolute number of such deaths, and do not view the numbers of deaths in response to the numbers of calls for assistance. Second, many of these statistics reflect all "disturbance" calls, which include domestic violence disturbances, barroom brawls, and noisy parties. There exists a perception among police that responding to domestic violence incidents does not constitute "real" police work (Breci and Simons, 1987).

Feldberg (1985) has suggested that the manner in which courts handle cases of partner violence may actually serve as a deterrent to arrest and intervention. Feldberg (1985) identified four primary styles of police response to a domestic violence situation: (1) avoidance, through which the officer threatens to arrest everyone if they continue to cause a disturbance; (2) punishment; (3) negotiation, including mediation; and (4) professional detachment, whereby the officer attempts to divert attention away from the crisis. Feldberg maintains that officers rely primarily on the first two modes of response if they do not trust that the courts will satisfactorily address the situation. If there is a lack of available social services, they are more likely, however, to adopt the third or fourth response style. Hirschel and colleagues (1992) similarly concluded from their historical review of the criminal justice system's approach to spousal abuse in the United States that officers continue to be reluctant to intervene in such situations possibly due to disappointment in the results to date of proarrest policies and as a result of the failure of the criminal justice system as a whole to address partner violence effectively.

The Prosecutorial Response

The "traditional" response of prosecutorial offices to instances of domestic violence was similar to that of the police. Prosecutors often perceived domestic violence cases as family matters that did not belong in the court (Welch, 1994). Consequently, there existed both low prosecution rates of domestic violence cases and high dismissal rates (Welch, 1994).

In an effort to reform such practices, some jurisdictions have adopted "no-drop" prosecutorial policies. Such policies provide that once a complaint has been filed, the victim of intimate partner violence may not withdraw it, despite threats or intimidation from the batterer (Development in the Law, 1993). However, such policies do not guarantee that the victim will cooperate and, absent such cooperation, the prosecutor may be forced to rely on existing police and medical reports. Additionally, the policies do not confer protection on the victim from actions of the batterer during the course of the criminal proceedings.

Prosecutors can require that men charged with partner violence present for treatment while the criminal charges are pending and can request that the judge order treatment. Research has indicated that the concurrent reliance on a law enforcement and a treatment approach may be effective:

> "[L]aw and order" and treatment approaches operate symbiotically to reduce further violence. Arrest serves both a didactic and deterrent function, showing the man that wife assault is unacceptable and will be punished by the state. Treatment then provides the opportunity for the man to learn new responses to the interchanges with his wife that formerly generated violent behavior. (Dutton and McGregor, 1991: 131).

Legislative Response

Mandatory Reporting

The majority of states have enacted laws that require that health care providers report to law enforcement and/or public health agencies cases involving domestic violence and/or injuries resulting from specified acts or weapons, such as gunshot wounds (Lund, 1999). As an example, California law requires that health care providers notify the local law enforcement agency to report injuries or wounds that they know or reasonably suspect could have resulted from assaultive or abusive acts. A written report, which includes the victim's name and whereabouts, the extent of the injuries, and the assailant's identity, must be forwarded to that agency within two days of receiving the information about the victim. (California Penal Code sections 11160-11163.2). Opponents of the law asserted that the law deprived battered women of the ability to decide for themselves whether police should intervene (Hyman, Schillinger, and Lo, 1995), while proponents argued that the law assisted in the identification and prosecution of batterers (Coulter and Chez, 1997). An interview-based study with 39 agencies in California found that reports of battering from health care providers constitute a small proportion of domestic violence caseloads, with emergency rooms providing the largest proportion of these (Lund, 1999). In general, neither the oral nor the written reports were provided to the agencies on a timely basis. Twenty-eight of the agencies had a standard protocol in place to handle telephone reports from providers. In many cases, the agencies were unable to match the reports that they received from health care providers with previous crime reports.

Mandatory Arrest

Despite the controversy surrounding the use of arrest as a deterrent to partner violence, many states now have policies which favor arrest (Bachman and Coker, 1995). For instance, New York's Family Protection and Domestic Violence Intervention Act of 1994 mandates arrest in domestic violence situations in which a police officer has reason to believe that certain felony or misdemeanor offenses have been committed or that a protective order has been violated (Chapter 222, New York Laws 786; see Walsh, 1995).

Numerous arguments have been advanced to support these legislative reforms, even in the absence of evidence linking arrest to reduced recidivism. Stark (1996) enumerated 5 reasons to maintain mandatory arrest policies: (1) to control police behavior; (2) to provide protection from immediate violence; (3) to provide a general deterrent effect among batterers in the general population, as opposed to a specific deterrent effect on the batterer involved in a particular incident; (4) to communicate to the public that domestic violence is a serious crime that will not be tolerated; and (5) to redistribute police resources to make them available to women on a more equal basis. A report issued to the National Institute of Justice emphasized the message communicated through such policies:

Even though arrest has not been shown to have particular deterrent value, and even if arrest may not have much punitive value, it may still constitute a more conscionable choice than non-arrest. Not to arrest may communicate to men that abuse is not serious and to women that they are on their own. It may communicate to children, who very often witness abuse of their mothers, that the abuse of women is tolerated, if not legitimated. It may communicate to the public at large that a level of violence which is unacceptable when inflicted by a stranger is accepted when inflicted by an intimate. (Hirschel, Hutchison, Kelley, and Pesackis, 1991).

Steinman's argument in favor of arrest clearly links the remedy of arrest to the underlying exchange theory:

Arrest imposes the most costs and no formal action imposes the fewest. The costs imposed by arrest include a brief time in jail or the chance of it and the possibility of being prosecuted and suffering court-mandated penalties like a fine or a jail term. Arrest may trigger indirect costs for offenders such as humiliation, divorce or separation from their partners, and loss of job (Steinman, 1991: 222).

Buzawa and Buzawa (1996), however, have argued that the policy of mandatory arrest cannot be justified, particularly in misdemeanor situations. They assert that mandatory arrest policies (1) increase the cost to public agencies because arrest costs are high and arrests require a substantial investment of time; (2) may result in adverse consequences, including an increased level of frustration among police officers due to their lack of discretion; (3) fail to consider the preferences of the victims; (4) increase the likelihood that judges will not consider domestic violence cases seriously because some of the arrests may be for *de minimus* offenses or may be frivolous; and (5) inadvisedly increase police power by permitting them to arrest both parties, thereby discouraging victims from reporting violent incidents.

Saccuzzo (1999) has examined mandatory arrest policies from the perspective of therapeutic jurisprudence. This orientation requires an examination of the concordance of the legal system's response to domestic violence with therapeutic goals, such as the rehabilitation of the assailants (see Simon, 1996). Therapeutic jurisprudence is premised on a cognitive approach to treatment, whereby attempts are made to modify unrealistic expectations and exaggerated perceptions (Saccuzzo, 1999). Simon (1996) has argued that the criminal justice system has fostered unrealistic expectations and perceptions, i.e. cognitive distortions in 4 domains: (1) the moral justification or euphemistic labeling of the violence; (2) the disavowal of responsibility (see chapter 7 on responses of the batterer); (3) the minimization of the effects of the violence; and (4) the dehumanization of the victim. Mandatory arrest policies serve to restructure cognitive distortions by emphasizing the victim's right to be free of such violence (Saccuzzo, 1999). A strong prosecutorial response following arrest denies the batterer support in trivializing his or her actions and the opportunity to maintain such behavior.

Permissive Arrest

Many jurisdictions now permit, but do not mandate, the warrantless arrest of batterers in certain circumstances (Welch, 1994). However, such statutes have been criticized as providing inadequate protection to abused women and failing to reduce the incidence of intimate partner violence (Welch, 1994). A study of Ohio's permissive arrest statute, enacted in 1978 (Ohio Revised Code sections 109.73, 109.77, 737.11, 1901.18, 1901.19, 1909.02, 2933.16, 1935.03, 2929.25-.26, 3113.31-32), found that the police provided victims with notice of certain rights in only 20 to 30 percent of the cases and that the police remained reluctant to effectuate an arrest if there was no physical evidence of abuse or if it was difficult to determine which party was the offender (Christoff, 1992). Additionally, there was no evidence to indicate that the statute had served to reduce the incidence of domestic violence. Subsequently, Ohio enacted a preferential arrest statute, which indicates that arrest is the preferred course of action under specified circumstances (Ohio Revised Code section 2935.032).

Judicial Response

The woman who is battered may herself face legal difficulties in both the criminal and civil contexts. In the criminal context, she may be facing charges of murder if she kills her abusive partner. In the civil context, she may have been confronted, both literally and figuratively, on an ongoing basis, by her abusive intimate in attempting to resolve issues relating to property division and child custody, should she decide to leave the relationship.

The Defense of Self-Defense

In general, a successful plea of self-defense to defend oneself against a charge of murder for the killing of another requires a reasonable belief on the part of the individual effectuating the killing that he or she was in imminent danger of great bodily harm or death at the time that he or she committed the defensive act. Additionally, the defendant must demonstrate that the only means of escape from such danger was through the use of deadly force. This requirement of objective reasonableness stems from a conceptualization of self-defense as it relates to one-time, face-to-face confrontations between men. However, it does not contemplate a situation involving the repeated beating and terrorization of a physically weaker individual socialized to refrain from violence by a physically stronger individual socialized to value strength and aggressiveness. As a result, a woman who kills her sleeping husband following yet another violent incident may be found to not be in imminent danger and her use of a gun against her partner may be judged to be unreasonable, resulting in a conviction for murder (*State v. Stewart*, 1988). A number of states, however, permit the reasonableness of a woman's actions to be judged on a subjective basis (*State v. Koss*, 1990; *State v. Leidholm*, 1983; *State v.*

Wanrow, 1977). Still others utilize a two-part test, whereby the individual must have believed that his or her life was in imminent danger (subjective belief) and that belief must have been objectively reasonable from the perspective of an ordinary, reasonable person in a similar situation (*People v. Aris*, 1989; *State v. Gallegos*, 1986; *State v. Kelly*, 1984; *State v. Norman*, 1989).

Some states permit a defense of imperfect self-defense, whereby an individual can be convicted of manslaughter rather than murder. The concept of self-defense acknowledges the individual's subjective belief that he or she was in imminent danger, but rejects the reasonableness of that belief. (*People v. Humphrey*, 1996; *In re Christian S.*, 1994).

These differences in the interpretation and application of self-defense are attributable to the differences among several competing paradigms of self-defense law: individualist models, which emphasize autonomy and the rights of the individual who is the target of aggression, thereby diminishing the need for proportionality in responding to the perceived danger; communitarian models, which stress the need for proportionality and the imminence of the danger, thereby considering the rights of the aggressor vis-à-vis the intended victim; and self-preservation models, which emphasize the instinct of self-preservation and reduce the importance of imminence and proportionality (Fletcher, 1988). Fletcher (1988: 27) has explained:

> The requirements of imminence, necessity, and proportionality, expressed in different languages, are found in virtually every legal system in the world. Yet these basic structural elements account for only the surface language of the law. Beneath the surface there surge conflicting moral and ideological forces that drive the interpretation of the law in particular directions. We may all be united in the terms in which we discuss self-defense, but we are divided in our loyalties to unarticulated theories that account for our willingness now to stretch the law broadly, now to interpret it narrowly. These deeper forces shaping our interpretation reflect the confrontation between passion and reason in the law.

The Admissibility of "Battered Woman Syndrome" as Evidence

Courts continue to be divided on the issue of whether evidence of "battered woman syndrome" is admissible in conjunction with an individual's claim of self-defense in the killing of an abusive partner. The court in *State v. Thomas* (1981) found that the lower court had ruled properly in excluding evidence of battered woman syndrome because it was irrelevant to the woman's claim of self-defense at the time she shot her abusive partner, because the subject of the expert testimony to be offered was within the competence of the jury, because the concept of the "battered wife syndrome" was not sufficiently developed scientifically to warrant testimony, and because the value of such testimony was outweighed by its potentially prejudicial effect. Since that time, numerous courts have admitted evidence relating to the battered woman syndrome (*State v. Allery*, 1984; *State v. Anaya*, 1981; *State v. Hennum*, 1989). However, even where such testimony is found to be relevant, the

court may exclude it if it finds that the expert proffering the testimony does not have
adequate credentials to do so. For instance, in *People v. White* (1980), the court
found that the testimony of the woman's treating physician regarding the tendency
of battered women to remain with their partners was not admissible. Although the
doctor was an experienced internist, he was not skilled in psychology and had not
had extensive experience with battered women.

Evidence of the battered woman syndrome has been used in criminal
proceedings to assist in the establishment of a batterer's guilt for the murder of his
partner. In the case of *State v. Baker* (1980), Baker was being tried for the first
degree murder of his wife. He pleaded not guilty by reason of insanity. Two
psychiatrists testified that he was legally insane at the time that he committed the
crime. Other family members testified to the repeated beatings he had inflicted on
his wife prior to her death. On cross-examination, one of the experts acknowledged
that Baker's marriage probably fell within the definition of "battered wife
syndrome." This provided an alternative explanation of the defendant's conduct;
the prosecution was essentially contending that the murder of his wife was but one
incident in a recurring pattern of domestic violence, that was not caused by mental
illness. The court found that such evidence was relevant to the defendant's claim of
insanity at the time the crime was committed.

Schneider (quoted in Gillespie, 1988: 180) has observed the potential and
inadvertent consequence of reliance on this defense: that "battered woman
syndrome" will be perceived as yet another example of woman's irrationality, albeit
legally excusable, rather than an explanation of the reasonableness of her behavior:

> "[B]attered woman syndrome" carries with it stereotypes of
> individual incapacity and inferiority which lawyers and judges may
> respond to precisely because they correspond to stereotypes of
> women which the lawyers and judges already hold. Battered
> woman syndrome does not mean, but can be heard as reinforcing
> stereotypes of women as passive, sick, powerless and victimized.
> Although it was developed merely to describe the common
> psychological characteristics which battered women share, and it is
> undoubtedly an accurate description of these characteristics,
> battered woman syndrome can be misused and misheard to
> enshrine the old stereotypes in a new form. This repeats an
> historic theme of treatment of women by the criminal law—
> women who are criminals are viewed as crazy or helpless or both.

Downs has spoken to the legal complexities and difficulties surrounding the use
of battered woman syndrome as a defense in the criminal context:

> Generally speaking, criminal acts are "justified" in law if self-
> defense of others is involved or if the larger social good would be
> promoted more by committing the act than by not committing it
> (for example, trespassing to save a baby from crawling into a
> swimming pool). Criminal acts are "excused" if the defendant is
> under "duress" or lacks the mental or emotional capacity to be
> blameworthy. Though the lines that distinguish justification and

excuse are not always clear... justification "speaks to the rightness of the act; an excuse to whether the actor is accountable for a concededly wicked act." Thus, self-defense is considered a right thing to do because of the defensive rights of the original target and the wickedness of the original aggressor. Excused acts are wrong in themselves, but we deem the perpetrator less blameworthy because of the extraordinary situational pressures he or she confronted (duress) or because of mental or related impairment (insanity). Self-defense and duress also involve a standard of reason that is lacking in incapacity excuses.

Essentially, Downs argues, battered woman syndrome may constitute both an excuse, thereby supporting the depiction of a battered woman as lacking capacity or as helpless, and a justification, thereby acknowledging responsibility even under difficult circumstances. Consequently, Downs asserts, reliance on the battered woman syndrome as an explanation for behavior provides little guidance in attempts to distinguish those who are culpable for their behavior from those who are not.

The Scope of Statutory Protections

Although some states' laws clearly protect intimate partners, regardless of whether their mate is of the same sex or of the opposite sex, the laws of others are often silent on this issue. Additionally, the criminal laws of some states are narrowly drawn and appear to apply to individuals assaulting only those individuals specifically enumerated by statute. A number of courts have read these provisions expansively, however. As an example, several courts have interpreted domestic violence statutes protecting persons living as a spouse as applicable to same-sex partners who function like a spouse (*State v. Hadinger*, 1991; *State v. Linner*, 1996). The state of Iowa charged Kellogg with the crime of domestic abuse assault, which is an aggravated misdemeanor under Iowa law (*State v. Kellogg*, 1996). The charge resulted from his battering of his live-in girlfriend. Although they lived in the same dwelling and shared financial responsibilities and had once had a romantic relationship, the romantic component of their relationship had ended and, at the time of the violent incident, had been maintaining separate bedrooms. The statute under which Kellogg had been charged defined assault as occurring between "family or household members who resided with each other at the time of the assault." "Family or household members" was further defined as "spouses, persons cohabiting, parents, or other persons related by consanguinity or affinity, except children under eighteen" (Iowa Code section 236.2(4)). The statute did not, however, define "cohabiting." The court refrained from interpreting the term to apply only to those who are married and, instead, enumerated several factors to be considered in determining whether individuals are cohabiting within the meaning of the criminal statute: (1) whether the individuals are having sexual relations; (2) whether the individuals share income or expenses; (3) whether there is joint use or ownership of the property; (3) whether the individuals involved hold themselves out as husband and wife; (4) the continuity of the relationship; and (6) the length of the relationship (*State v. Kellogg*, 1996).

What should be evident from the foregoing discussion is that no single remedy will "cure" the problem of intimate partner violence, regardless of how it is defined and what its underlying cause is perceived to be. Rather, a coordinated approach within and across numerous functions and institutions is required. Lerman's (1992: 221) description of the requisite linkages is instructive:

> Failure of coordination will cause the failure of any individual remedy. For example, if a statute requires the police to make arrests but the police department does not adopt a policy implementing the statute, the officers responding to calls may not even be aware of the statute. If a particular department adopts a policy implementing the statute, but the officers do not receive adequate training about the nature of woman abuse, they either may fail to make arrests or make inappropriate arrests. If the police are asked to make arrests but the prosecutor files charges in few of the arrest cases, the police may refuse to act, because they believed that making arrests in cases that will be dropped is a pointless exercise. If the prosecutor adopts a policy of aggressively prosecuting abuse cases but fails to provide victim advocacy services to maintain contact with victims, attend to their safety needs and help them to understand the law enforcement system, then the prosecutor is often doomed to frustration because the victims of abuse are less likely to remain available to testify. If the prosecutor sets up a good system within the office and obtains a high rate of convictions and guilty pleas, but the mental health community does not develop expertise on treatment of abusers and establish close communication with the courts, then most abusers will receive little effective attention. If the probation department fails to monitor abusers who have been convicted or who plead guilty to charges of spouse abuse, then there will be no deterrent to engaging in post-conviction recidivism.

CIVIL PROCEEDINGS

Restraining Orders

As indicated, battered partners may refrain from reporting their abuse to others for fear of reprisal by their intimate. Additionally, health care providers may often fail to identify victims of domestic violence as such, and may focus instead on the victim's other psychosocial problems, such as substance use and suicide attempts (Kurz, 1987; Randall, 1990; Stark, Flitcraft, Zuckerman, et al., 1981). Although as many as 25% of women presenting to hospital emergency departments may have been battered, only 2 to 8 percent are identified as such (Campbell, 1992). Many women may not reveal the actual cause of their injuries, and their batterers may go to great lengths to conceal it (Randall, 1990, 1991).

Such efforts to conceal the origin of the injuries and the actual nature of the intimate relationship may ultimately harm the battered individual in the context of proceedings to obtain a restraining order. For instance, a woman may legitimately fear retaliation for her efforts to leave the relationship (Browne and Williams, 1989). Absent documentation of past abuse or intimidation through complaints to the police or medical reports of presentation for the treatment of injuries, the victim may find it difficult to substantiate the basis for his or her request for a temporary restraining order against his or her intimate. Attempts to obtain an order may be further hindered by the law itself; state laws do not uniformly provide for civil protection orders to a woman who is pregnant with the batterer's child but does not yet have a live-born child with the abuser (*Gina C. v. Stephen F.*, 1991; *Woodin v. Rasmussen*, 1990) or to a woman who is dating, but not cohabiting with, the abusive partner (Klein and Orloff, 1993). Even if the victim is able to obtain a temporary restraining order, it may not be respected by the intimate partner. This is particularly true when it is a woman seeking judicial and law enforcement intervention. As an example, the California Committee on Gender Bias in the Courts noted that on the basis of statewide testimony

> Again and again, this committee heard testimony that police officers, district and city attorneys, court personnel, mediators, and judges—the justice system—treated the victims of domestic violence as if their complaints were trivial, exaggerated, or somehow their own fault. (Welling, Biren, Johnston, Kuehl, and Nunn, 1990, section 6, at 5)

The Quincy Court Domestic Violence Program, located in Massachusetts, serves as a model for domestic violence intervention programs. The program is premised on three fundamental goals: integration, communication, and the prioritization of domestic violence issues over other civil matters. The program comprises a separate restraining orders office to provide individual attention to women needing assistance in completing the requisite paperwork; full-time, specialized advocacy services by domestic violence clerks, who are often volunteers from nearby law schools and social work programs; expedited procedures for the presentation of restraining order requests; an accelerated enforcement program, whereby judges may revoke probation for restraining order violations without waiting for a new criminal trial and conviction; a tracking system whereby domestic violence complaints are forwarded to the district attorney's office by the police department; follow-up by counselors of the district attorney's office with the victim of the battering to inform him/her of the court procedures and provide referrals, specially trained staff at the district attorney's office, intensive monitoring of the batterer by the probation department, and linkages with a batterers' treatment program (Salzman, 1994).

Divorce and Custody Proceedings

Difficulties similar to those experienced in attempting to obtain restraining orders may arise in the context of custody proceedings. More than two-thirds of the states permit joint custody. Such arrangements essentially permit batterers to continue to assert their control, particularly because joint custody requires shared decision making on such issues as health, education, and extracurricular activities. The National Council of Juvenile and Family Court Judges cautioned against joint custody arrangements where the intimate relationship has involved abuse:

> Court orders which force victims to share custody with their abusers place both victims and children in danger... Continued aggression and violence between divorced spouses with joint custody has the most adverse consequences for children of any custody option (Family Violence Project, 1990: 26)

The Council has, in addition, noted the inappropriateness of mediation as a strategy for the resolution of custody issues in situations in which family violence has occurred:

> The pattern of power, control, and dominance by the abusive spouse which emerges over time in such relationships leaves the victim in a position of fear, dependence, and weakness. Even if the mediator is aware of the situation, it may be impossible to overcome the power imbalance between the two, such that any agreement reached will not truly have been voluntary. (Family Violence Project, 1990: 28)

A number of states require that evidence of spousal abuse be considered in determining custody issues. Children are often aware of intraparental violence that occurs (Geffner and Pagelow, 1990) and are harmed by it, either directly or indirectly (David and Carlson, 1987; Hughes, Parkingson, and Vargo, 1989; Wolfe, Jaffe, Wilson, and Zak, 1985). Additionally, children whose mothers are battered are significantly more likely to be battered than children of nonviolent homes (Stark and Flitcraft, 1985). (See chapter 8 for a discussion of the responses of children to intimate partner violence.)

Tort Suits

Traditionally, a married individual has been deemed by law to be immune from suit by his or her spouse. The rule of spousal immunity was originally formulated based upon the notion that a woman's identity was tied to that of her husband, thereby forming one legal unit (McCurdy, 1930). Many states have maintained this rule through to the present day due to concerns that tort actions between members of a married couple would provoke marital unrest and disharmony and fears that such lawsuits could, in fact, be collusive and represent attempts to defraud insurance companies (Ejercito, 1983; *Peters v. Peters*, 1981; *Shook v. Crabb*, 1979). Some states, such as Hawaii, however, permit one spouse to bring a lawsuit against the other for injuries sustained during an abusive relationship (Hawaii Revised Statutes section 663-1, 1984). This effectively recognizes that where abuse has occurred within a relationship and one spouse is so injured as to seek redress for those injuries, there is no marital harmony left to be protected and preserved.

THE RESPONSE OF UNITED STATES IMMIGRATION LAW

Prior to recent changes in the law, immigrant spouses were particularly vulnerable to intimate partner violence. They were often dependent upon their United States citizen or lawful permanent resident spouse for the filing of a petition with the Immigration and Naturalization Service (INS) that would initiate the process of obtaining permanent residence, popularly known as having a "green card." Undocumented spouses who challenged the violence in their households or threatened to report it were not infrequently threatened by their citizen or legally resident spouse with being turned over to the INS for deportation proceedings.

The Violence Against Women Act of 1994 attempted to address this situation by permitting both self-petitioning and a special form of cancellation of removal (a remedy to deportation) to abused spouses and children of United States citizens and lawful permanent residents. In addition, our interpretation of U.S. asylum law has been broadened to encompass domestic violence as a form of persecution and women as a particular social group. Each of these critical changes is discussed below.

Self-Petitioning

Under the self-petitioning provision, an abused spouse or child of a United States citizen or lawful permanent resident may file their own petition to commence the process of becoming a permanent resident, rather than having to depend on the abusive parent or spouse to file the petition. A spouse with an abused child may also file a petition for him- or herself and the child, based on the abuse suffered by the child.

In order to qualify for self-petitioning, the individual must demonstrate that he or she has been "battered" or has been the "subject of extreme cruelty," including "being the victim of any act or threatened act of violence, including any forceful detention, which results or threatens to result in physical or mental injury" (Immigration and Nationality Act section 204(a)). Acts of violence include "psychological or sexual abuse or exploitation, including rape, molestation, incest…or forced prostitution" and "other abuse actions…that, in and of themselves, may not initially appear violent but that are part of an overall pattern of violence" (Immigration and Nationality Act section 204(a)). Additional references should be consulted regarding the documentation of this abuse (Pendleton, 1997).

Additionally, the abuse must (1) have occurred during the marriage and (2) have been perpetrated by the self-petitioner's parent or spouse who was a lawful permanent resident or United States citizen both at the time the self-petitioner files the petition and at the time that the INS approves the petition. The marriage between the self-petitioner and the abuser must have been in good faith, i.e. not entered into to avoid the usual immigration process. The self-petitioner must be residing in the United States at the time that he or she files the petition and must have resided with the abusive spouse.

Cancellation of Removal

Cancellation of removal is a remedy to deportation (removal from the United States) that is potentially available from an immigration judge in the context of a removal proceeding. The applicant must demonstrate that (1) he or she was abused by a United States citizen or lawful permanent resident or is the parent of a United States citizen's permanent resident's child who was abused by the citizen or permanent resident; (2) the abuser was the spouse or parent at the time that the acts of domestic violence occurred; (3) at least a portion of the abuse occurred in the United States; (4) the applicant has been continuously physically present in the United States for at least three years; (5) the applicant has had good moral character during the three year period immediately preceding the date of application; and (6) deportation will result in extreme hardship (Immigration and Nationality Act section 240A).

Asylum

Asylum is potentially available to a foreign-born individual who is in the United States and is unwilling or unable to return to his or her country of nationality or, if he or she has no nationality, to his or her country of last habitual residence due to persecution or fear of persecution on account of race, religion, nationality, membership in a particular social group, or political opinion (Immigration and Nationality Act section 208). Other sources should be consulted for a detailed explanation of persecution, fear of persecution, application procedures, and the nature of the evidence that must be presented to support a claim for asylum (*INS v. Elias-Zacarias*, 1992; *Desir v. Ilchert*, 1988; *INS v. Cardoza Fonseca*, 1987; *Matter of Mogharrabi*, 1987; Hines, 1997).

A number of nonprecedential decisions by immigration judges have recognized domestic violence as a form of persecution. In *Matter of A and Z* (1994), the immigration judge granted asylum to a Jordanian woman who had suffered continual physical and verbal abuse from her husband during their 30-year marriage. The judge found that she was a member of the social group of women who challenged Jordan's traditions and government, and that she was unable to either divorce her husband or receive police protection. Similarly, a judge found in *Matter of M and K* (1995) that a woman from Sierra Leone had established her claim to asylum as a member of the social group of "women who have been punished with physical spousal abuse for attempting to assert their individual autonomy." A Bangladeshi woman was granted asylum in *Matter of Sharmin* (1996) on the basis of her husband's physical beatings in retaliation for her activities in the women's movement and her refusal to both remain indoors and to cease all communication with others.

A Guatemalan woman was granted asylum as a member of the social group of "Guatemalan women who become involved intimately with Guatemalan men who believe in male domination [and] are targeted by their male companions...through violence" (*Matter of A--P--*, 1996). The immigration judge specifically found that, despite horrific abuse, the Guatemalan police refused to protect her from her husband, who had been a soldier, and the courts had refused to grant her a divorce because her husband had refused to consent to one. The court described her abuse:

> He beat her often, and at many occasions, inflicting severe injury. He dislocated her jaw, nearly pushed out her eye, tried to cut off her hands with his machete, kicked her in the abdomen and vagina, and tried to force her to abort when she was pregnant with her second child by severely kicking her in the spine. He would drag her by her hair, use her head to break windows and mirrors, whip her with pistols and electrical cords, and threaten her with knives...A--P-- testified that she was severely sexually abused by her husband, both vaginally and anally, almost on a daily basis.... The sexual abuse severely injured A--P--, causing extensive hemorrhaging, excruciating abdominal pain and disease (*Matter of A--P--*, 1996, pp. 3-4).

7

RESPONSES OF THE BATTERER

A man says yes without knowing
how to decide even what the question is,
and is caught up, and then carried along
and never again escapes from his own cocoon;
and that's how we are, forever falling
into the deep well of other beings;
and one thread wraps itself around our necks,
another entwines a foot, and then it is impossible,
impossible to move except in the well—
nobody can rescue us from other people.

It seems as if we don't know how to speak;
it seems as if there are words which escape,
which are missing, which have gone away and left us
to ourselves, tangled up in snares and threads.
(Neruda, 1993: 73)

THE ACCOUNT

The assailant in an intimate partner violence situation may offer an account of his or her actions at various points in time: to the partner at the time of occurrence, to the law enforcement officer who is called to the scene, to the defense attorney, and to the judge and/or jury. The account may consist of such mechanisms as outright denial of the behavior, or consist of an excuse that attempts to justify it. Sykes and Matza (1957), in their work with deviant behavior, have referred to such denials of responsibility as a "technique of neutralization." These accounts may be used in an attempt to excuse or justify the conduct to the batterer him- or herself, to the victim of the assault, or to others, and/or to mitigate the consequences of the battering behavior.

Hearn (1996) has identified 9 types of accounts that male assaultive partners offer in response to an incident of battering: (1) denial, (2) forgetting, blanking out, and not knowing, (3) exclusion and inclusion, (4) minimization, (5) removal of the self and of intention, (6) excuses, (7) justifications, (8) confessions, and (9) combinations of talk. Denial is the most basic technique of neutralization; the batterer may deny that the incident ever happened, or that a portion of it never happened.

The following responses are also characteristic of denial:

- I didn't do it.
- I never touched her.
- I don't remember the incidents/It was so long ago.
- I was out of control./I was just seeing red./I didn't know what I was doing.
- I was drunk./I was high.
- I was in a blackout.
- I was in a "dry-drunk" blackout.
- I'm sober now so my anger isn't a problem for me anymore.
- I don't get angry anymore.
- Our real problem is that we just can't communicate.
- I don't have an anger and abuse problem.
- I'm not abusive.
- I'm not controlling (Decker, 1999: 23-24).

One man who was ultimately convicted of the attempted murder of his ex-wife explained what he was thinking as he repeatedly assaulted her in front of the police, without being stopped:

> I wasn't thinking. I don't even remember being there or what happened. All I saw was this blinding white light, nothing else. I don't remember anything else (Felder and Victor, 1996: 16, quoting Charles Thurman, 1988).

One man who had a history of battering his female partners explained about one relationship:

> Our relationship and our issues seemed dramatic, but I certainly didn't see myself as a batterer....I was intellectual. I believed in equality and feminism, and was immersed in the art culture. (Sid, quoted in Paymar, 2000: 93).

The technique of exclusion and inclusion refers to the batterer's definition of violence and what is excluded from coverage, thereby eliminating the battering incident. For instance, if physical violence is defined as more than a push, then holding, restraining, and pushing are not identified as acts of violence; the violent incident then never occurred. If physical violence did not cause visible injury, then it did not happen. If the violence was sexual, it was not violence, it was sex.

The mechanism of minimization similarly accomplishes the exclusion of certain acts from the category of violence. For instance, it was "only" a push; he "just" held her for a small moment. Other examples of minimization include the following:

- I only hit her once.
- I didn't really hurt her./She bruises easily.

- It's not that big a deal.
- I'm not nearly as bad as my dad was.
- This is nothing compared to what my friends do to their wives.
- I didn't hit her very hard.
- She's a big/strong woman. (i.e. "She can take it")
- I "kind of" pushed her.
- I just gave her a "little" shove.
- She "fell down" after I pushed her.
- She exaggerates.
- The police just overreacted.
- It didn't really happen that way (Decker, 1999: 24).

Removal of the self and of intention refers to such phrases as "I am not a violent person," essentially denying the possibility that a violent act could have occurred. The assaultive partner may also explain that the injury resulted from the female partner's own actions: "I didn't intend to hurt her. If she hadn't moved in that direction, my hand wouldn't have made contact with her face."

Excuses attempt to place the blame for the action on others. Excuses most frequently include the batterer's past, such as his mother or school; substances that affected him, such as drugs or alcohol; the behavior of the woman that made it impossible for him to avoid the action, e.g. nagging; and forces within the man that made him uncontrollable, such as a mental illness (Hearn, 1996). Andres English-Howard, convicted of the murder of his wife, recounted the events leading to his wife's killing:

> She was my, it got to the point where, where she was my...conscience....And Andrea knew what to say to, um, to make me react...
>
> I went in, I went into her room and, wanted to shut her, I wanted to shut her up...And she kept saying the one thing she could say to me that, um, that really made a difference was telling me to take responsibility for, take responsibility for my, my actions....
>
> So the next thing I, I knew, I found, I, I, I was on her. Like, like, like I grabbed her...I, I grabbed her neck...I wanted her to, I wanted her to shut up...She, um, she said, um, I, I grabbed her neck....I, I just grabbed her...Started to choke her...It shut her up. She was like my, my, my, she had become my conscience....
>
> And I grabbed her to shut her up. And she told me I was hurting her and I, it, it, did, I hear that. I mean, it didn't, it didn't mean anything....(Quoted in Jones, 2000: 120)

The killing, he explained, was the result of a cocaine-instilled delirium and the entreaties of his wife.

Justifications do not deny responsibility for the action, but they essentially argue that the battering act was necessary as a response to something. Common justifications include the female partner's infidelity; the female partner's lack of attention to her responsibilities, such as housework; and the failure of the female partner to restrict her movements and her autonomy in accordance with the batterer's dictates.   The following excerpts illustrate situations involving justification:

> With my wife—she gets on me about moving the furniture, that I'm not doing it right: "You always do this, you never do that, you never think about anyone else, you're only thinking about yourself...." The leg of the sofa breaks, now I'm the dummy who did it. She runs me down about money...."(Wexler, 2000: 12)

> There were times I would goad her by getting in her face, calling her particular names so she would strike first. When she did, it would give me the green light to knock the hell out of her. After all, she hit me first. I was never afraid of her. Sometimes I would laugh at her after she hit me. (Andy, quoted in Paymar, 2000: 11)

Confessions involve the acceptance of responsibility for the violence, but are often accompanied by a "naïve" explanation, such as "I beat her because I loved her so much."   Combinations of talk refers to the use of multiple mechanisms to account for the violence. Reliance on multiple techniques is not uncommon among men who have a long career of violence (Hearn, 1996).

As Downs (1996) has noted, one's response to a batterer's account is intimately linked to one's normative assumptions and to the narrative itself. Bennet and Feldman (1969: 6, 10, 32) observed the critical function that the narrative plays in determining the outcome to and for the batterer in the context of the criminal justice system:

> Perhaps the most significant application of the storytelling perspective involves clarifying the nature of bias in the justice process.   Stories are symbolic reconstructions of events and actions. People who cannot manipulate symbols within a narrative form may be at a disadvantage even when, as witnesses or defendants, they are telling the truth....
> The inadequate development of setting, character, means, or motive can, as any literature student knows, render a story's action ambiguous. In a novel or film, such ambiguity may be an aesthetic flaw. In a trial, it is grounds for reasonable doubt.

A number of studies lend support to the above observation.   Shields and Hannecke (1983) found in their study of male spouse assailants that 68 percent of the assailants attributed their behavior to externals causes or to alcohol. Dutton (1985) found in a study of 75 men who battered that 21 percent proffered excuses to explain their behavior. Several other researchers have found in their studies of men in treatment that several "techniques of neutralization" are common, including the minimization of the assault and its consequences, the attribution of blame to the victim, or the definition of the assaultive behavior as consistent with cultural norms (Sonkin, Martin, and Walker, 1985).

It has been hypothesized that a synergistic relationship exists between the willingness of the larger society to accept such accounts and the attribution of blame for the assaultive behavior to external causes (Collins, 1983). There is some empirical evidence to support this hypothesis. Saunders (1995) found in his study of 111 police officers' attitudes towards intimate partner violence that the officers' willingness to arrest assailants was related to the assailants' proffered justification for the assault. For instance, where assailants explained their behavior as a response to their partners' lack of sexual fidelity, the officer were much less likely to arrest the assailant.

In Brazil, the interplay between the assailant's account and the legal consequences of his actions is striking. The defendant in the 1990 spousal murder case in Apucarana was acquitted on the grounds that the murder constituted a legitimate defense of his honor because his wife had committed adultery. Brazil's highest court reversed the decision, holding that this did not constitute a defense of honor, but rather of "self-esteem, vanity, and the pride of the Lord who sees his wife as property." Despite this clear denunciation of murder as a legitimate response to adultery, the lower court again acquitted the husband on the grounds that he was defending his honor (Americas Watch, 1991: 18-19).

And, when the legal consequences fail to respond to the proffered account, others may bolster the account, hoping still to modify the response. A recent incident in Ohio provides an example. A Yemen-born man was convicted of and sentenced to a one year period of probation following his guilty plea to a charge of domestic violence, resulting from having hit his wife in the face. As a result of that conviction, he became subject to deportation from the United States because U.S. immigration law specifies that an immigrant can be deported if convicted of a crime that carries a sentence of one or more years in jail. The immigrant's wife had not pressed charges against her husband, but the Akron Police Department had (Sangiacomo, 1999). His lawyer, in commenting on the conviction, implicitly minimized violence against women in stating, "All it takes to make an immigrant deported is for an angry wife or girlfriend to file a police report for abuse. If he's convicted, he's gone."

RETALIATION

Batterers may retaliate against their victims for having reported the battering incident to the police, for having sought a restraining order, or for attempting to leave the relationship (Felder and Victor, 1996). Felder and Victor maintain that one of the most effective ways to prevent such retaliation is to institute mandatory prosecution:

> If men know from the beginning that, regardless of what threats they make to the victim, it makes no difference because it's out of the victim's hands, it's him against the state, the problem of intimidation or lying to drop the charges wouldn't be an issue. The reason a woman is in danger is because suddenly she has power and control over her batterer (Felder and Victor, 1996: 135, quoting Elizabeth Loewy, New York City district attorney).

TREATMENT

Treatment programs for men who batter women are relatively new. As recently as 1982, there were only 40 programs and services in the United States that were devoted specifically to men who batter women. Most of those utilizing such services were there through self-referral (Star, 1982). By 1985, the number of such programs has increased to 90 (Pirog-Good and Stets-Kealey (1985). It is now estimated that there may be hundreds of such programs nationally.

It is not unusual, however, for a violent partner to participate in treatment or rehabilitation as a condition of a court order, rather than on his or her own initiative (personal communication, Cuyahoga County Task Force on Domestic Violence). Dutton and Golant (1995: 13) have described the reaction of many men upon first entering into such a treatment program:

> The men who were referred to our treatment groups usually had never been in psychotherapy before and had thought it was for "sissies." Sent by the courts, they would rage and cry in their opening-night anxiety, some storming out, others attacking the justice system or their wives' actions that "caused" their violence. Others broke into tears of self-recrimination and remorse.

The outrage expressed by the abuser at the state involvement in his life may be even more extreme in instances in which the abuser is affluent and "well-connected" (Felder and Victor, 1996).

Dutton and Golant (1995) have suggested that a central theme of treatment must be the acceptance of personal responsibility for one's own behavior. Although critical, this step may be exceedingly difficult. Adams (1989: 84) has observed:

> [U]nfortunately, many abusive men enter counseling wanting guarantees of marital reconciliation and drop out promptly when guarantees are not given. This type of angry and manipulative behavior constitutes initial grief reaction to a loss that isn't yet accepted. The initial denial is accompanied by anger and accusations directed at the wife for abandoning and "humiliating" the man, and bargaining for her return with promises of change and/or counseling. If these ploys don't work, the man becomes depressed and feels unable to care for himself. In therapy, he is very dependent on the therapist for a "quick fix" or formula for creating the appearance of change.

Treatment is rendered even more difficult by various cultural and social structural supports for the battering of women. Tifft (1993) has noted the sex- and gender-based hierarchy that exists within our culture, our cultural support of patriarchal arrangements within families, and the reinforcement of hierarchical structure throughout our society, e g places of employment, which then defines expectations, behaviors, and relationships. Language is used to objectify and denigrate women, through the use of such terms as "bitch" and "cow" to describe women, the use of words such as "pussy-whipped" to describe and derogate men who show concern for their partners' feelings, and the use of expressions, such as "piece of ass," to characterize women as mere body parts.

Confrontation in group sessions may be used as a strategy to help the batterers gain a new perspective on their behavior. Participants are helped to distinguish conflict issues from feelings and from actions. Other researchers have emphasized the need to address not only anger management, communication skills, and self-esteem issues, but also the man's underlying attitudes towards women and issues relating to dependency and intimacy (Tifft, 1993). Adams (1989: 94) advised:

> The abusive man must be held accountable for his controlling behaviors and attitudes towards women....Any approach that focuses exclusively on individual or psychologic change is doomed to failure, since sexist attitudes and behaviors on the individual level are socially sanctioned and reproduced. It is essential to make these connections between the psychologic and political and to understand the ways that political structures and hierarchies shape individual feelings, attitudes, and behaviors. [Note: These arrangements are located in the family divisions of labor and decision-making arrangements as well as in the organization of other institutions of the society including the organization of the state and economy.] The work to eradicate male violence toward women demands both social and individual change, confrontation and compassion.

Sonkin and colleagues (1985) have recommended that treatment programs focus on (1) decreasing isolation and developing an interpersonal support system; (2) increasing feelings of personal power and self-esteem; (3) increasing the batterer's sense of responsibility for the violent behavior and awareness of the consequences of violent behavior; (4) developing communication, assertiveness, and stress-reduction skills; (5) developing an ability to empathize with the partner; (6) developing control over substance use; (7) increasing understanding of the relationship between violent behavior and sex-role behavior; and (8) encouraging individual or couple therapy. One judge who has presided over many cases involving partner violence deems it critical to treatment that batterers begin to understand why they batter and the battered begin to understand why they stay:

> Those men who are functioning on a higher intellectual level...we can safely assume are more affluent. They are the ones who will go about controlling their partners in a more methodical and subtle way, while others, less sophisticated and successful, will achieve the same results by functioning more viscerally. Logically, the batterer is usually married to or living with a woman who understands how he communicates, either with words or with actions. His techniques of control, therefore, depend only on what will make an impression on his partner, since she knows how to identify his desires, intentions, and threats. Whatever the method

that he chooses, however, power and control are not necessarily cognitive entities, which makes it so important that batterers be made to understand why they batter, while victims—all victims—must understand why they stay (Judge Virginia Knaplund, quoted in Felder and Victor, 1996: 206-207).

Cognitive restructuring has been integral to many of the treatment programs. Rational emotive therapy is premised on the belief that the batterer has irrational beliefs and expectations, which lead to irrational thoughts and, ultimately, to irrational behaviors (Edleson, 1984). For instance, a man may believe that he must be in control, but then feels out of control, and since he is not the one responsible because he is in control, his feeling out of control must be the result of his partner's behavior and he has no choice but to hit her because he is so upset. Various procedures for dissipating anger can be taught within the context of rational emotive therapy, including acknowledging the anger, assuming responsibility for making oneself angry, accepting oneself with the anger, identifying expectations related to the relationship, discriminating preferences from unreasonable demands of the partner, and working to dissipate and eliminate the anger through behavioral and emotive means (Ellis, 1976).

Another type of cognitive restructuring program focuses on the identification by the batterer of maladaptive thoughts and self-statements that precede, are contemporaneous with, and follow a decision to batter. The batterer is then taught to develop more appropriate thoughts and behaviors and practices them (Bolton and Bolton, 1987). Other programs utilize assertiveness training and relaxation skills to help the batterer respond to situations in which he might otherwise be violent. The batterer maintains a log in which he records any situations that provoked anger, the feelings that were aroused, and any self-statements (Edleson, 1985).

The Emerge Batterer Treatment Program, the first batterer treatment program in the country, incorporates many of these concepts. The program consists of 48 two-houir weekly sessions that are co-facilitated by male and fermale counselors. Enrollees sign a contract which specifies behavioral and attitudinal expectations of the program, attendance and payment requirements, and acknowledgement of contact between the program staff and victims, probation officers, and child protective workers (Adams, 1996). The first 8 weeks of the program are informational and provide basic education relating to definitions of violence, the effects of violence on victims and witnesses, and somatic and cognitive cues to violence. The remaining 40 weeks are devoted to individualized goals and homework assignments, as well as feedback through participation in groups (Adams, 1996).

It appears, however, that consensus with respect to the preferred mode of treatment does not exist. As indicated above, anger control therapy has been advocated by some clinicians. For instance, Dutton (1995) favors the use of anger management techniques when they are adapted appropriately to the relevant social milieu. Dutton further recognizes that although batterers participating in group anger management should be permitted to express their feelings of resentment, they may reinforce each other's feelings that a terrible injustice has been done to them, thereby minimizing the violence that they committed. This mode of therapy, however, has been rejected by a number of therapists because anger is often not the central issue in battering; rather, the need for control is pivotal. Cessation of physical violence is not synonymous with cessation of abuse, as the batterer may actually escalate his psychological abuse (Gondolf and Russell, 1986).

Couples therapy also has its supporters and detractors. Those who endorse it view wife assault from the perspective of a microsystem, rather than from an intrapsychic perspective. The family system determines the acceptability of behaviors and the power imbalances within the system (Dutton, 1995). Some researchers have asserted that, within this microsystem, battered wives may inadvertently reinforce the battering behaviors because of the low likelihood that they will retaliate, their acceptance of the battering as a response to stress, and adherence to a traditional ideology that includes, for instance, the belief that a woman should remain in a marriage regardless of the destructiveness of the relationship (Pagelow, 1984).

Others, however, have discredited couples therapy because it requires that women who have been battered be open with their partners, potentially subjecting themselves to greater risk (Gondolf and Russell, 1986). One woman described her fears and experience with couples therapy with her assaultive husband:

> We went to marriage counseling and it was a terrible experience. The counselor said I needed to be more accepting of him. I was angry because he was drinking a lot. The counselor said that on his days off, if he wanted to drink a case of beer in his own house I should accept that.
> *I was reluctant to bring up the violence and abuse, because I wasn't sure how my partner would react....*The one time I did mention the abuse it was basically discounted. When that happened, he felt totally validated. The counselor even said I needed to be more sexually receptive to him and not be so critical of his faults. (Paymar, 2000: 19; emphasis added).

Felder and Victor have described one situation that evidences the dangers the potential dangers of couples therapy:

> A successful investment banker arrived at an emergency room seeking treatment for cigarette burns on her hands and arms. "She told the nurse that her partner had a burn fetish...as if that were an acceptable explanation for her injuries." During the next six months, the woman appeared at the same emergency room on fifteen separate occasions with more severe burns to her face and body. Each time that the woman sought medical care, the nurse tried to convince her to get a restraining order to remove her partner from the condominium that they shared and that the woman owned and for which she alone paid all monthly maintenance fees. And each time the woman claimed that she and her partner were engaged in couple therapy to cure *him* of his burn fetish. The last time the nurse saw the woman, she was in the intensive care burn unit, suffering third-degree burns over 40 percent of her body. Her

partner with the burn fetish eventually scalded her with boiling water, leaving her permanently disfigured.

"The tragedy...is that this woman, by entering into couple therapy, gave her partner the message that she considered his burn fetish to be *their* problem" (Felder and Victor, 1996: 98, quoting a psychiatric clinical nurse named Trisha; emphasis in original).

Paymar has flatly stated that marriage counseling in the context of a violent relationship is both unethical and dangerous absent the following:

1. The man has successfully completed a reputable domestic abuse program that focuses on changing sexist beliefs and attitudes about controlling women.
2. A practitioner is convinced that the battering—violence, coercion, threats, initimidation, and psychological abuse—has ceased.
3. The battered woman has worked with a victims' advocate and has developed a safety plan to get help if her partner becomes abusive.
4. The battered wife feels safe.
5. The practitioner has discussed the risks associated with marriage counseling privately with the woman, and feels relatively sure abusive acts will not take place as the result of these sessions (Paymar, 2000: 19-20).

It has been asserted that men who are cyclical batterers are actually addicted to violence in much the same way as individuals might be addicted to nicotine or tobacco (Dutton and Golant, 1995). Consequently, treatment must incorporate and address the possibility of relapse. Accordingly, Dutton and Golant (1995) have recommended reliance on Prochaska and colleagues' (1992) model of behavior change, known as the transtheoretical model. This model presumes that individuals attempting to change behavior will pass through five stages: (1) precontemplation, (2) preparation, (3) action, (4) maintenance, and (5) termination. During the precontemplation stage, the individual has not yet acknowledged that a problem exists, although others may indicate such. During the contemplation stage, the individual will acknowledge that a problem is present. An individual will seek help during the preparation stage, and will undergo treatment during the action phase. The maintenance stage is characterized by the absence of violence, while the termination stage signifies that the individual has, indeed, effectuated behavior change and no longer needs to remain constantly vigilant (Dutton and Golant, 1995; Prochaska, DiClemente, and Norcross, 1992).

Batterers who have successfully changed their behavior have identified taking time-outs when angry, talking to themselves about restraint, and visualizing the reactions of other treatment program participants as helpful strategies (Gondolf, 1988). Research does not, however, support the view that these strategies are more helpful than any others (Gondolf, 1988).

In fact, treatment programs have not been evaluated to the extent that one might wish. Deschner's (1984) evaluation of an anger control program involving 32 women and 26 men found that, based on self-reports, the anger control training assisted the battering couples to reduce the intensity and frequency of their disputes. A Seattle-based controlled trial of 63 treated batterers and 26 wait-listed untreated controls found that the group that had participated in the treatment arm experienced a significant decrease on the measures of hostility and anger, as well as on measures of depression (Maiuro, Cahn, Vitaliano, and Zegree, 1986). Too, one of the difficulties in conducting an evaluation is the lack of agreement as to what constitutes successful treatment and the ethical issues associated with research designs that could potentially be used to evaluate the treatment's effectiveness. For instance,   controlled studies comparing treated and untreated batterers may raise not only serious ethical issues, but also potential legal issues as the receipt and completion of treatment may have a direct bearing on his legal position and there could be potential liability of the criminal justice system based on a battering victim's argument that the lack of treatment exposed her or him to an increased risk of a reoccurrence of the battering.

Many of the treatment programs that are available to batterers in general may not be as easily accessible to or effective with individuals from communities of color, due to the programs' location, their lack of a bilingual staff, and their lack of sensitivity with regard to cultural issues (Williams and Becker, 1994). To date, there have been few well done evaluations of treatment programs for batterers (personal communication, Cuyahoga County Task Force on Domestic Violence).

8

RESPONSES OF THE BATTERED

God, how well I remember that pain!
My soul, taken unawares
Jerked like a decapitated hen.... (Cassian, 1988a: 13)

Counts (1992) has identified six different strategies available to beaten women. Although these are based on her observations of wife-beating in Papua New Guinea, many are applicable in concept across many societies. Potential responses include: (1) leaving her husband and taking a lover or second husband [departure]; (2) taking the dispute to the public arena and charging her husband before the village or provincial court authorities [help-seeking]; (3) leaving her husband and returning to her own kin if her relatives do not intervene on her behalf [departure and help-seeking]; (4) exposing her husband to menstrual blood to cause his illness [retribution]; (5) committing suicide; and (6) fighting back [violence]. Additional approaches include isolation and social organization. Lateef (1992), based on her study of Indo-Fijian women, has identified yet another alternative strategy: acceptance or remaining with the batterer.

DEPARTURE

One of the possible responses to intimate partner violence is for the abused partner to leave. Leaving, however, is often a process, involving movement into and out of the abusive relationship (Limandri, 1987). A battered woman may leave her battering partner several times before she is able to leave permanently; it has been found that the average battered womanleaves her partner eight times before she leaves permanently (Felder and Victor, 1996). Schwartz (2000: 99) has described this process through the use of an allegory:

> There is a story about a snake, which serves as a metaphor for needing help and seeking therapy. Before therapy, you are walking down a road. You see a snake lying in the road and pick it up and begin to play with it, but being a snake, it bites you.
>
> During therapy, you are walking down this same road and see the snake again. You kick it with your shoe and sort of play with it, but you don't pick it up. You've learned through experience that it will bite you.
>
> At the end of therapy, you are once again walking down this same road and, as before, you see the same snake. This time, you cross to the other side of the road, avoiding it.

Women have described changes in themselves that have allowed them to ultimately leave their abusive partner: redefinition of abuse as they become angrier about their victimization (Ferraro and Johnson, 1983) and passage through a variety of phases of response to the abuse, including binding, enduring, disengaging, and recovering (Landenburger, 1989). Weldon (1999: 15), who suffered severe physical abuse from her ex-husband for many years, has described how she came to leave that abusive relationship:

> But there comes a time to stop pretending.
> The soul, I have learned, has its own agenda and knows the truth even if you dare not acknowledge it. When the slaps, bites, and punches are long since anesthetized in afterthought, there comes moment when, of its own volition, your soul says, "No more." You may not even hear it shout, or simply nod to its defiance, but it is there. And from that voice comes the solution and the strength, the voice no longer mute, the voice so clear it is deafening in its resolution.
> There is a last time. And though it begins the same, the end is different.

Nayala's (1997:48-49) decision making process was somewhat similar:

> One evening Kevin beat me for several hours, a cycle which had become utterly routine....Finally he hauled [our son] and several guns into the bedroom, vowing to kill my son if he heard any sound at all. I spent that night crouching in a corner at the farthest end of the house, holding my daughter in my arms and quieting her, my hand over her mouth, when she awoke whimpering. The next evening, Kevin beat me again and choked me unconscious. My last thought before blacking out was that this time I would die—leaving my children alone with this man....Too numb to feel fear, something finally snapped....[I] decided that if I lived through the night, I would take [the children] and run away.

Numerous factors have been found conducive to leaving an abusive relationship, including the availability of economic support (Strube and Barbour, 1984; Pfouts, 1978), the availability of support services (Snyder and Scheer, 1981), previous separations (Snyder and Scheer, 1981), and concerns for one's own safety and personal growth (Ulrich, 1991). Various other circumstances have been found to constitute additional barriers to leaving, including potential economic hardship (Gondolf et al., 1988), religious traditions (Ulrich, 1993), and love (Strube and Barbour, 1984).

Draper (1992), in her discussion of the responses of four !Kung women to battering by their husbands, noted that a decision to leave is frequently dependent on whether one has somewhere to go. In two of the four instances of battering described, the beating occurred away from kin. The wives had no adult children to whom they could flee and their parents were relatively poor. In contrast, the other two wives came from relatively wealthy families who could both intercede on their behalf and provide them with living accommodations.

Kerns (1992) found in her fieldwork in a Garifuna community in Belize that wife beating is quite rare because a woman who is beaten often has the means to leave and no compelling reason to stay. Unlike women in the United States, who often face numerous barriers to leaving, such as economic dependence, the absence of effective intervention or any intervention, social isolation, the lack of a reliable and accessible sanctuary, an ineffective criminal justice system, and an unsympathetic legal system, women in the Garifuna community are rarely dependent economically, can usually seek sanctuary with their families, and can generally rely on prompt and effective intervention by family members, who have the right and the duty to intervene.

NiCarthy (1997) has proposed that women contemplating departure from an abusive relationship utilize a series of questions to assist in deciding and in preparing for the future. These self-questions include recognition of one's worst fears resulting from leaving, recognition of one's worst fears as a result of staying, comparing the dangers resulting from each course of action, and balancing the recognized advantages and disadvantages of each path. She further recommends the development of a plan of action in either case.

HELP-SEEKING

Women who have been the victims of intimate partner violence may seek help in a variety of arenas, some of them formal and some informal. Unfortunately, little research has examined either factors related to a decision to seek help or patterns of help-seeking among physically abused women. A number of factors have been found to increase the likelihood that a battered woman will seek help: the severity and frequency of injury (Abel and Suh, 1987; Dobash and Dobash, 1979; Gelles, 1977) a higher educational level of the battered woman (Abel and Suh, 1987), younger age of the victim (West, Kantor, and Jasinski, 1998), and a greater ability of the victim to use English (West, Kantor, and Jasinski, 1998).

Schwartz (2000: 196) has observed both the internal dynamics that may impede a woman's search for help and the consequences that may arise as a result:

> Men can lash out, hit, swear, or kick the dog. Women internalize. Rather than try to punish our abuser, we punish ourselves. We might drink to the point of becoming an alcoholic, take drugs to numb our pain and sorrow, become promiscuous and sleep with any man who will have us, or end our life—*simply because we didn't reach out and seek help*. (Emphasis added.)

Barriers to Help-Seeking

Sorenson and Telles (1991) found that women's immigration status and minimal knowledge of English may be barriers to help seeking. Women may refrain from reporting instances of partner violence, fearing that they will be reported to the INS and deported from the United States. Sorenson (1996) has documented some of the difficulties that immigrant women reported during focus groups relating to violence:

> A much higher percentage of family violence may exist in a family where you run into harder situations and more difficult problems....(Korean American man, quoted in Sorenson, 1996: 132).

> I couldn't find a shelter and I did something which is taboo—I brought her [a battered woman] to my house...this man [the woman's husband] pulled a gun on both of us when I took her from the house with the children. We ran to my van [then] went to my house....A month later she was back with this man....Her fear was that she could not financially cope on her own. She was an immigrant woman [from Central America] who did not have her papers so she felt a fear that the authorities would pick her up and send her back...to her that was much worse than staying with a man that occasionally beats her. (Mexican American woman, quoted in Sorenson, 1996: 133)

The immigration experience itself may present a barrier to help-seeking. Le (1982) estimated that 40 percent of the female refugees traveling from Vietnam to other countries in 1980 had been raped by pirates at sea; 11 percent of these women were between the ages of 11 and 20. It has been hypothesized that women who survive such experiences may perceive dating violence as minimal in comparison and. consequently, may not report such violence (Kanuha, 1987).

Lesbians who have been battered by their lesbian partner may face difficulties at the hospital due to emergency room staff assumptions regarding her sexual orientation (Chrystos, 1996) and/or the potential consequences of disclosing her sexual orientation. As one researcher noted, it is not unusual for a lesbian victimized by her partner to

> ultimately decide against telling her full story. By coming out, a lesbian's sexual preference may be included as part of her permanent medical record, subject to review by unknown future insurers, physicians, nurses, and technicians (Hammond, 1989, quoted in Loring and Smith, 1994: 330).

Several women participating in the Cuyahoga County study, detailed in chapter 3, explained why it may be so difficult for a woman to seek help. One woman explained:

If you have intimacy with another person, with a person that you have nothing more, when you arrive at the point of sexual intimacy, the sexual intimacy surpasses the emotional, the physical, it surpasses all, it is all the relation that you have with whatever other human being. It changes you, your situation completely with that person, you don't see that when you are with this person you are different, your mind thinks differently, your body acts differently (Loue, unpublished data).

Physical and Mental Health Care

This discussion focuses on the receipt of physical and mental health care. Health consequences, such as physical injury and depression, were discussed previously in the context of forms of intimate partner violence.

Women who have been the victims of such violence have been found to utilize a large proportion of medical care, through emergency department services, clinic services such as chronic pain clinics (Bergman et al., 1992; Rath et al., 1989; Haber, 1985), and mental health services (Carmen et al., 1984; Stark et al., 1979).

Numerous barriers exist to the receipt of health care attention, however. A survey of 1,000 battered women found that health care practitioners were the least helpful of all professional help sources contacted (Brendtro and Bowker, 1989). Rather than addressing the totality of the situation, health practitioners may be more inclined to address only the medical signs and symptoms that are detectable (Stark and Flitcraft, 1988). Women who may have initially sought out the services of a health practitioner may refrain from returning due to the provider's negative or callous attitude (cf. Websdale, 1998). This characterization of physician response, however, is not surprising in view of the fact that few medical schools provide instruction relating to domestic violence (Holtz et al., 1989). Receipt of health care may be even more problematic for abused immigrants, who may refrain from seeking such services due to cultural beliefs (Capps, 1994; Frye and D'Avanzo, 1994; Uba, 1992; Moore and Boehnlein, 1991) and/or fear of being reported to the INS (Asch, Leake, and Gelberg, 1994).

Graham and Rawlings (1998) have suggested that women suffering from Stockholm syndrome may be more likely to loosen the bonds to the abuser if the conditions creating those bonds are themselves weakened. The fact that the woman has begun seeking treatment is one indication of potentially loosened bonds, since the therapy itself represents a reduction in her degree of isolation. Conditions may also be weakened through an assessment of possible alternative strategies for escape, the development of sources of caring and attention apart from those of the batterer, and the gradual characterization of the abuser's actions as abuse.

Decker (1999) has suggested that treatment for a battered woman should focus on (1) protection of herself and any children; (2) the development of awareness of community resources that may be available to her; (3) the initiation of a healing process to overcome the effects of the violence; (4) the development of stress management and interpersonal skills; (5) the development of an understanding of who she is as a woman; and (6) the re-establishment of her self-esteem.

Law Enforcement

Research indicates that the vast majority of women who suffer partner violence have never sought assistance from law enforcement. For instance, Roy (1977) found that approximately one-third of the women who called a domestic violence hotline had never called the police. Schulman (1981) found in a study of Kentucky women who were married to or living with a male partner that less than 10% of violent incidents between the partners had been reported to the police. Other studies have estimated that between 7% (Kantor and Straus, 1990) and half of all violent incidents (Bachman, 1994) are ever reported to the police.

Little empirical research has been conducted to explore the circumstances in which victims seek help from law enforcement and the legal system. Bachman and Coker (1995) found in their study of 1,535 female victims of intimate partner violence that victims were more likely to report a violent incident to the police if they were black, had sustained an injury as a result of the assault, and had not been victimized previously by the offender. (These same factors were also predictive of whether the police arrested the assailant.) Other research has indicated that women are more likely to seek police intervention if they have been abused for a longer period of time, have less education are of lower occupational status, and are married to men with alcohol-related difficulties (Abel and Suh, 1987). The severity of the injury also appears to be related to the likelihood that the police will be called (Kantor and Straus, 1990). Hutchison and colleagues (1994) found in their study of 18,712 domestic violence calls for police services in a large southern metropolitan area, conducted over a 17-month period, that currently married and cohabiting (unmarried) couples were equally likely to rely on police services. Almost one quarter of the calls were attributable to incidents between divorced partners, ex-cohabitants, or dating but not cohabiting partners. Almost one half of the victims were between the ages of 26 and 35 and approximately 80 percent of the calls were from women.

Research has identified various explanations by assaulted partners for their decision not to call the police in response to a violent incident. A study of data from the National Crime Survey from 1978 through 1982 found that women often refrained from calling the police because they felt that the violence was a personal matter, while a smaller proportion feared that they would suffer retaliation from their intimate if they called (Langan and Innes, 1986). An interview-based study of 137 women recruited from a Midwestern shelter found that nearly all of the women who had not contacted the police had been prevented from doing so, e.g. the assailant physically prevented them from calling, there was no phone. Women who reported being physically prevented from calling the police were found to have suffered from more severe abuse than women who gave other reasons for not seeking police assistance, e.g. thinking that the police would not help, fearing that they would suffer a reprisal if they called, and fear that the police would take away their children (Fleury, Sullivan, Bybee, and Davidson II, 1998). The fear of reprisal is not unfounded; one woman interviewed after the violent incident with her partner explained her subsequently inflicted injury: "Actually, I probably shouldn't have called the police. My husband got real mad at me for doing it and gave me this shiner" (Walter, 1981: 259).

Victims of physical violence have also refrained from seeking help from the police because of disappointment with the police response to past incidents of violence (Lerman, 1992). A recent study which focused on the aftermath of calls by victims to the police found that 8 weeks following the arrest at the scene of 24 assaultive male partners, 8 had entered guilty pleas, 2 had had the charges dismissed, and 14 had been released and were awaiting disposition of the charges, including 7 who had not been required to post a bond. Eighteen of the 24 individuals (75%) has spent fewer than 18 hours in jail. Of the 8 individuals who entered a guilty plea to domestic assault, 2 were ordered to perform 3 days of community service, 4 were ordered to participate in an anger management program, and 1 was ordered to undergo treatment for substance abuse (Brookoff, O'Brien, Cook, Thompson, and Williams, 1997). One woman participating in the Cuyahoga County study (see chapter 3) noted how a course of action was often difficult to determine for both the individuals involved and for the police, due to the complexity of many situations and the difficulty inherent in attempts to understand exactly who is the victim and who is the perpetrator:

> I don't know who is the victim and the perpetrator in the relationship so I would have to know that. They both need help....I think they should call the police. They should be stopped. I think they could both go for counseling. It depends on which one is the perpetrator or the victim. Could they both be perpetrators? I don't know. Yeah, that happens I think (Loue, unpublished data).

The Clergy

Adams (1993) has identified several barriers to seeking support from members of the clergy: the failure of clergy to address battering as a chronic problem, the minimization of the lethality of domestic and sexual violence, the acceptance by the clergy of inadequate counseling techniques as adequate, the redefinition of the batterer's criminal conduct as a psychological problem, the failure to maintain the confidences of the battered victim, identification of the male clergy figure with the male batterer, a willingness on the part of the clergy to believe the abuser's contriteness and a consequent emphasis on forgiveness as a remedy, and an overriding emphasis on the "covenant" of marriage. Paymar's account of the church-related experiences of a husband and wife during episodes of battering is instructive:

> [Wife]: I believed Chuck had the authority in the household based on our religious orientation. It was in the Scriptures, or at least in the way they were interpreted. We went to church three days a week for eleven years. When members of the congregation would see me battered they would say,"What did you do to make him so mad that he would beat you like that?" We finally quit the church after Chuck was ordered into counseling for battering me.

[Husband]: I beat M'Liss up once and her face was all swollen, her arms were bruised, and her glasses were broken, yet we still went to church. The word got to the pastor that I had beat her up. The preacher called me to his back room and asked me if I'd beaten her. I said, "Yes, I did." And he said, "If that's what it takes to keep her in line, well—" and he pointed to the door and I left. Nothing else was said. Our church would not tell the congregation that domestic abuse was wrong (Paymar, 2000: 35-36).

Despite such occurrences, some clergy urge that silence—the usual course of action among congregations in domestic violence situations—be broken. For instance, Fortune has cautioned clergy to consider how they portray the theme of forgiveness, to consider whether they have tacitly approved of domestic violence, and to avoid preaching about forgiveness in a way that equates forgiveness with "cheap grace" for perpetrators and reinforces shame and guilt among the victims and survivors of domestic violence (McClure and Ramsay, 1989: 3).

SUICIDE

Suicide is a not infrequent response to intimate partner violence. In South Africa, for instance, it has been estimated that violence occurs in 50 to 60 percent of all marriages. Of the women in such relationships, approximately 25 percent attempt suicide (Adams and Hickson, 1993). Suicide has been recognized as a culturally acceptable means out for women in India who have reached the end of their endurance of physical and emotional abuse. It may, in fact, be the only viable alternative to eventual murder by the husband or his family (Prasad, 1994). Counts (1987) has argued that in some Oceanic societies, such as Papua New Guinea, female suicide is a culturally recognized behavior that permits the "politically powerless…to revenge themselves on those who have made their lives intolerable." Mitchell (1992) found that Wape men in New Guinea may refrain from beating their wives because of the women's threats to commit suicide if their husbands shame them. Forty-one percent of Fijian Indian families in one study identified marital violence as the cause of suicide (Haynes, 1984). A study of 176 women who presented at a hospital emergency room following a suicide attempt found that 30% of the women had been battered and 22% had at least one documented incident of physical violence noted in their medical records (Stark and Flitcraft, 1996).

In the Romania study (chapter 3), suicide was presented as one solution to the violence. One woman recounted her own attempt:

[When I came home from the hospital after delivering the baby] my husband wanted to kill the baby. I took a lot of pills, I just wanted to die (Loue, unpublished data).

Schwartz (2000: 60-61) described her thoughts of suicide in response to her battering:

> I contemplated suicide regularly. I was so tired of feeling the way I had my entire life. Although I had accomplished some very exciting things in my life and had won impressive awards, none of these honors dispelled the belief that I was absolutely worthless.
>
> The only reason I didn't take my own life was my children... I believed that I didn't have the right to ruin my children's lives. Instead, I kept telling myself that there was a wonderful, happy life out there somewhere....

The suicide attempt, however, may ultimately lead to the woman's loss of custody of her children should she ultimately divorce, as the result of a judicial finding that she is not fit to care for the children (Stark and Flitcraft, 1996).

VIOLENCE

The amputation of John Bobbitt's penis by his wife Lorena has become infamous (Grindstaff and McCaughey, 1996). On June 23, 1993, Bobbitt returned home after a night out drinking with his friend. He woke his wife Lorena and raped her, and then fell asleep. She responded by cutting off his penis with a kitchen knofe and throwing it into a nearby vacant lot. Police recovered the severed organ based on Lorena's description of where she had thrown it, and surgeons re-attached it in a 9-hour operation. Lorena was ultimately acquitted of malicious wounding.

A number of studies have indicated that females murder male partners at a rate that is substantially less than murders of females by their male partners (Browne and Williams, 1989; Straus, 1986). It has been suggested that the vast majority of such murders result from self defense, retaliation, or desperation following years of physical abuse (Browne and Williams, 1989; Browne, 1987). Peggy Green, an inmate in Bedford Hills Prison in New York serving a sentence of 25 years to life for the murder of her intimate partner, explained how she finally decided to kill him:

> I was not a silent victim, I was not passive, and I learned my strength and anger very young. But striking out did me no good; but then nothing else did either. I went for help and no one listened. When I was being beaten, I went to the police and they sent me back home and I was beaten more. When I told the foster care workers about the foster fathers who were molesting me and their wives who were beating me, they defended them. And when I tried to tell the psychiatrists, they analyzed and asked lots of questions, but did nothing about the situation (Quoted in Felder and Victor, 1996: 176).

The acceptability to women of violence as a legitimate and/or desirable response to partner violence may depend on the actual and perceived existence of alternative solutions. For instance, in the Romania study (chapter 3), one participant observed:

In communism, the women had the same rights as a man,
everywhere she went. She was protected. But also she was
exploited. She was doing a lot of things and at home, too. There
was also a big problem because women couldn't have abortions.
Now the women have no rights, only the right to abortion. So, by
this point of view, we are in darkness. There is no protection
[from] violence. It is very difficult. The first who are fired [from
jobs] are women. The last to get jobs are women. Men just want
sex. So women become more violent because of this society.

ISOLATION

Not infrequently, women may self-isolate in an attempt to stop the violence. For
instance, if her partner claims that he hit her because she came home late from work
or school, she may cease those activities (Flitcraft, 1995).

Many times, however, the seemingly self-imposed isolation may be due to
coercion and fear. Goetting (1999: 130) described one such situation:

> Lee existed in total captivity. Tony dead-bolted her in the
> house when he was away (sometimes without food because she
> was "fat") and taped the edges of the door to alert him to
> tampering. Lee was instructed not to touch doors and windows.
> Tony sometimes took the phone with him. He would warn Lee
> that she could never escape, that he would find her and put her six
> feet under where she belonged. He was omnipresent. *Even when
> he was gone for days, she was afraid to leave*; she knew he would
> find her. *She had no money or car and had alienated her friends
> and son.* (Emphasis added.)

Common isolating behaviors of batterers include insistence on knowing who the
partner spoke with and what she did; phoning the victim's friends, family members,
and co-workers, resulting in their isolation to avoid such situations; discouraging
her from continuing in her education or employment; suddenly appearing at the
individual's place of work; acting jealous in public; undermining family social
activities; causing fights before the battered partner would leave the house to
discourage her from leaving; diabling the car; disconnecting the telephone; and
relocating to an isolated area (Paymar, 2000).

SOCIAL ORGANIZATION

Various women's movements have focused on violence against women. India's
women's movement provides a good example of this. The women's movement
there has organized rallies, protests, and mass meetings in an attempt to focus public
attention on the problem of intimate partner violence (Katzenstein, 1989). Although
many of the participants may not themselves have been abused, many of them have.
Various autonomous women's organizations in India have staged street plays about

dowry murders, rape, and other forms of domestic violence. Other organizations have provided legal help to women attempting to leave their abusive situations. Leaders within these movements have frequently used their connections to effectuate change, such as using governmental connections to arrange consultations regarding dowry violence.

A similar movement occurred in the United States during the 1970s. Feminist lawyers instituted numerous lawsuits against police departments for their refusal to arrest assaultive partners and against court personnel for denying battered women access to judges who could issue protective orders (Pleck, 1987). The National Organization for Women (NOW) in 1973 established the first task force on intimate partner violence. Various organizations established shelters for battered women. In 1976, there were about 20 such shelters throughout the United States; by 1982, there were approximately 300. Now, there are more than 2,000 community-based domestic violence programs in the United States, of which more than 1,300 provide shelter services to battered women (Dwyer, 1995; National Coalition Against Domestic Violence, 1999). Women's groups in Great Britain, Denmark, and Finland were also active in championing legal reforms and/or in establishing victims' services (Anon., 1985; Dwyer, 1995).

Many of these first shelters that were started in the United States were not "premeditated" ventures, but grew, instead, from political ideals and a grassroots movement (Brownmiller, 1999). Years later, the movement to protect battered women became the focus of social workers and others in professional careers. Brownmiller (1999: 275-276), noting the complexity of the issue, commented on the direction and the failings of the movement:

> It seemed to me that many of the battered women's advocates developed a bunker mentality marked by fixed and rigid positions partly because of the enormity of the violence they were confronting, immersed as they were in what amounted to a war zone. Shelter volunteers and staff workers heard war stories every day; they saw the bruises, the black eyes, the effects of the broken ribs. Identifying with the guarded, fearful personalities of the women they were championing, they oversimplified the complexities of male-female relations and publicly characterized batterers as all-powerful brutes, and the women in their sway as pure victims, even when they had reason to know better.
>
> The battered women's movement developed a serious blind spot in its refusal to take a hard look at the women who stayed in battering relationships or who returned to their deadly batterers again and again. "Fear," "economic dependence," and "society's lack of options" became the only permissible answers to the nagging question "Why doesn't she leave?"

ACCEPTANCE AND SELF-BLAME/REMAINING

Lateef (1992) found in her ethnographic examination of Indo-Fijian women that many not only accept a husband's right to physically discipline his wife, but also positively sanction this use of force. Men who do not beat their wives may become the subject of ridicule. The beatings generally stop when the sons are old enough to defend their mother. Ho (1990) similarly found in her study of domestic violence among Southeast Asians that Lao, Khmer, and Vietnamese women, particularly those who were first generation, accepted familial violence as a common occurrence.

The Romania study, detailed in chapter 3, found that many women accepted violence from their husbands as a "normal" response to a perceived deficiency in the wife's behavior or character. For instance, in a representative response to the vignette in which the husband forced his wife to have sex against her will, resulting in injury, one woman intimated that the problem was attributable to the wife:

> They need a psychologist to speak with them, not together but separately. The psychologist will find out the reason. Maybe the wife is afraid of sexual diseases. Because of stress, daily stress, from a lack of money and food, her job, a lot of children, and difficulty taking care of them, she is not in the mood to have sex.

A second woman, responding to the same vignette, commented:

> She must be treated for her [frigidity] by a specialist. The husband can also help her. I think in Romania it is possible to treat her problem because there are a lot of doctors who deal with such problems.

Forgiveness as a component of the acceptance and the decision to remain with the assaultive partner was a common theme. In response to the vignette in which the husband hit and bruised his wife, one woman began speaking of the vignette characters and then herself:

> If this is the first time or it is an accident, she must forgive him, but if it happened before or becomes a habit, then no. I did forgive [my husband] many times because such is life, you forgive. Afterwards, it was okay for a while and then we split up. If it becomes a habit then it is difficult to change. If he hits once or twice, you forgive again and again because there is nothing that can be done.

Despite this seeming acceptance of their fate, these wives may remain in their situations due to a lack of power or a perceived lack of power, rather than true acceptance. Few have any place to go if they leave. Most are economically dependent on their spouses. Many are concerned that they might lose their children if they leave or that they will bring shame to their families by doing so. One woman framed her course of action not as a decision to stay, but as a decision not to leave, explaining

> I didn't leave...because abuse wasn't supposed to happen to women like me....I didn't leave...because I believed I could fix

it....I didn't leave...because after a while I began to believe what Melvin kept telling me: that I was overreacting....I didn't leave... because there was nowhere to go for support....I didn't leave...because I grew accustomed to living a lie. ...(Weiss, 2000: 19-51)

In the United States, women who seemingly accept their violent fate may, in fact, be caught in a cycle of emotional dependency that is difficult to break. (This pattern has become variously known as the battered women's syndrome, the Stockholm syndrome, and traumatic bonding. (Graham et al., 1995.) Although the woman's continued relationship with her batterer appears to be voluntary, the underlying dynamic is hardly one of true acceptance.

There are several theories as to why abused partners continue to stay in the abusive relationships with their intimates. The first is premised on the theory of learned helplessness, which posits that the abused partner, usually the woman, remains because she has learned that her response to a beating does not affect what happens to her (Walker, 1979). Motivation is diminished as a result of the repeated beatings and passivity intensifies (Gondolf, 1988). Proponents of this theory assert that the way to assist the battered partner is to repeatedly show him or her the alternatives and the mechanisms necessary to effectuate an alternative (Okun, 1986).

The theory that women are actually active survivors rather than helpless victims has been proffered as an alternative theory to explain why abused women stay in their abusive relationships (Gondolf, 1988). Aspects of this theory are reminiscent of the investment theory, discussed in chapter 2. This theory argues that women stay not because of passivity, but because they have tried to leave and have been unable to effectuate a departure. The victim's efforts at help-seeking are thought to increase as the violence increases. Whether those help-seeking efforts will be effective is dependent on the individual's resources, his or her commitment to the relationship, the individual's perceptions of what is best for him or her and any children, and the individual's exposure to violence as a child (Gondolf, 1988).

Fagan and Browne (1994) have elucidated Sherif and Hovland's (1961) explanation of how a battered woman gradually assimilates the violent episodes into her experience, ultimately incorporating them into her "latitude of acceptance:"

The "latitude of acceptance" is the range of possibilities with which an individual is willing to agree or to which an individual can adapt. Latitudes are defined by end points, or anchors, that determine the extremes of the scale. Internal anchors are those originating within the individual, whereas external anchors are provided by outside factors or social consensus...According to social judgment theory, if stimuli continue to fall at the end of the continuum or even slightly above the end point, this will produce a shift of the range toward that anchor—or assimilation. However, if a stimulus is too far beyond the others, a contrast effect will ensue, and the stimulus will be perceived as being even more extreme than it really is (Fagan and Browne, 1994: 219-220).

The latitude of acceptance with respect to partner violence is affected by four factors: (1) the extent to which a woman has been socialized to accept the partner's behavior; (2) the extent to which she has had prior similar experiences; (3) the extent to which external stimuli were supportive or incompatible with the appropriateness of the events; and (4) the extent to which she feels trapped in her situation (Fagan and Browne, 1994).

Accounts by women who have been battered indicate that the basis of a decision to stay may vary, depending upon the individual and the frequency, severity, and duration of the battering in the relationship. Weldon (1999: xvi-xvii) explained why she initially remained with her battering spouse:

> I was vulnerable, naïve, blinded. I believed in a man I loved, and I did not believe he would keep hurting me. I stayed with him, and I chose not to see the man I married, the father of my three children, as a batterer who would always be a batter. I saw each instance as an isolated nightmare, all explained away, all forgiven. I didn't connect them to see the pattern.
>
> I excused his rage because I could not bear seeing him as he really was. That meant I would see myself as I was, and I refused to be a battered wife. But it was not until I could make that admission that the abuse could possibly end. It was not until I could say out loud what he had done that the carousel of pain would stop, and I could get off of the painted horse and walk away.

Weldon's (1999: 102-103) seeming acceptance of the violence in her life was closely linked to her idealization of love and conceptualization responsibility:

> I stayed because I didn't understand how you could walk away from someone you had once loved. I could not understand how you could be present in a hospital labor and delivery room with a person and later say you didn't love him anymore. How can it be so temporary? Love demands permanence. It was black and white. If you love, you stay. Like an obedient dog at the foot of the bed. Like people committed to each other.
>
> I believed life held certain constants, like the sun rising and the waves hitting the shore and staying married and in love forever. I believed that once you were married, you solved any problem that arose.

In contrast, Schwartz' (2000: 25) initial decision to remain with her abusive husband derived from her own insecurity, low self-esteem, and false pride:

> I had pride, but it was misdirected. Instead of focusing on important issues such as self-respect, inner peace, or living a normal, violence-free life, I would focus on what other people might think. A very short marriage, divorced again, being alone, growing old without a man, and being forced to start dating again. Although I felt I was a failure in every aspect of my life, I didn't

want others to view me in the same light. I had to hide the woman
I had become. In my mind, it was easier to live with violence than
admit I'd made yet another mistake.

One non-Hispanic woman participating in the Cuyahoga County study (chapter 3)
explained, in response to a vignette in which a wife attempted to stab her husband,
why leaving would be difficult for either partner:

He could call the police or she could realize that she needs help or
they could get help, he could leave, she could leave. Well, I think
it's very hard for people to leave. If he really is the perpetrator,
then he is highly unlikely to leave because he is happy with the
way things are, usually not as drained as the victim, still able to
function and carry on. She might just be too dog tired to leave or
to beaten down or too scared (Loue, unpublished data).

9

CHILDREN EXPOSED TO PARTNER VIOLENCE: THEIR RESPONSES

The flowers have been growing thorns for millions of years. For millions of years the sheep have been eating them just the same. And is it not a matter of consequence to try to understand why the flowers go to so much trouble to grow thorns which are never of any use to them? Is the warfare between the sheep and the flowers not important? ...And if I know—I, myself—one flower which is unique in the world, which grows nowhere but on my planet, but which one little sheep can destroy in a single bite some morning, without even noticing what he is doing—Oh!

(de Saint-Exupery, 1971: 24)

CHILDREN'S EXPOSURE TO PARENTAL/CAREGIVER VIOLENCE

There is currently no consensus with respect to the definition of either domestic violence or exposure to it, rendering it difficult to estimate accurately the number of children who can be said to have been exposed to it (Fantuzzo and Mohr, 1999). Fantuzzo and Mohr (1999: 22) have defined "exposure to domestic violence" through the use of examples, noting that it

> can include watching or hearing the violent events, direct involvement (for example, trying to intervene or calling the police), or experiencing the aftermath (for example, seeing bruises or observing maternal depression).

It has been estimated that at least 3.3 million children each year are exposed to violence between their parents (Carlson, 1984). In one study, approximately two-thirds of women who were battered indicated that their children were aware of most marital arguments (Holden and Ritchie, 1991), while almost half of the battered women in another study indicated that their children had directly observed marital aggression (O'Keefe, 1994). However, when multiple informants, such as parents and their children, are asked to estimate levels of exposure, agreement may be limited, indicating that abused women may underreport, deny, or be unaware of the level of their children's exposure to violence (O'Brien, John, Margoin, and Erel, 1994).

Children in violent households are three to nine times more likely to be injured and abused, either directly or in connection with their attempt to protect a parent from harm (Hall and Lynch, 1998). In anywhere from 60 to 75 percent of households in which a woman is battered, a child is also battered (Bowker, 1988; Fantuzzo, Boruch, Beriama, Atkins, and Marcus, 1997; McKibben, DeVos, and Newberger, 1989). A study based on the data obtained from police officers and female victims of intimate partner violence in the Spouse Assault Replication Program found that: (1) as compared to corresponding city demographics based on census data, children were disproportionately present in households in which there had been a substantiated assault of the female; (2) young children were disproportionately represented among those children present during the violence; (3) many of the households in which the violence occurred were characterized by poverty, were headed by a single female, and had a primary caregiver with a low level of education; and (4) the children in the violent households were often involved directly in the violent incident by calling for help, being identified as the catalyst for the dispute, and/or being physically abused by the assaultive adult ((Fantuzzo, Boruch, Beriama, Atkins, and Marcus, 1997).

Approximately 11 to 20 percent of adults remember from their childhood violent incidents that took place between a parent and an intimate other (Henning, Leitenberg, Coffey, Turner, and Bennett, 1996; Straus and Smith, 1990). In the 1975 National Family Violence Survey, 11% of respondents remembered at least one violent incident, while in the 1985 Survey, 13% remembered at least one violent episode (Straus, Gelles, and Steinmetz, 1980; Straus and Smith, 1990).

The violence that children witness may consist not only of hitting or throwing objects, but may encompass even more severe violence, such as attempted or effectuated stabbings or rape (Hyden, 1994). One woman, age 42 at the time of the interview, described one such incident that she witnessed as a child:

> My father was an alcoholic and he was drunk and he was beating up on my mother. It was an almost every day thing. One time he chased her down the street. She didn't have any clothes on and he was beating her and then he somehow took up a tool and almost fell on it. At the time I wished he would have died (Loue, unpublished data, interview conducted August 8, 1997).

Children may not only witness violence, but may also become the subject of violence themselves as they try to protect one parent from the other, or as a means of retaliation by one parent against the other (McCloskey, Figueredo, and Koss, 1995). The same woman described the punishment inflicted on her by her father as she tried to defend her mother, and her response:

> I took the beatings, the bruises, the hands over the light bulbs, stuff like that. My father had me hold my hands over a light bulb for two hours....He used to beat me with the iron, broomsticks. All it did was to teach me to hate. I hate the holy hell out of him because he robbed me of my life (Loue, unpublished data, interview conducted August 8, 1997).

Children may also experience aggression from the abused parent. Three explanations have been advanced to explain such behavior. First, "spill-over" aggression resulting from the marital violence may be directed against the child. Second, those who are victims of relationship violence come to understand that violence is an effective control mechanism and subsequently use violence with their children. Third, parents who are stressed are more likely than those who are not to adopt punitive, harsh, and/or negative behaviors towards their children (Holden, Stein, Ritchie, Harris, and Jouriles, 1998).

Children may be affected by partner violence indirectly, as well. For instance, a violent relationship between intimate partners may interfere with healthy child-raising practices, resulting in lack of warmth, inconsistent or harsh discipline, frequent disagreements regarding the children, poor communication between the parents and the children, and inconsistent styles of communication depending upon the presence or absence of a particular adult (Henning, Leitenberg, Coffey, Bennett, and Jankowski, 1997; Holden and Ritchie, 1991). A parent may become depressed in response to the partner conflict; depression has been demonstrated to be a significant factor affecting parenting (Patterson, 1990). A parent who fears for her own safety and who is hypervigilant with respect to her partner's moods may have little time or energy remaining to devote to a child (Hilton, 1992).

THE CHILD'S RESPONSE

How a child responds to the violence that he or she witnesses depends on various factors related to the violent incident itself, including the child's proximity to the threat of violence, the unexpectedness and duration of the experience, the child's relationship with the assailant and the victim, the physical integrity of the child, the severity and chronicity of the violence involved, the nature of the threats made, the presence or absence of a weapon (Holden, 1998; Humphreys, 1993). The child's response may also be affected by his or her developmental level (Davies, 1991), his or her age and gender, characteristics of the child (e.g. self-esteem) that may buffer the child, and the response of the child's battered mother (Holden, 1998; Humphreys, 1993). Khan's observations relating to trauma experienced by children is informative in this context:

> [T]he use of the word trauma in the concept of cumulative trauma should not mislead us into considering such breaches in the mother's role as a protective shield as traumatic at the time or in the context in which they happen. *They achieve the value of trauma only cumulatively and in retrospect* (Khan, 1963: 47; emphasis added).

Accordingly,

> each exposure may cause immediate traumatic reactions from which there is only incomplete recovery thus increasing the risk of significant deviation in the [child's] developmental trajectory....Each experience may also cause the child to be more vulnerable to adverse effects from successive exposures (Osofsky, Cohen, and Drell, 1995: 597).

Younger children may be more vulnerable to the emotional impact of the witnessed violence due to their own immaturity and inability to regulate their own responses (Davies, 1991). Exposure to violence in the family may interfere with a child's development of trust and normal exploratory behaviors (Osofsky, 1999; Wolfe and Korsch, 1994). A young child may sense the emotional unavailability of his or her mother and may respond accordingly. Infants who have been cared for at shelters for battered women have been noted to have poor health and sleeping difficulties and to engage in excessive screaming (Jaffe and Wolfe, 1990). Preschoolers may also express somatic complaints in response to the violence that they have witnessed and may feel guilt, believing that the violence would not have occurred if they had been "better" (Wolfe and Korsch, 1994).

In comparison, adolescents may be more able to view the partner violence as an issue of the partners and may experience less anxiety than younger children (Jaffe, Wolfe, and Wilson, 1990). However, some adolescents may assume additional responsibilities for childrearing and household chores, in an attempt to protect younger siblings and to maintain peace (Wolfe and Korsch, 1994). Studies are inconsistent with respect to the role of sex. Some studies have found that boys may be more likely than girls to respond with aggression to witnessing violence (Jaffe, Wolfe, and Wilson, 1990; Jouriles and LeCompte, 1991), while others have found that girls who had seen violent incidents between partners were more likely to be aggressive (Sternberg, Lamb, Greenbaum, Cicchetti, Dawud, Cortes, Krispin, and Lorey, 1993).

Young children who witness the murder of a parent have been found to display symptoms of post-traumatic stress disorder (PTSD) (Malmquist, 1986). Symptom criteria for PTSD include the re-experiencing of the trauma, persistent avoidance of trauma-related stimuli or psychological numbing, and symptoms of increased arousal that did not exist prior to the traumatic event; these symptoms must be present for a minimum of one month. Symptoms in children include regression to an earlier stage of development, nightmares, and difficulties in concentration (American Psychiatric Association, 1994). Young children witnessing the murder later displayed somatic complaints and had fantasies about restraining the perpetrator or assisting the victim. Some children became passive and inhibited, while others became argumentative and acted out (Malmquist, 1986). Adolescents were more likely to react to the homicide through rebelliousness, impulsiveness, and pessimism regarding the future (Malmquist, 1986). At least one study, though, has found that neither the intensity nor the frequency of the parental violence is associated with the child's development of PTSD (Kilpatrick and Williams, 1998).

Continued exposure to violence may result in children's desensitization to violence and the development of a perception of violence as normal (Jones, 1997). Children who witness family violence may display symptoms characteristic of post-traumatic stress disorder (PTSD) (Kilpatrick and Williams, 1997; McCloskey and Walker, 2000; Yates, 1996). Children may attempt to deal with the violent situation by blunting their tension and agitation, a process known as aversive arousal (Dutton and Golant, 1995). If the child feels that he or she is unable to control the situation, he or she may escape or withdraw, either emotionally or physically, such as to the child's bedroom. However, if the child is unable to remove him- or herself from the situation, the child may experience learned helplessness; the child must try to subdue his own anger towards the assailant, but may also simultaneously feel shame at his own inability to control the situation (Dutton and Golant, 1995).

Alternatively, the child witnessing chronic violence that is beyond his or her control may dissociate, as if he or she has split mind and body and is watching his or her body from outside of itself. The child is essentially cut off from his or own feelings, effectively psychically numbing him-/herself (Dutton and Golant, 1995). Should learned helplessness or dissociation prove inadequate to address the apparently uncontrollable violence, the child may run away, become ill, or attempt suicide in an attempt to lessen the pain (Dutton and Golant, 1995).

A child who witnesses violence between partners may display a number of symptoms. These include behavioral manifestations, such as aggression, tantrums, acting out, truancy, and delinquency; physical symptoms, such as failure to thrive, regressive behaviors, eating disorders, poor motor skills, and psychosomatic illnesses; emotional responses, such as anxiety, depression, withdrawal, low self-esteem, and anger; and cognitive difficulties, such as poor performance in school and delays in language development (Wildin, Williamson, and Wilson, 1991). Additionally, children who are witnesses to partner violence may be at greater risk of developing adjustment problems, compared with children whose parents are not violent (Fantuzzo, DePaola, Lambert, Martino, Anderson, and Sutton, 1991).

However, there is not a one-to-one correspondence between exposure to family violence and the development of emotional and/or behavioral problems (Quay and Peterson, 1979; Rosenbaum and O'Leary, 1981). A number of factors have been found to mediate negative effects of the environment including the mother's low level of depression (Garmezy, 1985), a higher socioeconomic status, and peer and sibling relationships (Rutter, 1987; Sameroff, 1995). Some children appear to be "resilient" and may not develop any symptoms associated with exposure to violence (Jones, 1997). Key factors that appear to contribute to a child's resilience include the presence of a caring adult and a child's internal resources, such as average or above-average intellectual development and good attention and interpersonal skills (Marans and Cohen, 1993; Masten, 1994; Masten, Best, and Garmezy, 1990; Rutter, 1994). More rarely, severely traumatized children may assume a "superman" or "batman" response, whereby they "become major helpers and organizers of others in distress as a way of dealing with their own trauma" (Osofsky, Cohen, and Drell, 1995: 597).

RESPONSES TO THE CHILD WITNESS

Crisis and Mental Health Interventions

Wolak and Finkelhor (1998) have suggested that intervention on behalf of the child witness may be necessary in situations in which the parents or partners are not adequately addressing their violent situation. Crisis intervention may entail conducting a lethality assessment, formulating a safety plan, training children in safety procedures, reporting child abuse if it is occurring, and providing crisis counseling. In noncrisis situations, however, the following procedures have been recommended: screening children for partner violence, assessing children who have been exposed to partner violence, reporting child abuse as appropriate and indicated by law, assigning a worker to the child, coordinating services for the child with other professionals, considering child custody issues that may arise, and providing parenting education to the parent(s) regarding the effects of violence on child witnesses (Wolak and Finkelhor, 1998).

Groves (1999) has advocated the development of mental health interventions for child witnesses of domestic violence. These interventions should be designed to promote an open discussion of the child's experiences, to help children understand and cope with their emotional responses to the violence, to promote children's acquisition of positive behaviors, to reduce the symptoms that children may be experiencing in response to the violence. Mental health services should also help the family to create a safe and stable environment for the child and, in situations in which that is not possible, to assist the abused parent to obtain safety for her- or himself and the children (Groves, 1999). Such interventions may be provided in the context of group or individual counseling (Peled and Davis, 1995; Silvern, Karyl, and Landis, 1995).

Several projects illustrate the use of an individually-focused model. The Boston Medical Center houses the outpatient, non-shelter-based Child Witness to Violence Project. This model encourages children to discuss the events that they have witnessed and to identify the feelings that they associate with such incidents. The program involves children's teachers and caregivers in both the assessment and intervention processes (Groves, 1994). The Child Trauma Research Project of San Francisco General Hospital focuses on helping preschoolers and their mothers to deal with the effects of violence and to improve their ability to function as a family unit (Lieberman, Van Horn, Grandison, and Pekarsky, 1997). Unlike the Child Witness to Violence Project, which has adapted its approach from models developed for the treatment of PTSD, the Child Trauma Research Project utilizes a psychodynamic approach.

Counseling services may also be provided in the context of shelter programs for battered women and their children. As of 1997, approximately 72 percent of shelters offered children's services, ranging from mental health counseling to recreational activities (National Coalition Against Domestic Violence, 1997).

The Legal System

As of 1997, 44 states and the District of Columbia required that courts consider domestic violence as a factor in rendering custody determinations (Kurtz, 1997). However, the legal system has failed to respond adequately to the needs of children who have witnessed domestic violence. For instance, as of 1997, 28 states had statutes that favored an award of custody to the parent who was most likely to encourage contact between the child and the other parent (Kurtz, 1997), essentially penalizing battered women who wished for obvious reasons to discontinue contact with their abusers. Not surprisingly, researchers have found that children who refuse to visit a noncustodial parent following the parents' separation or divorce are significantly more likely than non-refusing children to have a parent who has displayed a high level of violence, including violence against the other partner (Racusin, Copans, and Mills, 1994). Children witnesses of domestic violence are often excluded from states' statutory definitions of persons who may request a restraining order against the battling parents (Lemon, 1999).

THE CHILD GROWS UP

Numerous studies have demonstrated that children who either witness violence between their parents or who experience violence directly are more likely to be aggressive as children (Dodge, Pettit, and Bates, 1994; Thornberry, 1994), and, in adult life, commit violence against their spouses (Fagan, Stewart, and Hansen, 1983; Hotaling and Sugarman, 1986). One man's description of his behavior as a child who observed frequent violence between his parents is illustrative:

> All through my childhood, I was very rough. I would beat up on my younger brother and my older brother would beat up on me. One time in the seventh grade I got into a fight with a kid at school. I remember being scared of him because he was kind of a bully, but I couldn't back down. When we fought, I smashed his face into the brick wall of the school. I remember feeling very powerful, especially with all the kids around me saying how great I was. Also, to have beaten up this kid who I perceived to be so tough felt good.
>
> I was violent with girls from the time I started dating. My first steady girlfriend was Terri. Once we were at a party and everyone was drinking. I wanted her to drink and have fun, but she didn't want to. We got into an arument in the car and I grabbed her by the throat and pushed her up against the door and told her she was going to do what I wanted her to do. When I let go of her, she slapped me. I slapped her back especially hard and got into a total rage. I punched the window and broke it and left her crying in the car (Jim, quoted in Paymar, 2000: 58).

Girls who have witnessed abuse as children are more likely to be abused by a male partner in adult life. One woman who as a child had witnessed her father abuse her mother recounted one of her own experiences with an abusive intimate during her adult life:

> So I went with this guy....We were doing good until one time he sucker punched me and I almost lost my eye. So I said by. My mother told me, she always tells me, once you let a man hit you, it's continuously....Well, me and my mother, we talked not too long ago and I asked her, how could you always take those beatings. I said did you love him? She never loved him....Her mother would always take her away from my father but he would always con her mother, Oh, I'm doing good, I'm not drinking. You know my mother would always go back because of being scared. You know, a lot of it was he had scared her to death, she

wouldn't budge without asking, she didn't take a piss without his permission. She always told me you let a man hit you once, they do it for the rest of your life....[My ex-partner] tore the shit out of my apartment (Loue, unpublished data, interview August 8, 1997).

One man, who battered his intimate partner, looked back after having been in treatment and reflected on what he believed witnessing the violence had done to his children:

My adult children have all had experiences with chemical dependency and domestic abuse. My two girls have been in abusive relationships. Even though we've talked about what it was like for them growing up in our household, and how their lives have been affected by my violence, they've made some bad decisions, just like I did. My daughters have both been in treatment. I continue to talk with them about what I know about substance abuse, but they aren't ready to make the changes necessary to get sober.

My son Joe...was having problems with his girlfriend....He understands how he may have been influenced by what he saw as a child, and he recognizes his own behavior is abusive... (Dave, quoted in Paymar, 2000: 194).

10

LOOKING TOWARDS THE FUTURE: RESEARCH, PREVENTION, AND THE PROVISION OF SERVICES

Our greatest glory consists not in never falling, but in rising every time we fall.

Ralph Waldo Emerson

Never doubt that a small group of thoughtful and committed citizens can change the world. Indeed it's the only thing that ever has.

Margaret Mead

Despite our apparently extensive knowledge relating to intimate partner violence, there is much that we do not know. Yet the information that we lack may be critical to the prevention of partner violence and its sequelae.

RESEARCH

Assessing Violence

Researchers have, unfortunately, presumed that a level of homogeneity exists both across and within groups. Lockhart (1985: 40) has observed, for instance, that

> [r]acial comparisons made by ...researchers [may have been] based on an implicit assumption that all groups in this country are homogeneous, regardless of their ppolitical, socio-historical, and economic experiences. Researchers who ignore the fundamentally different realities of racial groups commit serious methodological and theoretical errors.

For instance, researchers who are unaware of the cultural expectations placed on many women may fail to ask questions that are key to understanding why men batter and why women remain. Existing measures are subject to numerous limitations, including the failure to include non-white groups in their development, the failure to assess the context in which the violence occurs, and the failure to assess the nature and the severity of the resulting injuries. The exclusion of non-white populations from the development of instruments may result in an inability to measure their experiences adequately and to interpret their reports accurately. Prevention models premised on the reality of one group may prove ineffective for others, precisely because of key elements of differing realities. Accordingly, improved measures are needed to assess partner violence.

Second, the scope and the depth of research relating to partner violence have been relatively limited. Research has tended to focus on three areas: the identification of the victim, offender, and incident characteristics; the response of the criminal justice and health care systems; and the social structures and cultural norms that tacitly allow battering to occur (Miller, 1989). Research efforts have, in general, failed to address such critical questions as the following:

- Are screening mechanisms developed to identify battered women and assaultive male partners similarly sensitive and specific in their identification of battered men and assaultive females? Are other screening mechanisms needed?
- Do changes in policy impact on violent behavior or the reporting of violent behavior or both?
- Do mandatory and pro-arrest policies disproportionately affect individuals by ethnicity or socioeconomic class? For instance, do poorer women refrain from calling the poice or seeking medical attention because the household will lose critical income if the battering partner is jailed?
- What is the long-term effectiveness of various treatment modalities on the behavior of the batterer?
- What are the short- and long-term impacts of various treatment modalities on the family system, e.g., the batterer, the battered and the child-witness/victim?
- To what extent does the impact of partner violence on children depend upon the frequency, duration, and/or severity of that violence? What factors mediate that impact?
- What coping strategies are used by children in families in which partner violence exists?
- Do children who initially appear to be "resilient" later develop social, emotional, or behavioral difficulties and, if so, are there identifiable predictors of such difficulties that are amenable to intervention?
- What are the effects on children of seeing a parent arrested by authority figures, such as the police, in response to domestic violence?
- What theoretical models are available to explain adequately same-sex violence and female-male violence?

The relative lack of attention to female-female violence, female-male violence, and male-male violence has resulted in the nonexistence of data that is critical to the formulation of policy and the development of service programs.

Such questions cannot be addressed adequately absent the utilization of an integrative perspective. Such an approach has been rare, despite the complexity and cross-disciplinary nature of partner violence. All too often, research has been either quantitative or qualitative in nature, rather than integrating these strategies to provide a more coherent description and explanation. Studies have often been cross-sectional in design, rather than longitudinal, thereby limiting our understanding of predictors and mediators of violence and the cessation of violence. Research has often failed to integrate the theoretical models and methodologies of the numerous disciplines relevant to partner violence, such as epidemiology, psychology, and ethics, resulting in research that is often narrower in scope and shallower in depth than that which could be maximally achieved.

PREVENTION EFFORTS

Heretofore, prevention efforts have generally failed to distinguish between primary, secondary, and tertiary prevention efforts, although this distinction is critical. Primary prevention efforts would seek to prevent partner violence before its occurrence. We have developed numerous screening mechanisms for the identification of individuals who have been battered, and we have learned what factors may be associated with first and subsequent episodes of partner violence. However, we have failed to apply this knowledge to develop adequate mechanisms to identify individuals and/or couples at high risk of committing or suffering violence before that violence occurs. Such a screening could be conducted, for instance, in the context of an annual physical examination or gynecological examination. Concomitantly, we have failed to develop adequate programs which effectively help individuals to avoid violence within their intimate relationships before the violence begins. Rather, we have focused on the formulation of strategies to prevent the reoccurrence of violence—secondary prevention—and, to a lesser extent, to mediate its consequences—tertiary prevention.

Prevention efforts that seek fundamental change in the nature of the relationship and society must necessarily acknowledge and address differences in perceptions of the "self"and the "other" that may exist between men and women. The Gilligan-Kohlberg debate on the nature of moral development is instructive in this regard.

Gilligan formulated the "ethic of care" based upon empirical observations indicating that men tend to resolve situations utilizing an ethic of rights, with an emphasis on fairness, while women tend to rely on an ethic of caring that focuses on needs, care, and the prevention of harm (Gilligan, 1982). Gilligan maintained that society had placed a greater value on individual achievement, thereby devaluing the caretaking roles fulfilled by women:

> The very traits that have traditionally defined the "goodness" of women, their care for and sensitivity to the needs of others, are those that mark them as deficient in moral development. The infusion of feeling into their judgments keeps them from developing a more independent and abstract ethical conception in which concern for others derives from principles of justice rather than from compassion and care (Gilligan, 1977: 484).

She argued that two different modes of social experience must be recognized:

> The failure to see the different reality of women's lives and to hear the differences in their voices stems in part from the assumption

that there is a single mode of social experience and interpretation. By positing instead two different modes, we arrive instead at a more complex rendition of human experience. (Gilligan, 1982: 173-174)

Gilligan (1982) delineated three levels in the development of an ethic of care and responsibility: orientation to individual survival, goodness as equated with self-sacrifice, and nonviolence. There are two transitions between levels. The first reflects movement from selfishness to responsibility for others and occurs between the first two levels. The second transition, occurring between the second and third levels, reflects increasing attention to oneself as well as to others.

Gilligan's paradigm is to be contrasted with that of Kohlberg's model of the development of moral judgment, which Gilligan argued had represented men's development, not human development. In contrast to Gilligan's phenomenological orientation, Kohlberg's model emphasized rationality. Gilligan's paradigm emphasized the self as connected and attached, relational, whereas Kohlberg viewed the self as individual and separate. Kohlberg's (1976; Colby and Kohlberg, 1987) model reflected three levels and six stages. The levels, from lowest to highest, were termed the preconventional, the conventional, and the postconventional or principled. Stages 1 and 2, that of heteronomous morality and individualism, instrumental purpose and exchange, consist of compliance with rules in order to avoid punishment and compliance with rules when it is for one's own benefit. The third and fourth stages, placed at level 2, consist of mutual interpersonal expectations, interpersonal conformity, and the maintenance of social system and conscience. Adherence to rules during these stages is a function of meeting the expectations of others or of a pre-existing agreement. Stage 5 focuses on individual rights and social contract, while stage 6 entails universal ethical principles. Adherence to and compliance to rules rests on the existence of a social contract and self-chosen ethical principles.

Blum (1993) has cogently enumerated seven major differences between the Kohlberg and Gilligan formulations of morality.

1.   Gilligan's moral self is defined by its historical connections and relationships, whereas Kohlberg's moral self attempts to achieve an impersonal standpoint that defines the moral point of view.
2.   Gilligan conceives of the self, the other, and the situation as particularized, whereas Kohlberg does not.
3.   Gilligan views the acquisition of knowledge of the other person as a complex task that requires reliance on specifically moral capacities. Kohlberg emphasizes, in contrast, the acquisition of knowledge of the other as an empirical process.
4.   Gilligan conceives of the self in relation to others; those relationships are not necessarily as result of choice. Kohlberg, though, views the individual as an autonomous, independent agent.
5.   Gilligan's concept of morality involves a consideration of cognition, emotions and action, whereas Kohlberg views morality as a function of rationality, with emotions playing only a secondary, if any, role.

6. Gilligan views the appropriateness of action in a particular situation as nonsubjective and premised on standards of care and responsibility. Kohlberg, however, views the principles of right action as universal.
7. For Gilligan, moral action expresses and sustains the connections with others, while Kohlberg's ultimate moral concern is with morally right action and principle.

The difference between these perspectives is perhaps best understood through example. Gandhi is known for his philosophy of nonviolence, but he wreaked psychological violence on his family and the children of the ashram. Although Gandhi asserted that truth "excludes the use of violence because man is not capable of knowing the absolute truth and therefore is not competent to punish" (Erikson, 1969: 241; see Gilligan, 1993: 104), Gandhi, unable to recognize the relativity of truth, imposed his truth on others and consequently did violence to their integrity (Erikson, 1969; Gilligan, 1993). Gilligan further illustrates these differences through the use of an example from the Bible. Abraham stands ready to sacrifice his son as a demonstration of the "integrity and supremacy of his faith" (Gilligan, 1993: 104). In contrast, the woman who pleads for her child before Solomon is willing to relinquish her claim to the child in order to spare his life. Gandhi and Abraham exemplify the "ethics of an adulthood that [have] become principled at the expense of care..." (Gilligan, 1993: 105).

The experience of a man who was battered by his wife and whose own ethic was founded upon caring illustrates well how these differences can affect the dynamic between partners and the course of action that an individual chooses:

> She was able to appeal to my own sense of 'ethics.' I held to the idea that I was a kind person. I would have had to become a mean, horrible person to throw her out of my house or call the police when the violence started. It was the 'love and care' piece that kept me there, got me to allow things to happen (Jones, 2000:156)

The distinction between an ethic of caring and an ethic based upon abstract principle is similarly reflected in a student's account of the interactions between her parents:

> My mother never really abused my father or anything, like stabbing him or shooting him...He was so unreasonable. He didn't ever talk about anything...He started talking to her and he would go and grab her arm, rip her clothes off her. My brother would get in the middle. My father was a preacher. Two married people are not supposed to get divorced or something like that. It's in the Bible somewhere...I guess he was slow. He's now accepting the fact that it's time for her to live her life. He can't run her life. It was making the whole family miserable (Ward, 1988: 198).

If prevention efforts at the primary and secondary levels are to succeed they must focus not only on helping batterers to understand the impact of their behavior on those around them and the "wrongness" of those behaviors, as many programs do, but they must also address the underlying differences in the participants' perception of and response to particular situations. For instance, suppose that a man comes home from work, expecting that dinner will be on the table at 6 p.m. as his wife had promised. It is not. His immediate emotional response is anger, but he has learned through counseling that violence is an inappropriate response. "Understanding" may consist of seeing that hitting someone causes a visual bruise; causing bruises is wrong because it hurts someone else and may result in legal consequences. This is a far different understanding than the following thought process: "My wife agreed with me this morning that dinner would be ready. Something must have happened for dinner to not be ready as promised. I wonder if she is okay." Both responses are physically nonviolent. The difference lies in the emotional accompaniment. In the first, the man retains a sense of "rightness:" what was promised was not delivered and his anger is justifiable. In the second, a sense of caring takes precedence over a sense of being right.

A distinct, but related, issue is that of role definition. Empirical research relating to violence in the context of heterosexual intimate relationships indicates that rigidity of men's and women's role definition is often one element in the development of violent conflict. How differences in role definition can be recognized, addressed, and resolved proactively at both the level of the couple and trhe community is less clear and remains a critical issue. Less apparent still, and also demanding of attention, is the contribution of role definition to violence between intimate partners of the same sex.

THE PROVISION OF SERVICES

Measuring Success

In the treatment context, we have failed to develop a uniform standard by which to measure success. Numerous criteria could potentially provide a basis for the measurement of "success": completion of a treatment program, as evidenced by attendance; absence of any additional reports of abuse with the current partner; absence of any additional reports of partner violence within a specified period of time, such as five years; reduced frequency and/or severity of violence episodes; and/or adoption of one or more alternative strategies for the resolution of conflict. Similasrly, no consensus has been reached regarding the standard for the "successful" treatment of the battered individual. Again, numerous measures could be employed, including a reduction in the severity and frequency of violent episodes experienced; departure from the abusive relationship; and/or engagement in a subsequent nonviolent relationship. We must also develop measures by which to evaluate success at apopulation level. Numerous possibilities exist, including decreased incidence and prevalence rates of violence; decreased rates of morbidity and mortality due to partner violence; and/or an increased rate of completion of treatment programs by batterers.

Registries

The development of registries for intimate partner violence could provide significant contributions to the prevention of violence, the provision of appropriate services, and the formulation of grounded and effective policy. Registries have been used in a variety of disease contexts as a data resource to support both treatment and prevention efforts (Godard, Knoppers, Glass, Grenon, Bouchard, Bouvier, Goulet, and Gauvreau, 1994; Myrhoj, Bernstein, Bisgaard, Svendsen, Sondergaard, Mohr, Dahl, and Bulow, 1994; Smith, Osuch, and Linver, 1995) and have been suggested for use in the context of domestic violence (Bowen and Sedlak, 1985). Domestic violence registries, once established, could be used as a resource to assist in the identification of risk factors for domestic violence, estimate the incidence and prevalence of intimate partner violence, and identify factors that appear to mediate reoccurrences of violence (Bowen and Sedlak, 1985).

Numerous impediments exist to the establishment of such registries, however. These include the lack of consensus with respect to a definition of intimate partner violence, logistical and methodological difficulties associated with the reporting of incidents to the registry, and the costs associated with such a massive undertaking. Ethical issues must also be considered including the extent to which information contained in the registry will remain confidential, e.g. whether the information may be accessed without identifiers and for research purposes only, or whether it may be accessed for use in a criminal context for use in prosecutions, and the extent to which information in the registry may be linked to other sources of information, such as police and medical reports, drivers' licenses, etc. (see Newcombe, 1994). Potential legal liability must be addressed for improper disclosures and harm that may result therefrom.

CONCLUSION

A journey of a thousand miles begins with a single step.
Lao-Tzu, *The Way of Lao-Tzu*

This has been a book about responsibility—of individuals who batter, of those who are physically abused, of professionals who must address intimate partner violence in the context of their professional lives, and of systems that provide care and services to those who are violent and to those who are the objects of that violence. Ultimately, we are all inextricably linked to each other through community. By implication, then, there are many unseen and unheard others who potentially bear responsibility in the context of partner violence: the neighbor who hears screams in the night, the teacher who sees the grade school child depressed and anxious, the manicurist who sees the woman's bruised arms. Violence will not stop unless and until we are willing to speak out against it and to provide a refuge in both time and space to those escaping from it. It is critical to this effort that we develop and commit the resources necessary to maximize the safety and security of those members of our communities who are in need of sanctuary.

REFERENCES

Abbey A. (1991). Acquaintance rape and alcohol consumption on college campuses: How are they linked? *Journal of American College Health, 39*, 165-169.

Abel EM, Suh EK. (1987). Use of police services by battered women. *Social Work, 32*, 526-528.

Adams CJ. (1993). "I just raped my wife! What are you going to do about it, Pastor": The church and sexual violence. In E Buchwald, P Fletcher, M Roth (Eds.). *Transforming a Rape Culture* (pp. 57-86). New York: Milkweed Editions.

Adams D. (1996). Guidelines for doctors in identifying and helping their patients who batter. *Journal of the American Medical Women's Association, 51*, 123-126.

Adams D. (1989). Stages of anti-sexist awareness and change for men who batter. In LJ Dickstein, CC Nadelson (Eds.). *Family Violence* (pp. 61-98). Washington, D.C.: American Psychiatric Press.

Adams D. (1988). Treatment models of men who batter: A profeminist analysis. In K Yllo, M Bograd (Eds.). *Feminist Perspectives on Wife Abuse* (pp. 176-200). Beverly Hills, California: Sage.

Adams I, Hickson J. (1993). Wife-beating among coloureds in South Africa and its impact on the marital relationship. *International Journal of Sociology of the Family, 23*, 117-137.

Akers RL. (1996). Is differential association/social learning cultural deviance theory? *Criminology, 34*, 229-247.

Akhmatova A. (1940). Rupture. In Akhmatova A. (1988). *Anna Akhmatova: Poems* (pp. 147-148). Moscow: Raduga Publishers.

Alpert EJ. (1995). Violence in intimate relationships and the practicing internist: New 'disease' or new agenda? *Annals of Internal Medicine, 123*, 774-781.

Alvarez A. (1977). The development of the Puerto Rican child. Unpublished manuscript. Cited in L. Comas-Diaz. (1988). Mainland Puerto Rican women: A sociocultural approach. *Journal of Community Psychology, 16*, 21-31.

American Psychiatric Association. (1994). *Diagnostic and Statistical Manual of Mental Disorders* (4th ed). Washington, D.C.: Author.

American Veterinary Medical Association. (1997). *The Veterinarian's Role in Animal Welfare.* Schaumberg, Illinois: American Veterinary Association.

Americas Watch. (1991). *Criminal Injustice: Violence Against Women in Brazil.* New York: Human Rights Watch.

Andison FS. (1977). TV violence and viewer aggression: A cumulation of study results: 1956-1976. *Public Opinion Quarterly, 41*, 314-331.

Andrade AR. (1992). Machismo: A universal malady. *Journal of American Culture, 5*, 33-41.

Anon. (2000, April). Cum sa iti bati nevasta...fara sa lasi urme [How to beat your wife without leaving marks]. *Playboy*, 100-101.

Anon. (1996). In Harm's Way? Domestic Violence, AFDC Receipt, and Welfare Reform in Massachusetts. Cited in Corlett, JR (1999, June 9). Women, domestic violence, and welfare. *Human Services Agenda of Northeast Ohio, 3*, 1-5.

Anon. (1985). Responses to wife abuse in four countries. *Response, 8*, 15-18.

Anon. (1985, June 23). See cops let husband beat her, woman says: $3.5m suit sets national precedent. *The Record*, at A2.

Arbuckle J, Olson L, Howard M, Brillman J, Anctil C, Sklar D. (1996). Safe at home? Domestic violence and other homicides among women in New Mexico. *Annals of Emergency Medicine, 27*, 210-215.

Arias I, Samios M, O'Leary KD. Prevalence and correlates of physical aggression during courtship. *Journal of Interpersonal Violence, 2*, 82-90.

Arkow P. (1995). *Breaking the Cycles of Violence: A Practical Guide.* Anaheim, California: The Latham Foundation.

Asch S, Leake B, Gelberg L. (194). Does fear of immigration authorities deter tuberculosis patients from seeking care? *Western Journal of Medicine, 161*, 373-376.

Asencio MW. (1999). Machos and sluts: Gender, sexuality and violence among a cohort of Puerto Rican adolescents. *Medical Anthropology Quarterly, 13*, 107-126.

Attala JM, Bauza K, Pratt H, Viera D. (1995). Integrative review of effects on children of witnessing domestic violence. *Issues in Comprehensive Pediatric Nursing, 18*, 163-175.

Attorney General's Task Force on Family Violence. (1984). *Attorney General's Task Force on Family Violence: Final Report.* Washington, D.C.: United States Department of Justice.

Aubry TD, Tefft B, Currie RF. (1995). Public attitudes and intentions regarding tenants of community mental health residences who are neighbors. *Community Mental Health Journal, 31,* 39-52.

Babcock JC, Waltz J, Jacobson NS, Gottman JM. (193). Power and violence: The relation between communication patterns, power discrepancies, and domestic violence. *Journal of Consulting and Clinical Psychology, 61,* 40-50.

Bachman R. (1994). *Violence Against Women.* [Bureau of Statistics, United States Department of Justice, NCJ Pub. No. 145325]. Washington, D.C.: Government Printing Office.

Bachman R, Coker AL. (1995). Police involvement in domestic violence: The interactive effects of victim injury, offender's history of violence, and race. *Violence and Victims,* 10, 91-106.

Bach-y-Rita G. (1982). The Mexican-American: Religious and cultural influences. In RM Becerra, M Karno, JI Escobar (Eds.). *Mental Health and Hispanic Americans: Clinical Perspectives* (pp. 29-40). New York: Grune and Stratton.

Bainbridge WR. (1989). The religious ecology of deviance. *American Sociological Review, 54,* 288-295.

Balakrishnan C, Imell LL, Bandy AT, Prasad JK. (1995). Perineal burns in males secondary to spouse abuse. *Burns,* 21, 34-35.

Balistreri v. Pacifica Police Department, 855 F.2d 1421 (9th Cir. 1988), amended and superseded by 901 F.2d 696 (1990).

Ballard DT, Blair GD, Devereaux S, Valentine LK, Horton AL, Johnson BL. (1990). A contemporary profile of the incest perpetrator. Background characteristics, abuse history, and use of social skills. In AL Norton, BL Johnson, LM Roundy, & D Williams (Eds.). *The Incest Perpetrator: A Family Member No One Wants to Treat* (pp. 54-64). Newbury Park, California: Sage.

Bandura A. (1983). Psychological mechanisms of aggression. In RG Green, EI Donnerstein (Eds.). *Aggression: Theoretical and Empirical Review* (pp. 1-40). New York: Academic Press.

Bandura A. (1979). The social learning perspective: Mechanisms of aggression. In H Tich (Ed.). *Psychology of Crime and Justice* (pp. 198-236). New York: Holt, Rinehart, and Winston.

Bandura A. (1977). *Social Learning Theory.* Englewod Cliffs, New Jersey: Prentice-Hall.

Barkan SE, Gary LT. (1996). Woman abuse and pediatrics: Expanding the web of detection. *Journal of the American Medical Women's Association, 51,* 96-100.

Barry H. III, Child IL, Bacon MK. (1967). Relation of child training to subsistence economy. In CS Ford (Ed.). *Cross-Cultural Approaches* (pp. 146-158). New Haven: HRAF.

Bartalone v. County of Berrien, 643 F. Supp. 574 (W.D. Mich. 1986).

Bates L, Redman S, Brown W, Hancock L. (1995). Domestic violence experienced by women attending an accident and emergency department. *Australian Journal of Public Health, 19,* 292-299.

Beck SR, Freitag SK, Singer N. (1996). Ocular injuries in battered women. *Ophthalmology, 103,* 148-151.

Becker HS. (1973). *Outsiders: Studies in the Sociology of Deviance.* New York: Free Press.

Beirne P, Quinney R. (Eds.). *Marxism and the Law.* New York: John Wiley and Sons.

Belknap J. (1995). Law enforcement officers' attitudes about the appropriate responses to woman battering. *International Review of Victimology,* 4, 47-62.

Belknap J, McCall KD. (1994). Woman battering and police referrals. *Journal of Criminal Justice, 22,* 223-236.

Bell CC, Jenkins EJ, Kpo W, Rhodes H. (1994). Response of emergency rooms to victims of interpersonal violence. *Hospital and Community Psychiatry, 45,* 142-146.

Bell D. (1985). Domestic violence: Victimization, police intervention, and disposition. *Journal of Criminal Justice, 13,* 525-534.

Bell RB. (1971). *Social Deviance.* Homewood, Illinois: Dorsey.

Bell ST, Kuriloff PJ, Lottes I. (194). Understanding attributions of blame in stranger rape and date rape situations: An examination of gender, race, identification, and students' social perceptions of rape victims. *Journal of Applied Psychology, 24,* 1719-1734.

Belsky J. (1980). Child maltreatment: An ecological integration. *American Psychologist, 35,* 320-335.

Bennet WL, Feldman MS. (1981). *Reconstructing Reality in the Courtroom: Justice and Judgment in American Culture.* New Brunswick, New Jersey: Rutgers University Press.

Ben-Yehuda N. (1985). *Deviance and Moral Boundaries: Witchcraft, the Occult, Science Fiction, Deviant Science, and Scientists.* Chicago: University of Chicago Press.

Ben-Yehuda N. (1990). *The Politics and Morality of Deviance: Moral Panics, Drug Abuse, Deviant Science, and Diverse Stigmatization.* Albany: State University of New York Press.

Bergman B, Brismar B. (1993). Assailants and victims: A comparative study of wife-beaters and battered males. *Journal of Addictive Diseases, 12,* 1-10.

Bergman B, Brismar B, Nordin C. (1992). Utilisation of medical care by abused women. *British Journal of Medicine, 305,* 27-28.

Berk RA, Berk SF, Newton PJ, Loseke D. (1984). Cops on call: Summoning the police to the scene of spousal violence. *Law & Society Review, 18*, 479-498.

Berk RA, Campbell A, Klap R, Western B. (1992). A Bayesian analysis of the Colorado Springs spouse abuse experiment. *Journal of Criminal Law & Criminology, 83*, 170-200.

Berk RA, Fenstermaker S, Newton PJ. (1988). An empirical analysis of police responses to incidents of wife battery. In GT Hotaling, D Finkelhor, JT Kirkpatrick, MA Straus. *Coping with Family Violence: Research and Policy Perspectives* (pp. 158-168). Newbury Park, California: Sage.

Bernard C, Schlaffer E. (1992). Domestic violence in Austria: The institutional response. In E.C. Viano (Ed.). *Intimate Violence: Interdisciplinary Perspectives* (pp 243-253). Washington, D.C.: Hemisphere Publishing Corporation.

Bersani CA, Chen H. (1988). Sociological perspectives on family violence. In V.B. Hasselt, RL Morrison, AS Bellack, M. Hersen, eds. *Handbook of Family Violence* (p. 57-86). New York: Plenum.

Bettelheim B. (1943). Individual and mass behavior in extreme situations. *Journal of Abnormal and Social Psychology, 38*, 417-432.

Bierstedt R. (1963). *The Social Order* (2nd ed.). New York: McGraw-Hill.

Billingham RE. (1987). Courtship violence: The patterns of conflict resolution strategies across seven levels of economic commitment. *Family Relations, 36*, 283-289.

Birch HG, Gussow JD. (1970). *Disadvantaged Children: Health, Nutrition, and School Failure.* New York: Harcourt, Brace, and World.

Birenbaum A, Sagarin E. (1976). *Norms and Human Behavior.* New York: Praeger.

Black D. (1976). *The Behavior of Law.* New York: Academic Press.

Blood RO, Wolfe DM. (1960). *Husbands and Wives: The Dynamics of Married Living.* Glencoe, Illinois: Free Press.

Blum LA. (1993). Gilligan and Kohlberg: Implications for moral theory. In MJ Larrabee (Ed.). *An Ethic of Care: Feminist and Interdisciplinary Perspectives* (pp. 49-68). New York: Routledge.

Blumer H. (1969). *Symbolic Interactionism: Perspective and Method.* Englewood Cliffs, New Jersey: Prentice Hall.

Bogdan R, Taylor S. (1987). Toward a sociology of acceptance: The other side of the study of deviance. *Social Policy, 18*, 34-39.

Bograd M. (1990). Feminist perspectives on wife abuse: An introduction. In K. Yllo, M. Bograd (Eds.). *Feminist Perspectives on Wife Abuse* (pp. 11-27). Newbury Park, California: Sage.

Bograd M. (1988). How battered women and abusive men account for domestic violence: Excuses, justifications or explanations? In GT Hotaling, D Finkelhor, JT Kirkpatrick, MA Straus (Eds.). *Coping with Family Violence: Research and Policy Perspectives* (p. 60-70). Newbury Park, California: Sage.

Bolton FG, Bolton SR. (1987). *Working with Violent Families.* Beverly Hills, California: Sage.

Bologna HJ, Waterman CK, Dawson CJ. (1987, July). Violence in gay male and lesbian relationships: Implications for practitioners and policy makers. Presented at the Third National Conference for Family Violence Researchers, Durham, North Carolina. Cited in Loring MT, Smith RW. (1994). Health care barriers and interventions for battered women. *Public Health Reports,109*, 328-338.

Booth A, Dabbs J. (1993). Testosterone and men's marriages. *Social Forces, 47*, 334-355.

Bowen GL, Sedlak AJ. (1985). Toward a domestic violence surveillance system: Issues and prospects. *Response, 8*, 2-7.

Burgos NM, Diaz-Perez YI. (1986). An exploration of human sexuality in the Puerto Rican culture. *Journal of Social Work and Human Sexuality, 4*, 135-150.

Bourgois P. (1996). In search of masculinity: Violence, respect, and sexuality among Puerto Rican crack dealers in East Harlem. *British Journal of Criminology, 36*, 412-427.

Bourque L. (1989). *Defining Rape.* Durham, North Carolina: Duke University Press.

Bowker LH. (1986). Law enforcement. In LH Bowker. *Ending the Violence: A Guidebook Based on the Experience of 1000 Battered Wives* (p. 56-65). Holmes Beach, Florida: Learning Publications.

Bowker LH. (1988). On the relationship between wife beating and child abuse. In K Yllo, M Bograd (Eds.). *Feminist Perspectives on Wife Abuse.* Newbury Park, California: Sage.

Breci MG. (1987). Police officers' values on intervention in family fights. *Police Studies, 10*, 192-202.

Breci MG, Murphy JE. (192). What do citizens want police to do at domestics: Enforce the law or provide services? *American Journal of Police, 11*, 53-68.

Breci MG, Simons RL. (1987). An examination of organizational and individual factors that influence police response to domestic disturbances. *Journal of Police Science and Administration, 15*, 93-104.

Brendtro M, Bowker L. (1989). Battered women: How can nurses help? *Issues in Mental Health Nursing, 10*, 169-180.

Brookoff D, O'Brien KK, Cook CS, Thompson TD, Williams C. (1997). Characteristics of participants in domestic violence: Assessment at the scene of domestic assault. *Journal of the American Medical Association, 277,* 1369-1373.

Brown JK. (1992). Introduction: Definitions, assumptions, themes, and issues. In DA Counts, JK Brown, JC Campbell (Eds.). *Sanctions and Sanctuary: Cultural Perspectives on the Beating of Wives* (pp. 1 -18). Boulder, Colorado: Westview Press, Inc.

Browne A. (1987). *When Battered Women Kill.* New York: Macmillan and Free Press.

Browne A, Williams KR. (1989). Explaining the effect of resource availability and the likelihood of female-perpetrated homicides. *Law and Society Review,* 23, 75-94.

Browne A, Williams KR. (1993). Gender, intimacy, and lethal violence: Trends from 1976 through 1987. *Gender and Society,* 7, 78-98.

Brownmiller S. (1999). *In Our Time: Memoir of a Revolution.* New York: Dial Press/Random House Inc.

Bruynooghe R et al. (1989). Study of Physical Violence Against Belgian Women. Departement des Sciences et Humaines et Sociales, Limburgs Universitair Centrum, Belgium. Cited in A Garcia (1991). *Sexual Violence Against Women: Contribution to a Strategy for Countering the Various Forms of Such Violence in the Council of Europe Member States.* Strasbourg, France: European Committee for Equality Between Men and Women.

Burgess RL, Akers RL. (1966). A differential association-reinforcement theory of criminal behavior. *Social Problems, 14,* 128-147.

Burgio LD, Sinnott J, Janosky JE, Hohman MJ. (192). Physicians' acceptance of behavioral treatments and pharmacotherapy for behavioral disturbances in older adults. *Gerontologist, 32,* 546-551.

Burke PJ, Stets JE, Pirog-Good MA. (1989). Gender identity, self-esteem, and physical and sexual abuse in dating relationships. In MA Pirog-Good and JE Stets (Eds.). *Violence in Dating Relationships: Emerging Social Issues* (pp. 72-93). New York: Praeger Publishers.

Buss DM, Shackelford TK. (1997). Human aggression in evolutionary psychological perspective. *Clinical Psychology Review, 17,* 605-619.

Buzawa ES, Austin TL, Buzawa CG. (1995). Responding to crimes of violence against women: Gender differences versus organizational imperatives. *Crime & Delinquency, 41,* 443-466.

Buzawa ES, Buzawa CG. (1996). Domestic Violence: The Criminal Justice Response, 2nd ed. Newbury Park, California: Sage.

Bullock LF, McFarlane J. (1989). The birthweight/battering connection. *American Journal of Nursing, 89,* 1153-1155.

California Penal Code §§ 11160-1116.32.

Cameron MO. (1964). *The Booster and the Snitch.* New York: Free Press.

Campbell J. (1992). Prevention of wife battering: Insights from cultural analysis. *Response, 80,* 19-24.

Campbell JC. (1992). "If I can't have you, no one can." Power and control in homicide of female partners. In J. Radford & D. Russell (Eds.). *Femicide: The Politics of Woman Killing* (pp. 99-113). Boston: Twayne.

Campbell JC. (1992). Review of nursing research on battering. In CM Sampselle (Ed.). *Violence Against Women: Nursing Research, Education, and Practical Issues* (pp. 69-81). New York: Hemisphere Press.

Campbell JC, Torres S, Ryan J, King C, Campbell DW, Stallings RY, Fuchs SC. (1999). Physical and nonphysical partner abuse and other risk factors for low birth weight among full term and preterm babies: A multiethnic case-control study. *American Journal of Epidemiology, 150,* 714-726.

Capps LL. (1994). Change and continuity in the medical culture of the Hmong in Kansas City. *Medical Anthropology Quarterly, 8,* 161-177.

Caputo RK. (1991). Police classification of domestic-violence calls: An assessment of program impact. In DD Knudsen & JL Miller (Eds.). *Abused and Battered: Social and Legal Responses to Family Violence* (pp. 147-151). New York: Aldine de Gruyter.

Carlson BE. (1984). Children's observations of interparental violence. In AR Roberts (Ed.). *Battered Women and Their Families* (pp. 147-167). New York: Springer.

Carmen E, Riecker P, Mill T. (1984). Victims of violence and psychiatric illness. *American Journal of Psychiatry, 141,* 378.

Cassian N. (1988). The blood. In A. Deletant, B. Walker (Trans.). *Call Yourself Alive: The Love Poems of Nina Cassian* (p. 13). London: Forest Books.

Cassian N. (1988). Escape. In A. Deletant, B. Walker (Trans.). *Call Yourself Alive: The Love Poems of Nina Cassian* (p. 14). London: Forest Books.

Castro de Alvarez C. (1990). AIDS prevention program for Puerto Rican women. *Puerto Rico Health Sciences Journal, 9,* 37-41.

Cazenave NA, Straus MA. (1979). Race, class, network embeddedness and family violence: A search for potent support systems. *Journal of Comparative Family Studies, 10,* 280-300.

Ceaucescu N. (1985, Dec. 26). Decret No. 411.

Ceaucescu N. (1966, Sept. 29). Decret No. 770.

Ceaucescu N. (1986). *Der Spiegel*. Oct. 20: 217-218.

Chagnon NA. (1968). *Yanomamo: The Fierce People*. New York: Holt, Rinehart, and Winston.

Chambliss LR, Bay RC, Jones RF III. (1995). Domestic violence: An educational imperative? *American Journal of Obstetrics and Gynecology, 172*, 1035-1038.

Chaney CK, Saltzstein GH. (1998). Democratic control and bureaucratic responsiveness: The police and domestic violence. *American Journal of Political Science, 42*, 745-768.

Chapter 222, New York Laws 786 (McKinney)(revised at ch. 224 § 1 [1994] New York Laws 808).

Chelmowski M, Hamberger LK. (1994). Screening men for domestic violence in your medical practice. *Wisconsin Medical Journal, 93*, 623-626.

Chesler P. (1989). *Women and Madness*. San Diego: Harcourt, Brace, Jovanovich.

Chimbos PD (1998). Spousal homicides in contemporary Greece. *International Journal of Contemporary Sociology, 39*, 213-223.

Chin KL. (1994). Out-of-town brides: International marriage and wife abuse among Chinese immigrants. *Journal of Comparative Family Studies, 25*, 53-69.

Christensen E. (1975). The Puerto Rican woman: The challenge of a changing society. *Character Potential*, 89-96.

Christensen EW . (1979). The Puerto Rican woman: A profile. In E Acosta-Belen, E Hidalgo Christensen (Eds.). *The Puerto Rican Woman*. New York: Praeger.

Christoff JP. (1992). Ohio's domestic violence laws: Recommendations for the 1990s. *Ohio Northern University Law Review, 19*, 163-198.

Chrystos: "What did he hit you with? The doctor said. (1986). In K. Lobel (Ed.). *Naming the Violence* (00. 19-20). Seattle, Washington: Seal Press.

Clinard MB, Meier RF. (1979). *The Sociology of Deviant Behavior*. (5th ed.). New York: Holt, Rinehart, and Winston.

Cockerham WC. (1999). Health and Social Change in Russia and Eastern Europe. New York: Routledge.

Cogan R, Porcerelli JH. (196). Object relations in abusive partner relationships: An empirical investigation. *Journal of Personality Assessment, 66*, 106-115.

Cohen AK. (1955). *Delinquent Boys: The Culture of the Gang*. Glencoe, Illinois: Free Press.

Cohen D, Llorente M, Eisdorfer C. (1998). Homicide-suicide in older persons. *American Journal of Psychiatry, 155*, 390-396.

Cohn EG, Sherman LW. (1986). *Police Policy on Domestic Violence, 1986*. Washington, D.C.: Crime Control Institute.

Colby A, Kohlberg L. (1987*)*. *The Measurement of Moral Judgment*, Vol. I. *Theoretical Foundations and Research Validation*. Cambridge, London: Cambridge University Press.

Coleman DH, Straus MA. (1983). Alcohol abuse and family violence. In E Gottheil, KA Druley, TE Skoloda, HM Waxman (Eds.). *Alcohol, Drug Abuse, and Aggression* (pp. 104-124). Springfield, Illinois: Charles C. Thomas.

Coleman DH, Straus MA. (1986). Marital power, conflict, and violence. *Violence and Victims, 1*, 141-157.

Coleman VE. (1990). *Violence Between Lesbian Couples: A Between Groups Comparison*. Doctoral Dissertation (University Microfilms No. 9109022). Cited in CM West. (1998). Leaving a second closet: Outing partner violence in same-sex couples. In JL Jasinski and LM Williams (Eds.). *Partner Violence: A Comprehensive Review of 20 Years of Research* (pp. 163-183). Thousand Oaks, California: Sage.

Coleman VE. (1994). Lesbian battering: The relationship between personality and the   perpetuation of violence. *Violence and Victims, 9*, 139-152.

Collins JJ Jr. (1983). Alcohol use and expressive interpersonal violence: A Proposed explanatory model. In E Gottheil, KA Druley, TE Skoloda, HM Waxman (Eds.). *Alcohol, Drug Abuse and Aggression* (pp. 5-25). Springfield, Illinois: Charles C. Thomas.

Comas-Diaz L. (1988). Mainland Puerto Rican women: A sociocultural approach. *Journal of Community Psychiatry, 16*, 21-31.

Conrad P, Schneider JW. (1980). *Deviance and Medicalization*. St. Louis: CV Mosby Company.

Cook CA, Harris KJ. (1995). Attributions about spouse abuse in cases of bidirectional battering. *Violence and Victims, 10*, 143-151.

Cook PW. (1997). *Abused Men: The Hidden Side of Domestic Violence*. Westport, Connecticut: Praeger.

Coser LA. (1969). Alienation and anomie. In LA Coser, B Rosenberg (Eds.). *Sociological Theory*, 3rd ed. (pp. 503-505). New York: Macmillan.

Coulter MA, Chez RA. (1997). Domestic violence victims support mandatory reporting: For others. *Journal of Family Violence, 12*, 349-356.

Council on Ethical and Judicial Affairs, American Medical Association. (1992). Physicians and domestic violence: Ethical considerations. *Journal of the American Medical Association, 267*, 3190-3193.

Council on Scientific Affairs, American Medical Association. (1992). Violence against women: Relevance for medical practitioners. *Journal of the American Medical Association, 267*, 3184-3189.

Counts DA. (1992). "All men do it": Wife beating in Kaliai, Papua New Guinea. In DA Counts, JK Brown, JC Campbell eds. *Sanctions and Sanctuary: Cultural Perspectives on the Beating of Wives* (pp. 63-76). Boulder, Colorado: Westview Press, Inc.

Counts D. (1987). Female suicide and wife abuse: A cross-cultural perspective. *Suicide and Life Threatening Behavior, 17*, 194-204.

Counts DA, Brown JK, Campbell JC, eds. (1992). *Sanctions and Sanctuary: Cultural Perspectives on the Beating of Wives*. Boulder, Colorado: Westview Press, Inc.

Courtright PB. (194). The iconographies of sati. In JS Hawley (Ed.). *Sati, The Blessing and the Curse: The Burning of Wives in India* (pp. 27-49). Oxford: Oxford University Press.

Covington J. (1986). Self-esteem and deviance: The effects of race and gender. *Criminology, 24*, 105-138.

Cramer E, McFarlane J, Parker B, Soeken K, Silva C, Reel S. (1998). Violent pornography and abuse of women: Theory to practice. *Violence and Victims, 13*, 319-332.

Cromwell RE, Olson DH. (1975). *Power in Families*. New York: Wiley.

Cuklanz LM. (2000). *Rape on Prime Time: Television, Masculinity, and Sexual Violence*. Philadelphia: University of Pennsylvania Press.

Cullen FT, Cullen JB. (1978). *Toward a Paradigm of Labeling Theory*. Lincoln, Nebraska: University of Nebraska.

Dabbs JM Jr, Morris R. (1990). Testosterone, social class, and antisocial behavior in a sample of 4,462 men. *Psychological Science, 1*, 209-211.

David HP. (1990a). Ceaucescu's psychological legacy: A generation of unwanted children. *Psychology International, 1*, 6-7.

David HP. (190b). Romania ends compulsory childbearing. *Entre Nous, 14*, 9-10.

David HP. (1990c). Romania ends compulsory childbearing. *Population Today, 18*: 4-10.

David HP, Baban A. (1996). Women's health and reproductive rights: Romanian experience. *Patient Education and Counseling, 28*, 235-245.

David HP, Wright NH. (1971). Abortion legislation: The Romanian experience. *Studies in Family Planning, 2*, 205-210.

Davidson T. (1978). *Conjugal Crime: Understanding and Changing the Wife Beating Pattern*. New York: Hawthorn.

Davies D. (1991). Intervention with male toddlers who have witnessed parental violence. *Families in Society, 72*, 515-524.

Davis GE, Leitenberg H. (1987). Adolescent sex offenders. *Psychological Bulletin, 101*, 417-427.

Davis LV, Carlson BE. (1987). Observation of spouse abuse: What happens to the children? *Journal of Interpersonal Violence, 2*, 278-291.

Davis NJ. (1975). *Social Construction of Deviance*. Dubuque, Iowa: William C. Brown.

Davis RC, Taylor G. (1997). A proactive response to family violence: The results of a randomized experiment. *Criminology, 35*, 307-333.

De La Cancela V. (1986). A critical analysis of Puerto Rican machismo: Implications for clinical practice. *Psychotherapy, 23*, 291-196.

De la Vega E. (1990). Considerations for reaching the Latino population with sexuality and HIV/AIDS information and education. *SIECUS Report, 18*, 1-8.

De Saint-Exupery A. (1971). *The Little Prince* (K. Woods Trans., 50th Anniversary Ed.) San Diego: Harcourt Brace & Company.

Deal JE, Wampler KS. (1986). Dating violence: The primacy of previous experiences. *Journal of Social and Personal Relationships, 3*, 457-471.

Decker DJ. (1999). *Stopping the Violence: A Group Model to Change Men's Abusive Attitudes and Behaviors*. New York: The Haworth Maltreatment and Trauma Press.

DeFleur ML, Antonio WV, DeFleur NL, Adamic CH. (1977). *Sociology: Human Society*, 2nd ed. Glenview, Illinois: Scott, Foresman.

Denisoff R, McCaghy CH. (1973). *Deviance, Conflict, and Criminality* Chicago: Rand McNally.

Denzin NK. (1984). Toward a phenomenology of domestic, family violence. *American Journal of Sociology, 90*, 483-513.

Deschner J. (1984). *The Hitting Habit: Anger Control for Battering Couples*. New York: Free Press.

DeShaney v. Winnebago County Department of Social Services, 489 U.S. 189 (1989).

Desir v. Ilchert, 840 F.2d 723 (9th Cir. 1988).

Deutsch H. (1930). The significance of masochism in the mental life of women. *International Journal of Psychoanalysis, XI*, 48-60.

Developments in the law: Legal responses to domestic violence. (1993). *Harvard Law Review, 106*, 1498-1620.

DeYoung Y, Zigner EF. (1994). Machismo in two cultures: Relation to punitive childrearing practices. *American Journal of Orthopsychiatry, 64*, 386-395.

DiVale WT, Harris M. (1976). Population, warfare, and the male supremacist complex. *American Anthropologist, 78*, 521-538.

Dobash RE, Dobash R. (1979). *Violence Against Wives*. New York: Free Press.

Dodge KA, Pettit GS, Bates JE. (1994). Socialization mediators of the relation between socioeconomic status and child conduct problems. *Child Development, 65*, 649-655.

Dohrenwend BP. (1959). Egoism, altruism, anomie, and fatalism: A conceptual analysis of Durkheim's types. *American Sociological Review, 24*, 466-473.

Douglas J. (1977). Shame and deceit in creative deviance. In E Sagarin (Ed.). *Deviance and Social Change*. Newbury Park, California: Sage.

Downs DA. (1996). *More Than Victims: Battered Women, the Syndrome Society, and the Law*. Chicago: University of Chicago Press.

Dunford FW. (1992). The measurement of recidivism in cases of spouse assault. *Journal of Criminal Law & Criminology, 83*, 120-136.

Draper P. (1992). Room to maneuver: !Kung women cope with men. In DA Counts, JK Brown, JC Campbell (Eds.). *Sanctions and Sanctuary: Cultural Perspectives on the Beating of Wives* (pp. 43-61). Boulder, Colorado: Westview Press, Inc.

Du Bois B. (1983). Passionate scholarship: Notes on values, knowing and method in feminist social science. In G Bowles, RD Klein (Eds.). *Theories of Women's Studies*. London: Routledge & Kegan Paul.

Duffy SJ, McGrath ME, Becker BM, Linakis JG. (1999). Mothers with histories of domestic violence in a pediatric emergency department. *Pediatrics, 103*, 1007-1013.

Duminy FJ, Hudson DA. (1993). Assault inflicted by hot water. *Burns, 19*, 426-428.

Durkheim E. (1951). *Suicide*. New York: Free Press.

Dutton DG. (1995). *The Domestic Assault of Women: Psychological and Criminal Justice Perspectives*. Vancouver: University of British Columbia Press.

Dutton DG. (1985). An ecologically nested theory of male violence towards intimates. *International Journal of Women's Studies, 8*, 404-413.

Dutton DG, Golant SK. (1995). *The Batterer: A Psychological Profile*. New York: Basic Books.

Dutton DG, McGregor BMS. (1991). The symbiosis of arrest and treatment for wife assault: The case for combined intervention. In M Steinman (Ed.). *Woman Battering: Policy Responses* (pp. 131-154). Cincinnati: Anderson Publishing Co.

Dutton DG, Painter S. (1993). Emotional attachments in abusive relationships: A test of traumatic bonding theory. *Violence and Victims, 8*, 105-120.

Dutton DG, Painter SL. (1981). Traumatic bonding: The development of emotional attachments in battered women and other relationships of intermittent abuse. *Victimology: An International Journal, 1*, 139-155.

Dutton DG, van Ginkel C, Starzomski A. (1995). The role of shame and guilt in the intergenerational transmission of abusiveness. *Violence and Victims, 10*, 121-131.

Dutton MA. (1992). *Empowering and Healing the Battered Woman: A Model for Assessment and Intervention*. New York: Springer.

Dworkin A. (1981). *Pornography: Men Possessing Women*. New York: G.P. Putnam Sons.

Dwyer DC. (1995). Response to the victims of domestic violence: Analysis and implications of the British experience. *Crime and Delinquency, 41*, 527-540.

Edgerton RB. (1973). *The Cloak of Competence*, revised ed. Berkeley, California: University of California Press.

Edgerton RB. (1976). *Deviance: A Cross-Cultural Perspective*. Menlo Park, California: Benjamin Cummings Publishing Company.

Edgerton RB. (1985). *Rules, Exceptions, and Social Order*. Berkeley, California: University of California Press.

Edleson JL. (1985). Violence is the issue: A critique of Neidig's assumptions. *Victimology, 9*, 483-489.

Edleson JL. (1984). Working with men who batter. *Social Work, 29*, 237-242.

Edwards SSM. (1986). *The Police Response to Domestic Violence in London*. London: Central London Polytechnic.

Egeland B, Jacobritz D, Stroufe AL. (1988). Breaking the cycle of abuse. *Child Development, 59*, 1080-1088.

Eigenberg HM, Scarborough KE, Kapeler VE. (1996). Contributory factors affecting arrest in domestic and non-domestic assaults. *American Journal of Police, 15*, 27-54.

Eisenstat SA, Bancroft L. (1999). Domestic violence. *New England Journal of Medicine, 341*, 886-892.

Eisikovits ZC, Guttmann E, Sela-Amit M, Edleson JL. (1993). Women battering in Israel: The relative contributions of interpersonal factors. *American Journal of Orthopsychiatry, 63*, 313-317.

Ejercito AE. (1983). Peters v. Peters: Is there really a choice of law under Hawaii's interest analysis? *University of Hawaii Law Review, 5*, 113-133.

Ellis A. (1976). Techniques of handling anger in marriage. *Journal of Marriage and Family Counseling, 2*, 305-315.

Ellis D. (1987). Policing wife-abuse: The contribution made by "domestic disturbances" to deaths and injuries among police officers. *Journal of Family Violence, 2*, 319-333.

Else L, Wonderlish SA, Beatty WW, Christie DW, Staton RD. (1993). Personality characteristics of men who physically abuse women. *Hospital and Community Psychiatry, 44*, 54-58.

Erchak GM, Rosenfeld R. (1994). Societal isolation, violent norms, and gender relations: A reexamination and extension of Levinson's model of wife beating. *Cross-Cultural Research, 28*, 111-133.

Erez E. (1986). Intimacy, violence, and the police. *Human Relations, 39*, 265-281.

Erikson EK. (1969*). Gandhi's Truth*. New York: W.W. Norton.

Erikson KT. (1962). Notes on the sociology of deviance. *Social Problems, 9*, 307-314.

Erikson RV, Baranek PM, Chan JBL. (1987). *Visualizing Deviance: A Study of News Organizations*. Toronto: University of Toronto Press.

Eron LD, Huesmann LR, Lefkowitz MM, Walder LO. (1972). Does television violence cause aggression? *American Psychologist, 27*, 253-263.

Europa Publications Limited. (1992). *The Europa World Yearbook*, Vol. II. London: Staples Printers Rochester Limited.

Europa Publications Limited. (1993). *The Europa World Yearbook*, Vol. II. London: Staples Printers Rochester Limited.

Fagan JA. (1990). Intoxication and aggression. In JQ Wilson, M Tonry (Eds.). *Drugs and Crime*, vol. 13: *Crime and Justice: An Annual Review of Research* (pp. 241-320). Chicago: University of Chicago Press.

Fagan J, Browne A. (1994). Violence between spouse and intimates: Physical aggression between women and men in intimate relationships. In AJ Reiss Jr, JA Roth (Eds.). *Understanding and Preventing Violence. Vol. 3. Social Influences* (pp. 115-292). Washington, D.C.: National Academy Press.

Fagan JA, Stewart D, Hansen K. (1983). Violent men or violent husbands? Background factors and situational correlates of domestic and extra-domestic violence. In D Finkelhor, R Gelles, G Hotaling, M Straus (Eds.). *The Dark Side of Families: Current Family Violence Research*. (pp. 49-67). Beverly Hills, California: Sage Publications.

Family Violence Project. (1990). *Family Violence: Improving Court Practices. Recommendations from the National Council of Juvenile and Family Court Judges' Family Violence Project*. Washington, D.C.: United States Department of Justice.

Fantuzzo J, Boruch R, Beriama A, Atkins M, Marcus S. (1997). Domestic violence and children: Prevalence and risk in five major U.S. cities. *Journal of the Academy of Child and Adolescent Psychiatry, 36*, 116-122.

Fantuzzo JW, DePaola LM, Lambert L, Martino T, Anderson G, Sutton S. (1991). Effects of interparental violence on the psychological adjustment and competencies of young children. *Journal of Consulting and Clinical Psychology, 59*, 258-265.

Fantuzzo JW, Mohr WK. (1999). Prevalence and effects of child exposure to domestic violence. *Domestic Violence and Children, 9*, 21-32.

Farley N. (1996). A survey of factors contributing to gay and lesbian domestic violence. In CM Renzetti and CH Miley (Eds.).*Violence in Gay and Lesbian Domestic Partnerships* (pp. 35-42). Binghamton, New York: Haworth.

Farmer F. (1994). Will there really be a morning? Excerpted in JL Geller, M Harris. *Women of the Asylum* (pp. 314-325). . New York: Anchor Books.

Feder L. (1997). Domestic violence and police response in a pro-arrest jurisdiction. *Women & Criminal Justice, 8*, 79-98.

Feder L. (1996). Police handling of domestic calls: The importance of offender's presence in the arrest decision. *Journal of Criminal Justice, 24*, 481-490.

Feldberg M. (1985). Police discretion and family disturbances: Some historical and contemporary reflections. In EH Newberger, R Bourne (Eds.). *Unhappy Families: Clinical and Research*

Perspectives on Family Violence (pp. 121-129). Littleton, Massachusetts: PSG Publishing Company.

Felder R, Victor B. (1996). *Getting Away with Murder: Weapons for the War Against Domestic Violence.* New York: Simon and Schuster.

Feldhaus KM, Koziol-McLain J, Amsbury HL, Norton IM, Lowenstein SR, Abbott JT. (1997). Accuracy of 3 brief screening questions for detecting partner violence in the emergency department. *Journal of the American Medical Association, 277,* 1357-1361.

Feldman SD (Ed.). (1978). *Deciphering Deviance.* Boston: Little Brown.

Felson RB. (1996). Mass media effects on violent behavior. *Annual Review of Sociology, 22,* 103-128.

Felson RB, Ribner SA, Siegel MS. (1984). Age and the effect of third parties during criminal violence. *Sociology and Social Research, 68,* 452-462.

Ferraro KJ, Johnson JM. (1983). How women experience battering: The process of victimization. *Social Problems, 30,* 325-337.

Ferris LE, Norton PG, Dunn EV, Gort EH, Degani N. (1997). Guidelines for managing domestic abuse when male and female partners are patients of the same physician. *Journal of the American Medical Association, 278,* 851-857.

Fiebert MS. (1996). College students' perception of men as victims of women's assaultive behavior. *Perceptual and Motor Skills, 82,* 49-50.

Fildes J, Reed L, Jones N, Martin M, Barrett J. (1992). Trauma: The leading cause of maternal death. *Journal of Trauma, 32,* 643-645.

Finch J. (1987). Research note: The vignette technique in survey research. *Sociology, 21,* 105-114.

Finkelhor D, Yllo K. (1980). Forced sex in marriage: A preliminary research report. Presented at the Annual Meeting of the American Sociological Association, New York.

Finkelhor D, Yllo K. (1983). Rape in marriage: A sociological view. In D Finkelhor, RJ Gelles, GT Hotaling, MA Straus (Eds.). *The Dark Side of Families: Current Family Violence Research* (pp. 119-130). Beverly Hills: Sage.

Finn MA, Stalans LJ. (195). Police referrals to shelters and mental health treatment: Examining their decisions in domestic assault cases. *Crime & Delinquency, 41,* 467-480.

Fletcher G. (1988). *A Crime of Self-Defense: Bernard Goetz and the Law on Trial.* New York: Free Press.

Fleury RE, Sullivan CM, Bybee D, Davidson WS II. (1998). What happened depends on whom you ask: A comparison of police records and victim reports regarding arrests for woman battering. *Journal of Criminal Justice, 26,* 53-59.

Fleury RE, Sullivan CM, Bybee D, Davidson WS II. (1998). "Why don't they just call the cops?": Reasons for differential police contact among women with abusive partners. *Violence and Victims, 13,* 333-346.

Fliszar GM, Clopton JR. (195). Attitudes of psychologists in training towards persons with AIDS. *Professional Psychology: Research and Practice, 26,* 274-277.

Flitcraft AH. (1995). Clinical violence intervention: Lessons from battered women. *Journal of Health Care for the Poor and Underserved, 6,* 187-197.

Flitcraft AH, Hadley SM, Hendricks-Matthews MK, McLeer SV, Warshaw C. (1992). *Diagnostic and Treatment Guidelines on Domestic Violence.* Chicago: American Medical Association.

Fortune MM. (1998). Preaching forgiveness? In JS McClure, NJ Ramsay (Eds.). *Telling the Truth: Preaching About Sexual and Domestic Violence* (pp. 49-57). Cleveland, Ohio: United Church Press.

Freeman J. (1995). Domestic violence: The law and physician liabilities. *Iowa Medicine, 85,* 70-75.

Freidson E. (1966). Disability as a social deviance. In MB Sussman (Ed.). *Sociology and Rehabilitation* (pp. 71-99). Washington, D.C.: American Sociological Association.

Freire P. (1978). *Pedagogy* of the Oppressed. New York: Penguin.

French F, Wilke AS, Mayfield L, Woolley B. (1985). The physician's role in covering deviance: Assisting the physically handicapped. *Psychological Reports, 57,* 1255-1259.

Frieze IH, Browne A. (1989). Violence in marriage. In L Ohlin, M Tonry (Eds.). *Family Violence,* vol. 11: *Crime and Justice: An Annual Review of Research.* Chicago: University of Chicago Press.

Freund KM, Bak SM, Blackhall L. (1996). Identifying domestic violence in primary care practice. *Journal of General Internal Medicine, 11,* 44-46.

Frieze JH. (1980, Sept.). The causes and consequences of marital rape. Presented at the Annual Meeting of the American Psychological Association, Montreal.

Fromm E. (1973). *The Anatomy of Human Destructiveness.* New York: Fawcett.

Frye B.A., D'Avanzo C. (1994). Themes in Managing Culturally Defined Illness in the Cambodian Refugee Family. *Journal of Community Health Nursing, 11,* 89-98.

Fyfe JJ, Klinger DA, Flavin JM. (197). Differential police treatment of male-on-female spousal violence. *Criminology, 35*, 455-473.

Gabler M, Stern SE, Misreandino M. (1998). Latin American, Asian, and American cultural differences in perceptions of spousal abuse. *Psychological Reports, 83*, 587-592.

Gaffney KF, Choi E, Yi K, Jones GB, Bowman C, Tavangar NN. (197) Stressful events among pregnant Salvadoran women: A cross-cultural comparison. *Journal of Obstetric, Gynecologic, and Neonatal Nursing, 26*, 303-310.

Ganley AL, Harris L. (1978). Domestic violence: Issues in designing and implementing programs for male batterers. Paper presented at the 86th Annual Convention of the American Psychological Association, Toronto, Canada. Cited in JC Babcock, J Waltz, NS Jacobson, JM Gottman. (1993). Power and violence: The relation between communication patterns, power discrepancies, and domestic violence. *Journal of   Consulting and Clinical Psychology, 61*, 40-50.

Garmezy N. (1985). Stress resistant children: The search for proitective factors. In JE Stevenson (Ed.) *Recent Research in Developmental Psychopathology* (pp. 213-233). Oxford, England: Pergammon Press.

Gartin PR. (1995). Examining differential officer effects in the Minneapolis domestic violence experiment. *American Journal of Police, 14*, 93-110.

Geffner R, Pagelow MD. (1990). Mediation and child custody issues in abusive relationships. *Behavioral Sciences and the Law, 8*, 151-159.

Gelles RJ. (1993). Alcohol and other drugs are associated with violence: They are not its cause. In RJ Gelles, DR Loseke (Eds.). *Current Controversies on Family Violence* (pp. 182-196). Newbury Park, California: Sage.

Gelles RJ. (1989). Child abuse and violence in single parent families: Parent absence and economic deprivation. *American Journal of Orthopsychiatry, 59*, 492-501.

Gelles RJ. (1983). An exchange/social theory. In D Finkelhor, RJ Gelles, GT Hotaling, MA Straus, eds. *The Dark Side of Families: Current Family Violence Research* (pp. 151-165). Beverly Hills, California: Sage.

Gelles RJ. (1987). *Family Violence*. Newbury Park, California: Sage.

Gelles RJ. (1977). No place to go: The social dynamics of marital violence. In M. Roy (Ed.). *Battered Women: A Psychosociological Study of Domestic Violence*. New York: Van Nostrand Reinhold.

Gelles RJ. (1994). Research and advocacy: Can one wear two hats? *Family Process, 33*, 93-96.

Gelles RJ, Straus MA. (1979). Determinants of violence in the family. Toward a theoretical integration. In WR Burr, FI Nye, SK Steinmetz, M Wilkinson (Eds.). *Contemporary Theories About the Family* (pp. 549-581). New York: Free Press.

Gil RM, Vasquez CI. (1996). *The Maria Paradox: How Latinas Can Merge Old World Traditions with New World Self-Esteem*. New York: Berkeley Publishing.

Gilberg T. (1979). Rural transformation in Romania. In I. Volgyes (Ed.). *The Peasantry of Eastern Europe*. New York: Pergamon,.

Gillespie CK. (1988). *Justifiable Homicide: Battered Women, Self-Defense, and the Law*. Columbus, Ohio: Ohio State University Press.

Gilligan C. (1977). Concepts of the self and of morality. *Harvard Educational Review, 47*, 481-517.

Gilligan C. (1982*). In a Different Voice: Psychological Theory and Women's Development*. Cambridge, Massachusetts: Harvard University Press.

Gilligan C. (1993). *In a Different Voice: Psychological Theory and Women's Development*. Cambridge, Massachusetts: Harvard University Press.

Gina C. v. Stephen F., 576 N.Y.S.2d 776 (Fam. Ct. 1991).

Giraldo P. (1972). El machismo como fenomeno psicocultural [Machismo as a psychocultural phenomenon]. *Revista Latino-Americana de Psicologia, 4*, 295-309.

Gitlin T. (1980). *The Whole World Is Watching*. Berkeley, California: University of California Press.

Godard B, Knoppers BM, Glass K, Grenon M, Bouchard R, Bouvier M, Goulet J, Gauvreau D. (1994). Ethical issues involved in establishing a registry for familial Alzheimer's disease. *Alzheimer Disease and Associated Disorders, 8*, 79-93.

Goddard H. (1912). *The Kallilak Family*. New York: Macmillan.

Goetting, A. (1999). *Life Stories of Women Who Left Abusive Men*. New York: Columbia University Press.

Goffman E. (1961). *Asylums*. Garden City, New York: Anchor Books.

Gondolf EN, Fisher ER. (1988). *Battered Women as Survivors: An Alternative to Treating Learned Helplessness*. Lexington, Massachusetts: Lexington Books.

Gondolf EW. (1988). How some men stop their abuse: An exploratory program evaluation. In GT Hotaling, D Finkelhor, JT Kirkpatrick, MA Straus (Eds.). *Coping with Family Violence: Research and Policy Perspectives* (pp. 129-144). Newbury Park, California: Sage.

Gondolf EW, Fisher E, McFerron JR. (1988). Racial differences among shelter residents: A comparison of Anglo, Black, and Hispanic battered women. *Journal of Family Violence, 3,* 39-51.

Gondolf EW, Russell D. (1986). The case against anger control treatment programs for batterers. *Response, 9,* 2-5.

Goode W. (1971). Force and violence in the family. *Journal of Marriage and the Family, 33,* 624-636.

Goodman A. (2000). Answering their call: Verizon Wireless' Denny Strigl and the victims of domestic abuse. *Delta Sky, July,* 112-114.

Goodman LA, Koss MP, Russo NF. (1993). Violence against women: Physical and mental health effects. Part I. Research findings. *Applied and Preventive Psychology, 2,* 79-89.

Goring C. (1913). *The English Convict.* London: His Majesty's Stationery Office.

Gove WR. (1982). The formal reshaping of deviance. In MM Rosenberg, RA Stebbins, A Turowitz (Eds.). *The Sociology of Deviance* (pp. 175-201). New York: St. Martin's Press.

Graham DLR, Rawlings EI. (1998). Bonding with abusive dating partners: Dynamics of Stockholm Syndrome. In B Levy (Ed.). *Dating Violence: Young Women in Danger* (pp. 119-135). Seattle: Seal Press.

Graham DLR, Rawlings EJ, Ihms K, Latimer D, Foliana J, Thompson A, Suttman K, Farrington M, Hacker R. (1995). A scale for identifying "Stockholm syndrome" reactions in young dating women: Factor structure, reliability, and validity. *Violence and Victims, 10,* 3-22.

Grasmick HG, Blackwell BS, Bursik Jr RJ, Mitchell S. (1993). Changes in perceived threats of shame, embarrassment, and legal sanctions for interpersonal violence, 1982-1992. *Violence and Victims, 8,* 313-325.

Greenberg D (Ed.). (1981). *Crime and Capitalism.* Palo Alto, California: Mayfield Publishing Company.

Grindstaff L, McCaughey M. (1996). Re-membering John Bobbitt: Castration anxiety, male hysteria, and the phallus. In A Myers, S Wight (Eds.). *No Angels: Women Who Commit Violence* (pp. 142-160). London: Pandora.

Groves B. (1994). The child witness to violence project. *Discharge Planning Update, 14,* 14-18.

Groves BM. (1999). Mental health services for children who witness domestic violence. *Domestic Violence and Children, 9,* 122-132.

Gunderson, J.G. (1984). *Borderline Personality Disorder.* Washington, D.C.: American Psychiatric Association.

Gutmann MC. (1996). *The Meanings of Macho: Being a Man in Mexico City.* Berkeley, California: University of California Press.

Haber J. (1985). Abused women and chronic pain. *American Journal of Nursing, 85,* 1010-1012.

Hadley SM. (1992). Working with battered women in the emergency department: A model program. *Journal of Emergency Nursing, 18,* 18-23.

Hall D, Lynch MA. (1998). Violence begins at home: Domestic strife has lifelong effects on children. *British Medical Journal, 316,* 1551.

Hamberger KL, Hastings JE. (1988). Characteristics of male spouse abusers consistent with personality disorders. *Hospital and Community Psychiatry, 39,* 763-760.

Hammond N. (1989). Lesbian victims of relationship violence. *Women Therapy, 8,* 89-105.

Hanneke CR, Shields NM, McCall GJ. (1986). Assessing the prevalence of marital rape. *Journal of Interpersonal Violence, 1,* 350-362.

Harlan L. (1994). Perfection and devotion: Sati tradition in Rajasthan. In JS Hawley, ed. *Sati: The Blessing and the Curse: The Burning of Wives in India* (pp. 79-91). New York: Oxford University Press.

Harsanyi DP. (1993). Women in Romania. In N Funk, M Mueller (Eds.). *Gender Politics and Post-Communism* (pp. 39-52). New York: Routledge.

Hart B. (1993). Battered women and the criminal justice system. *American Behavioral Scientist, 36,* 624-638.

Hart B. (1986). Lesbian battering: An examination. In K Lobel (Ed.). *Naming the Violence: Speaking Out About Lesbian Battering* (pp. 173-189). Seattle, Washington: Seal Press.

Hart BJ. (1997). Arrest: What's the big deal. *William & Mary Journal of Women & the Law, 3,* 207-221.

Hart SD, Dutton DG, Newlove T. (1992). The prevalence of personality disorder among wife assaulters. *Journal of Personality Disorders, 7,* 328-340.

Hartzell KN, Botek AA, Goldberg SH. (1996). Orbital fractures in women due to sexual assault and domestic violence. *Ophthalmology, 103,* 953-957.

Harwood A. (1987). *Rx: Spiritist as Needed: A Study of a Puerto Rican Community Mental Health Resource.* Ithaca, New York: Cornell University Press.

Hawaii Revised Statutes § 663-1 (1984).

Hawkins R, Tiedeman G. (1975). *The Creation of Deviance: Interpersonal and Organizational Determinants.* Columbus, Ohio: Merrill.

Hawley JS. (1994). Introduction. In JS Hawley (Ed.). *Sati, The Blessing and the Curse: The Burning of Wives in India* (pp. 3-26). Oxford: Oxford University Press.

Haynes RH. (1984). Suicide in Fiji: A preliminary study. *British Journal of Psychiatry*, 145, 433- 438.

Hearn J. (1996). Men's violence to known women: Men's accounts and men's policy developments. In B Fawcett, B Featherstone, J Hearn, C Toft. (Eds.). *Violence and Gender Relations: Theories and Interventions* (p. 9-114). Thousand Oaks, California: Sage.

Heilbrun C. (1990). *Hamlet's Mother and Other Women*. New York: Columbia University Press.

Helton AS, Snodgrass FG. (1987). Battering during pregnancy: Intervention strategies. *Birth, 14*, 142-147.

Henning K, Leitenberg H, Coffey P, Bennett T, Jankowski MK. (1997). Long-term psychological adjustment to witnessing interparental physical conflict during childhood. *Child Abuse and Neglect, 21*, 501-515.

Henning K, Leitenberg H, Coffey P, Turner T, Bennett RT. (1996). Long-term psychological and social impact of witnessing physical conflict between parents. *Journal of Interpersonal Violence, 11*, 35-51.

Herman JL. (1992). *Trauma and Recovery: The Aftermath of Violence: From Domestic Abuse to Political Terror*. New York: Basic Books,

Hilberman E. (1980). Overview: The "wife-beater's wife" reconsidered. *American Journal of Psychiatry, 2*, 460-470.

Hilton NZ. (1992). Battered women's concerns about their children witnessing wife assault. Journal of *Interpersonal Violence, 7*, 77-86.

Hirschel JD, Hutchison III IW. (1992). Female spouse abuse and the police response: The Charlotte, North Carolina experiment. *Journal of Criminal Law and Criminology, 83*, 73-119.

Hirschel JD, Hutchison III IW, Dean CW, Kelley JJ, Pesackis CE. (1991). *Charlotte Spouse Assault Replication Project:Final Report*. Washington, D.C.: National Institute of Justice.

Hirschel JD, Hutchison III IW, Dean CW, Mills AM. (1992). Review essay on the law enforcement response to spouse abuse: Past, present, and future. *Justice Quarterly, 9*, 247-283.

Hirschi T. (1969). *The Causes of Delinquency*. Berkeley, California: University of California Press.

Hirschi T, Gottfredson MR. (Eds.). (1994). *The Generality of Deviance*. New Brunswick, New Jersey: Transaction Books.

Ho CK. (1990). An analysis of domestic violence in Asian-American communities: A multicultural approach to counseling. In LS Brown, MPP Root (Eds.). *Diversity and Complexity in Feminist Therapy* (pp. 129-150). New York: Haworth Press.

Holden GW. (198). Introduction: The development of research into another consequence of family violence. In GW Holden, R Geffner, EN Jouriles (Eds.). *Children Exposed to Marital Violence: Theory, Research, and Applied Issues* (pp. 1-18). Washington, D.C.: American Psychological Association.

Holden, G.W. & Ritchie, K.L. (1991). Linking extreme marital discord, child rearing, and child behavior problems: Evidence from battered women. *Child Development, 62*, 311-327.

Holden GW, Stein JD, Ritchie KL, Harris SD, Jouriles EN. (1998). Parenting behaviors and beliefs of battered women. In GW Holden, R Geffner, EN Jouriles (Eds.). *Children Exposed to Marital Violence: Theory, Research, and Applied Issues* (pp. 289-334). Washington, D.C.: American Psychological Association.

Hollos M. (1976). Conflict and social change in a Norwegian mountain community. *Anthropological Quarterly, 49*, 239-257.

Holloway M. (1994). Trends in women's health: A global view. *Scientific American*, 77-83.

Holtz H, Hames C, Safran M. (1989). Education about domestic violence in U.S. and Canadian medical schools, 1987-1988. *Morbidity and Mortality Weekly Report, 38*, 17.

Hord C, David HP, Donnay F, Wolf M. (1991). Reproductive health in Romania: Reversing the Ceaucescu legacy. *Studies in Family Planning, 22*, 231-240.

Horney K. (1935). The problem of feminine masochism. *Psychoanalytic Review, 12*, 241-257.

Hotaling GT, Sugarman DB. (1986). An analysis of risk markers in husband to wife violence: The current state of knowledge. *Violence and Victims, 1*, 101-124.

Huesmann LR, Eron LD. (1986). The development of aggression in American children as a consequence of television violence viewing. In LR Huesmann, LD Eron (Eds.). *Television and the Aggressive Child: A Cross-National Comparison* (pp. 45-80). Hillsdale, New Jersey: Erlbaum.

Hughes HM. (1988). Psychological and behavioral correlates of family violence in child witnesses and victims. *American Journal of Orthopsychiatry, 58*, 77-90.

Hughes HM. (1986). Research with children in shelters: Implications for clinical services. *Children Today, 15*, 21-25.

Hughes HM, Parkingson D, Vargo M. (1989). Witnessing spouse abuse and experiencing physical abuse: A "double whammy"? *Journal of Family Violence, 4*, 197-209.

Humphreys J. (1993). Children of battered women. In JC Campbell & J Humphreys (Eds.). *Nursing Care of Survivors of Family Violence*. St. Louis: Mosby.

Hutson HR, Anglin D, Yarbrough J, Hardaway K, Russell M, Strote J, Canter M, Blum B. (1998). Suicide by cop. *Annals of Emergency Medicine, 32*, 665-669.

Hutchison IW, Hischel JD, Pesackis CE. (1994). Family violence and police utilization.. *Violence and Victims, 9*, 299-313.

Hyden M. (1994). *Woman Battering as a Marital Act*. New York: Oxford University Press.

Hyman A, Schillinger D, Lo B. (1995). Laws mandating reporting of domestic violence: Do they promote patient well-being? *Journal of the American Medical Association, 273*, 1781-1787.

Ikels C. (190). The resolution of intergenerational conflict: Perspectives of elders and their family members. *Modern China, 16*, 379-406.

Immigration and Nationality Act of 1952, Pub. L. No. 82-414, 66 Stat. 163, codified as amended at 8 U.S.C. section 1101 *et seq*.

In re Christian S., 7 Cal. 4th 768 (1994).

INS v. Cardoza-Fonseca, 480 U.S. 421 (1987).

INS v. Elias-Zacarias, 502 U.S. 478 (1992).

Island D, Letellier P. (1991). *Men Who Beat the Men Who Love Them: Battered Gay Men and Domestic Violence*. New York: Harrington Park.

Israel FL. (Ed.). (1977). *The State of the Union: Messages of the Presidents, 1790-1966*, vol. 2. New York: Chelsea House.

Jacobson N. (1993, October). Domestic Violence: What Are the Marriages Like? American Association for Marriage and Family Therapy: Anaheim, California. Quoted in DG Dutton and SK Golant. (1995). *The Batterer: A Psychological Profile*. New York: Basic Books.

Jaffe P, Wolfe DA. (1990). *Children of Battered Women*. Newbury Park, California: Sage.

Jaffe PG, Wolfe DA, Wilson SK. (1990). *Children of Battered Woman*. Newbury Park, California: Sage.

Jang D, Lee D, Morello-Frosch R. (1990). Domestic violence in the immigrant and refugee community: Responding to the needs of immigrant women. *Response*, 13, 2-7.

Jenkins JH, Cofresi N. (1998). The sociosomatic course of depression and trauma: A cultural analysis of suffering and resilience in the life of a Puerto Rican woman. *Psychosomatic Medicine, 60*, 439-447.

Joint Center for Poverty Research and Institute for Policy Research. (1998). Domestic violence and women's employment. Cited in JR Corlett (1999, June 9). Women, domestic violence, and welfare. *Human Services Agenda of Northeast Ohio, 3*, 105.

Joint Commission on Accreditation of Healthcare Organizations. (1992). *Accreditation Manual for Hospitals*. Oakbrook Terrace, Illinois: Joint Commission on Accreditation of Healthcare Organizations.

Jolin A. (1983). Domestic violence legislation: An impact assessment. *Journal of Police Science and Administration, 11*, 451-456.

Jolin A, Moose CA. (1997). Evaluating a domestic violence program in a community policing environment: Research implementation issues. *Crime & Delinquency, 43*, 279-297.

Jones FC. (1999). Community violence, children and youth: Considerations for programs, policy, and nursing roles. *Pediatric Nursing, 23*, 131-139.

Jones KB. (2000). *Living Between Danger and Love: The Limits of Choice*. New Brunswick, New Jersey: Rutgers University Press.

Jouriles EN, LeCompte SH. (1991). Husbands' aggression towards wives and mothers' and fathers' aggression toward children: Moderating effects of child gender. *Journal of Consulting and Clinical Psychology, 57*, 453-455.

Kaiser L. (1995). *Survey of Accident and Health and Life Insurers Relating to Insurance Coverage for Victims of Domestic Violence*. Harrisburg, Pennsylvania: Commonwealth of Pennsylvania, Pennsylvania Insurance Department.

Kantor GK, Jasinski JL, Aldarondo E. (1994). Sociocultural status and incidence of marital violence in Hispanic families. *Violence and Victims, 9*, 207-222.

Kantor GK, Straus MA. (1987). The "drunken bum" theory of wife eating. *Social Problems, 34*, 213-230.

Kantor GK, Straus MA. (1990). Response of the victims and the police to assaults on wives. In MA Straus, RJ Gelles (Eds.). *Physical Violence in American Families: Risk Factors and Adaptations to Violence in 8,145 Families* (pp. 473-488). New Brunswick, New Jersey: Transaction Publishers.

Kanuha V. (1987). Sexual assault in Southeast Asian communities: Issues in intervention. *Response, 10*, 4-6.

Katzenstein MF. (1989). Organizing against violence: Strategies of the Indian women's movement. *Pacific Affairs*, 62, 53-71.

Kaufman J, Kantor G, Straus MA. (1987). The "drunken bum" theory of wife beating. *Social Problems,* *34*, 213-230.

Kaufman J, Zigler E. (1987). Do abused children become abusive parents? *American Journal of Orthopsychiatry*, 57, 316-331.

Kelly L. (190). How women define their experiences of violence. In K Yllo, M Bograd (Eds.). *Feminist Perspectives on Wife Abuse* (pp. 114-132). Newbury Park, California: Sage.

Kerns V. (1992). Preventing violence against women: A Central American Case. In DA Counts, JK Brown, JC Campbell eds. *Sanctions and Sanctuary: Cultural Perspectives on the Beating of Wives* (pp. 125-138). Boulder, Colorado: Westview Press, Inc.

Kilpatrick KL, Williams LM. (1997). Post-traumatic stress disorder in child witnesses to domestic violence. *American Journal of Orthopsychiatry, 67*, 639-644.

Kilpatrick KL, Williams LM. (1998). Potential mediators of post-traumatic stress disorder in child witnesses to domestic violence. *Child Abuse and Neglect, 22*, 319-330.

Kim K, Cho Y. (1992). Epidemiological survey of spousal abuse in Korea. In EC Viano, ed. *Intimate Violence: Interdisciplinary Perspectives*. Washington, D.C.: Hemisphere Publishing.

Kitsuse JL. (1962). Societal reaction to deviant behavior: Problems of theory and method. *Social Problems, 9*, 247-256.

Klein CF, Orloff LE. (1993). Providing legal protection for battered women: An analysis of state statutes and case law. *Hofstra Law Review, 21*, 801-1189.

Kligman G. (1992). The politics of reproduction in Ceaucescu's Romania: A case study in political culture. *Eastern European Political Science, 6, 364-419.*

Klingbeil KS, Boyd VD. (1984). Emergency room intervention: Detection, assessment, and treatment. In AR Roberts (Ed.). *Battered Women and Their Families* (pp. 27-28). New York: Springer.

Knight RA, Hatty SE. (1992). Violence against women in Australia's capital city. In E.C. Viano (Ed.). *Intimate Violence: Interdisciplinary Perspectives* (pp. 255-263). Washington, D.C.: Hemisphere Publishing Corporation.

Kohlberg L. (1976). Moral stages and moralization: The cognitive-developmental approach. In T. Lickona (Ed.), *Moral Development and Behavior: Theory, Research, and Social Issues* (pp. 31-53). New York: Holt, Rinehart, and Winston.

Kornblit AL. (1994). Domestic violence--An emerging health issue. *Social Science and Medicine, 39,* 1181-1188.

Kornhauser RR. (1978). *Social Sources of Delinquency: An Appraisal of Analytic Models*. Chicago: University of Chicago Press.

Koss MP, Goodman LA, Browne A, Fitzgerald LF, Keita GP, Russo NF. (1994). *No Safe Haven: Male Violence Against Women at Home, at Work, and in the Community*. Washington, D.C.: American Psychological Association.

Krugman SD, Wissow LS. (1998). Helping children with troubled parents. *Pediatric Annals, 27*, 23-29.

Kurt JL. (1995). Stalking as a variant of domestic violence. *Bulletin of the Academy of Psychiatry and Law, 23*, 219-230.

Kurtz LR. (1997). Protecting New York's children: An argument for the creation of a rebuttable presumption against awarding a spouse abuser custody of a child. *Albany Law Review, 60*, 1345-1375.

Kurz D. (1987). Emergency department responses to battered women: Resistance to medicalization. *Social Problems, 34*, 69-81.

Kurz D, Stark E. Not-so-benign neglect. In K Yllo, M Bograd (Eds.) *Feminist Perspectives on Wife Abuse* (pp. 249-266). Newbury Park, California: Sage.

Lamb S. (1999). Constructing the victim: Popular images and lasting labels. In In S Lamb (Ed.). *New Versions of Victims: Feminists Struggle with the Concept* (pp. 108-138). New York: New York University Press.

Lambeck M. (1992). Like teeth biting tongue: The proscription and practice of spouse abuse in Mayotte. In DA Counts, JK Brown, JC Campbell (Eds.). *Sanctions and Sanctuary:Cultural Perspectives on the Beating of Wives* (pp. 157-171). Boulder, Colorado: Westview Press, Inc.

Lamberty C, Coll CG. (1994). Overview. In C Lamberty, CG Coll (Eds.). *Puerto Rican Women and Children: Issues in Health, Growth, and Development* (pp. 1-10). New York: Plenum Press.

Landau RE. A survey of teaching and implementation: The veterinarian's role in recognizing and reporting abuse. *Journal of the American Veterinary Medical Association, 215*, 328-331.

Landenburger K. (1989). A process of entrapment in and recovery from an abusive relationship. *Issues in Mental Health Nursing, 10*, 209-227.

Laner MR. (1989). Competition and combativeness in courtship: Reports from men. *Journal of Family Violence, 4*, 47-62.

Langan PA, Innes CA. (1986). Preventing domestic violence against women. *The Criminal Justice Archive and Information Network, Fall*, 1-3.

Langford DR. (1990). Consortia: A strategy for improving the provision of health care to domestic violence survivors. *Response, 13*, 17-19.

Lanza ML, Carifio J. (192). Use of a panel of experts to establish validity for patient assault vignettes. *Evaluation Review, 17*, 82-92.

Lanza-Kaduce L, Greenleaf RG, Donahue M. (1995). Trickle-up report writing: The impact of a proarrest policy for domestic disturbances. *Justice Quarterly, 12*, 525-542.

Larrain S. (1993). *Estudio de Frecuencia de la Violencia Intrafamiliar y La Condicion de la Mujer en Chile* [Study of the Frequency of Intrafamilial Violence and the Condition Women in Chile]. Pan-American Health Organization.

Lateef S. (1992). Wife abuse among Indo-Fijians. In DA Counts, JK Brown, JC Campbell (Eds.). *Sanctions and Sanctuary: Cultural Perspectives on the Beating of Wives* (pp. 185-201). Boulder, Colorado: Westview Press, Inc.

Lauderdale P, Parker J, Smith-Cunnien P, Inverarity J. (1984). External threat and definition of deviance. *Journal of Personality and Social Psychology, 46*, 1058-1068.

Le N. (1982). The Asian perspective on rape. Proceedings from Conference on Rape and Women of Color, Edgewater Uptown Community Mental Health Center, Rape Victim Assistance Program, June.

Lemert EM. (1951). *Social Pathology*. New York: McGraw Hill.

Lemon NKD. (1999). The legal system's response to children exposed to domestic violence. *Domestic Violence and Children, 9*, 67-83.

Lenski G, Lenski J. (1970). *Human Societies: An Introduction to Macrosociology*. New York: McGraw-Hill.

Lerman LG. (1992). The decontextualization of domestic violence. *Journal of Criminal Law & Criminology, 83*, 217-240.

Lester D. (1987). Wife abuse and psychogenic motives in nonliterate societies. *Perceptual and Motor Skills, 64*, 154.

Letellier P. (1994). Gay and bisexual male domestic violence victimization: Challenges to feminist theory and responses to violence. *Violence and Victims, 9*, 95-106.

LeVine BA. (1982). *Culture Behavior, and Personality*, 2nd ed. New York: Alsine Publishing Company.

Levinson D. (1989). *Family Violence in Cross-Cultural Perspective*. Newbury Park, California: Sage Publications.

Levinson D, Malone M. (1980). *Toward Explaining Human Culture*. New Haven: HRAF.

Lie G, Gentlewarrior S. (1991). Intimate violence in lesbian relationships: Discussion of survey findings and practice implications. *Journal of Social Services Research, 15*, 41-49.

Lieberman A, Van Horn P, Grandison D, Pekarsky J. (1997). Mental health assessment of infants, toddlers, and preschoolers in a service program and a treatment outcome research program. *Infant Mental Health Journal, 18*, 158-170.

Limandri BJ. (1987). The therapeutic relationship with abused women. *Journal of Psychosocial Nursing, 25*, 9-16.

Linz D, Malamuth N. (1993). *Pornography*. Newbury Park, California: Sage.

Lobel K. (1986). Introduction. In K. Lobel (Ed.). *Naming the Violence: Speaking Out About Lesbian Battering* (pp. 1-7). Seattle, Washington: Seal Press.

Lockhart L, White BW. (1989). Understanding marital violence in the black community. *Journal of Interpersonal Violence, 4*, 421-436.

Lockhart LL. (1985). Methodological issues in comparative racial analyses: The case of wife abuse. *Social Work and Abstracts, 21*, 35-41.

Lockhart LL, White BW, Causby V, Isaac I. (1994). Letting out the secret: Violence in lesbian relationships. *Journal of Interpersonal Violence, 9*, 469-492.

Lombroso C. (1911). Introduction. In G Lombroso-Ferrero (Eds.). *Criminal Man According to the Classification of Cesare Lombroso*. New York: Plenum.

Loue S, Faust M. (1998). Intimate partner violence among immigrants. In S Loue (Ed.). *Handbook of Immigrant Health* (pp. 521-544). New York: Plenum Press.

Lund LE. (1999). What happens when health practitioners report domestic violence injuries to the police? A study of the law enforcement response to injury reports. *Violence and Victims 14*, 203-214.

Lynn BW. (1986). "Civil rights" ordinances and the Attorney General's Commission: New developments in pornography regulation. *Harvard Civil Rights-Civil Liberties Law Review, 21*, 27-_.

MacAndrew C, Edgerton R. (1969). *Drunken Comportment: A Social Explanation*. Chicago: Aldine.

MacKinnon C. (1984). Not a moral issue. *Yale Law and Policy Review, 2*, 321-345.

180

REFERENCES

MacKinnon CA. (1997). Rape: On coercion and consent. In K Conboy, N Medina, S Tanbury (Eds.). *Writing on the Body: Female Embodiment and Feminist Theory* (pp. 42-58). New York: Columbia University Press.

Maiuro RD, Cahn TS, Vitaliano PP, Zegree JB. (1986). Anger control treatment for men who engage in domestic violence: A controlled outcome study. Paper presented at the annual conference of the Western Psychological Association, Seattle, Washington. Cited in DG Dutton. (1995). *The Domestic Assault of Women: Psychological and Criminal Justice Perspectives.* Vancouver: University of British Columbia Press.

Makepeace JM. (1981). Courtship violence among college students. *Family Relations, 30,* 97-102.

Malaysia Women's Aid Organisation. (1992). *Draft Report of the National Study on Domestic Violence.* Kuala Lumpur: Women's Aid Organisation.

Malmquist CP. (1986). Children who witness parental murder: Posttraumatic aspects. *Journal of the American Academy of Child and Adolescent Psychiatry, 25,* 320-325.

Marans S, Cohen D. (1993). Children and inner-city violence: Strategies for intervention. In L Leavitt, N. Fox (Eds.). *Psychological Effects of War and Violence on Children* (pp. 281-302). Hillsdale, New Jersey: Lawrence Erlbaum.

Margolies L, Leeder E. (1995). Violence at the door: Treatment of lesbian batterers. *Violence Against Women, 1,* 139-157.

Marin BV. (1990). AIDS prevention for non-Puerto Rican Hispanics. *NIDA Research Monograph, 93,* 35-52.

Marshall LL. (1992). Development of the Severity of Violence Against Women Scales. *Journal of Family Violence, 7,* 103-121.

Marshall LL, Rose P. (1987). Gender, stress, and violence in adult relationships of a sample of college students. *Journal of Social and Personal Relationships, 4,* 299-316.

Marshall WL, Ecles A, Barbaree HE. (1991). The treatment of exhibitionists: A focus on sexual deviance versus cognitive and relationship features. *Behavior Research and Therapy, 29,* 129-135.

Martin D. (1976). *Battered Wives.* New York: Simon and Schuster.

Martin SE. (1992). The epidemiology of alcohol-related interpersonal violence. *Alcohol Health and Research World, 16,* 230-237.

Martin SL, English KT, Clark KA, Cilenti D, Kupper KL. (1996). Violence and substance use among North Carolina pregnant women. *American Journal of Public Health, 86,* 991-998.

Martin SL, Tsui AO, Maitra K, Marinshaw R. (1999). Domestic violence in northern India. American *Journal of Epidemiology, 150,* 417-426.

Masten AS. (1994). Resilience in individual development: Successful adaptation despite risk and adversity. In MC Wang, EW Gordon (Eds.). *Educational Resilience in Inner-City America: Challenges and Prospects* (pp. 3-25). Hillsdale, New Jersey: Lawrence Erlbaum.

Masten AS, Best KM, Garmezy N. (1990). Resilience and development: Contributions from the study of children who overcame adversity. *Development and Psychopathology, 2,* 425-444.

Matlaw JR, Spence DM. (1994). The hospital elder assessment team: A protocol for suspected cases of elder abuse and neglect. *Journal of Elder Abuse and Neglect, 6,* 23-37.

Matter of A and Z, A72 190 893, A72 793 219 (IJ Dec. 20, 1994)(Arlington).

Matter of A--P--, A73 753 922 (IJ Sept. 20, 1996)(San Francisco).

Matter of M and K, A72 374 558 (IJ Aug. 9, 1995)(Arlington).

Matter of Mogharrabi, 19 I. & N. Dec. 439 (BIA 1987).

Matter of Sharmin, A73 556 833 (IJ Sept. 27, 1996)(New York).

Matthews WJ. (1984) Violence in college couples. *College Student Journal, 18,* 150-158.

Mazza D, Dennerstein L, Ryan V. (1996). Physical, sexual, and emotional violence against women: A general practice-based prevalence study. *Medical Journal of Australia, 164,* 14-17.

May ET. (1975). The pursuit of domestic perfection: Marriage and divorce in Los Angeles, 1890-1920. Unpublished doctoral dissertation, University of California.

McCloskey LA, Figueredo AJ, Koss MP. (1995). The effects of systemic family violence on children's mental health. *Child Development, 66,* 1239-1261.

McCloskey LA , walker M. (2000). Posttraumatic stress in children exposed to family violence and single-event trauma. *Journal of the Academy of Child and Adolescent Psychiatry, 39,* 108-115.

McClure JS. (1998). Preaching about sexual and domestic violence. In JS McClure, NJ Ramsay (Eds.). *Telling the Truth: Preaching About Sexual and Domestic Violence* (pp. 110-119). Cleveland, Ohio: United Church Press.

McClure JS, Ramsay NJ. (1989). Introduction: Poured out like water. In JS McClure, NJ Ramsay (Eds.). *Telling the Truth: Preaching About Sexual and Domestic Violence* (pp. 1-7). Cleveland, Ohio: United Church Press.

McClure M. (1994). Sermon, May 5. Quoted in JS McClure (1998). Preaching about sexual and domestic violence. In JS McClure, NJ Ramsay (Eds.). *Telling the Truth: Preaching About Sexual and Domestic Violence* (pp. 110-119). Cleveland, Ohio: United Church Press.

McFarlane J. (1989). Battering during pregnancy: Tip of an iceberg revealed. *Women's Health, 15*, 69-84.

McFarlane J, Parker B, Soeken K, Bullock L. (1992). Assessing for abuse during pregnancy: Severity and frequency of injuries and associated entry into prenatal care. *Journal of the American Medical Association, 267*, 3176-3178 .

McFarlane J, Greenberg L, Weltge A, Watson M. (1995). Identification of abuse in emergency departments: Effectiveness of a two-question screening tool. *Journal of Emergency Nursing, 21*, 391-94.

McFarlane J, Parker B, Soeken K, Silva C, Reed S. (1999). Severity of abuse before and during pregnancy for African American, Hispanic, and Anglo women. *Journal of Nurse-Midwifery, 44*, 139-144.

McFarlane J, Wiist W, Watson M. (1998). Predicting physical abuse against pregnant Hispanic women. *American Journal of Preventive Medicine, 15*, 134-138.

McGee L, Newcomb MD. (1992). General deviance syndrome: Expanded hierarchical evaluations at four ages from early adolescence to adulthood.

McGrath JE. (1970). A conceptual formulation of stress. In JE McGrath (Ed.). *Social Psychological Factors in Stress* (pp. 10-21). New York: Holt, Rinehart, and Winston.

McHenry, P.C., Julian, T.W., Julian, T.W., & Gavazzi, S.M. (1995). Toward a biopsychosocial model of domestic violence. *Journal of Marriage and the Family, 57*, 307-320.

McKibben L, DeVos E, Newberger E. (1989). Victimization of mothers of abused children: A controlled study. *Pediatrics, 84*, 531-535.

McKinley DG. (1964). *Social Class and Family Life*. London: Free Press.

McKinney K. (1986). Perceptions of courtship violence: Gender difference and involvement. *Free Inquiry Into Creative Sociology, 14*, 61-66.

McLeod DM. (1995). Communicating deviance: The effects of television news coverage of social protest. *Journal of Broadcasting and Electronic Media, 39*, 4-19.

McLeod M. (1984). Women against men: An examination of domestic violence based on an analysis of official data and national victimization data. *Justice Quarterly 1*, 171-193.

Mead GH. (1934). *Mind, Self, and Society*. Chicago: University of Chicago Press.

Melhuus M. (1996). Power, value, and the ambiguous meanings of gender. In M Melhuus, KA Stolen. *Machos, Mistresses, Madonnas: Contesting the Power of Latin American Gender Imagery* (pp. 230-259). London: Verso.

Mercer JR. (1973). *Labeling the Retarded*. Berkeley, California: University of California Press.

Merton RK. (1964). Anomie, anomia, and social interaction. In M Clinard (Ed.). *Anomie and Deviant Behavior*. Glencoe, Illinois: Free Press.

Merton RK. (1959). Social conformity, deviation, and opportunity structures: A comment on the contributions of Dubin and Cloward. *American Sociological Review, 24*, 177-189.

Merton RK. (1968). *Social Theory and Social Structure*. New York: Free Press.

Mignon SI, Holmes WM. (1995). Police response to mandatory arrest laws. *Crime & Delinquency, 41*, 430-442.

Mikawa JK, Morones PA, Gomez A, Case HL, Olsen D, Gonzalez Huss MJ. (1992). Cultural practices of Hispanics: Implications for the prevention of AIDS. *Hispanic Journal of Behavioral Sciences, 14*, 421-433.

Miller LJ. (1990). Violent families and the rhetoric of harmony. *British Journal of Sociology, 41*, 263-288.

Miller SL. (1989). Unintended side effects of pro-arrest policies and their race and class implications for battered women: A cautionary note. *Criminal Justice Policy Review, 3*, 299-317.

Milner JS, Chilamkurti, C. (1991). Physical child abuse perpetrator characteristics: A review of the literature. *Journal of Interpersonal Violence, 6*, 345-366.

Mirande A. (1997). *Hombres & Machos: Masculinity and Latino Culture*. Boulder, Colorado: Westview Press.

Mississippi State Medical Association. (1995). Diagnostic and treatment guidelines on domestic violence. *Journal of the Mississippi State Medical Association, 36*, 331-348.

Mitchell RG. (1984). Alienation and deviance: Strain theory reconsidered. *Social Inquiry, 54*, 330-345.

Mitchell, W. (1992). Why Wape men don't beat their wives: Constraints towards domestic tranquility in a New Guinea society. In DA Counts, JK Brown, JC Campbell (Eds.). *Sanctions and Sanctuary: Cultural Perspectives on the Beating of Wives* (pp. 89-98). Boulder, Colorado: Westview Press, Inc.

Mixon, D. (1995). The Domestic Abuse Act: The physician's role. *Journal of the Arkansas Medical Society, 92*, 218-220.

Moore, L.J., Boehlein J.K. (1991). Treating Psychiatric Disorders Among Mien refugees from Highland Laos. *Social Science and Medicine, 32*, 1029-1036.

Morley, R. (1994). Wife beating and modernization: The case of Papua New Guinea. *Journal of Comparative Family Studies, 25*, 25-51.

Mosher DL. (1991). Macho men, machismo, and sexuality. *Annual Review of Sex Research, 2*, 199-247.

Mullen, P.E., Romans-Clarkson, S.E., Walton, V.A., & Herbison, P.E. (1988). Impact of sexual and physical abuse on women's mental health. *Lancet, 1*, 841.

Murdock GP. (1949). *Social Structure*. New York: Macmillan.

Murphy Y, Murphy RF. (1974). *Women of the Forest*. New York: Columbia University Press.

Murty KS, Roebuck JB. (1992). An analysis of crisis calls by battered women in the city of Atlanta. In E.C. Viano (Ed.). *Intimate Violence: Interdisciplinary Perspectives* (pp. 61-70). Washington, D.C.: Hemisphere Publishing Corporation. '

Myrhoj T, Bernstein I, Bisgaard ML, Svendsen LB, Sondergaard JO, Mohr J, Dahl S, Bulow S. (1994). The establishment of an HNPCC register. *Anticancer Research, 14*, 1647-1650.

Nandy A. (1994). Sati as profit versus sati as spectacle: The public debate on Roop Kanwar's death. In JS Hawley (Ed*.*). *Sati, The Blessing and the Curse: The Burning of Wives in India*. Oxford: Oxford University Press.

Narasimhan S. (1990). *Sati: Widow Burning in India*. New York: Doubleday.

Naroll R. (1970). What we have learned from cross-cultural surveys. *American Anthropologist, 72*, 1227-1288.

National Clearinghouse for the Defense of Battered Women. (1990). Statistics Packet. Cited in Browne SM (1995). Due process and equal protection challenges to the inadequate response of the police in domestic violence situations. *Southern California Law Review, 68*, 1295-1334.

National Coalition Against Domestic Violence. (1999*).* About the National Coalition Against Domestic Violence. Denver, Colorado: National Coalition Against Domestic Violence.

National Coalition Against Domestic Violence. (1997). *1997 National Directory of Domestic Violence Programs: A Guide to Community Shelter, Safe Home, and Service Programs*. Washington, D.C.: National Coalition Against Domestic Violence.

National Committee for Injury Prevention and Control. (1989). *Injury Prevention: Meeting the Challenge*. New York: Oxford University Press.

National Institute of Mental Health. (1992). *Family Violence. National Workshop on Violence: Analysis and Recommendations*. Report prepared by K.D. O'Leary and A. Browne. Rockville, Maryland: Violence and Traumatic Stress Research Branch, National Institute of Mental Health, National Institutes of Health, United States department of Health and Human Services.

Neruda P. (1993). Emerging. In A Reid (Trans.). *Pablo Neruda: Extravagaria*. Austin, Texas: University of Texas Press.

Newcombe HB. (1994). Cohorts and privacy. *Cancer Causes and Control, 5*, 287-291.

NiCarthy, G. (1997). *Getting Free: You Can End Abuse and Take Back Your Life*. Seattle: Seal Press.

Norton LB, Peipert JF, Zierler S, Lima B, Hume L. (1995). Battering in pregnancy: An assessment of two screening methods. *Obstetrics and Gynecology, 85*, 321-325.

Novello AC, Rosenberg M, Saltzman L, Shosky J. (1992). A medical response to domestic violence. *Journal of the American Medical Association, 267*, 3132.

Nyala H. (1997). *Point Last Seen: A Woman Tracker's Story of Domestic Violence and Personal Triumph*. New York: Penguin Books.

Obeso P, Bordatto O. (1979). Cultural implications in treating the Puerto Rican female. *American Journal of Drug and Alcohol Abuse, 6*, 345-353.

O'Brien M, John RS, Margolin G, Erel O (194). Reliability and diagnostic efficacy of parent's reports regarding children's exposure to marital aggression. *Violence and Victims, 9*, 45-62.

Ofei-Aboagye RO. (1994). Altering the strands of the fabric: A preliminary look at domestic violence in Ghana. *Signs*, 19, 924-938.

Ohio Revised Code §§ 109.73, 109.77, 737.11, 1901.18-.19, 1909.02, 2919.25-.26, 2933.16, 2935.03, 2935.032, , 3113.31-.32.

O'Keefe M. (1994). Adjustment of children from martially violent homes. *Families in Society, 75*, 403-415.

Okun L. (1986). *Woman Abuse: Facts Replacing Myths*. Albany: State University of New York Press.

Oldenburg VT. (194). The Roop Kanwar case: Feminist responses. In JS Hawley (Ed.). *Sati, The Blessing and the Curse: The Burning of Wives in India* (pp. 101-130). Oxford: Oxford University Press.

O'Leary KD. (1988). Physical aggression between spouses: A social learning theory perspective. In V.B. Hasselt, R.L. Morrison, A.S. Bellack, M. Hersen, (Eds.). *Handbook of Family Violence* (pp. 31-55). New York: Plenum.

O'Leary KD. (1993). Through a psychological lens: Personality traits, personality disorders, and levels of violence. In RJ Gelles, DR Loseke (Eds.). *Current Controversies on Family Violence* (pp. 7-30). Newbury Park, California: Sage.

O'Leary KD, Arias I. (1988). Assessing agreement of reports of spouse abuse. In GT Hotaling, D. Finkelhor, JT Kirkpatrick, & MA Straus (Eds.). *Family Abuse and Its Consequences: New Directions for Research* (pp. 218-227). Newbury Park, California: Sage.

Olson L, Huyler F, Lynch AW, Fullerton L, Werenko D, Sklar D, Zumwalt R. (1999). Guns, alcohol, and intimate partner violence: The epidemiology of female suicide in New Mexico. *Crisis, 20,* 121-126.

Orcutt JD. (1983). *Analyzing Deviance.* Homewood, Illinois: Dorsey Press.

Oriel KA, Fleming MF. (1998). Screening men for partner violence in a primary care setting: A new strategy for detecting domestic violence. *Journal of Family Practice, 64,* 493-398.

Osofsky JD. (1999). The impact of violence on children. *Domestic Violence and Children, 9,* 33-49.

Osofsky JD, Cohen G, Drell M. (1995). The effects of trauma on young children: A case of 2-year-old twins. *International Journal of Psycho-Analysis, 76,* 595-607.

Pagelow M. (1984). *Family Violence.* New York: Praeger.

Pan HS, Neidig PH, O'Leary KD. (1994). Predicting mild and severe husband-to-wife physical aggression. *Journal of Consulting and Clinical Psychology, 62,* 975-981.

Panitz DR, McConchie RD, Sauber SR, Fonseca JA. (1983). The role of machismo and the Hispanic family in the etiology and treatment of alcoholism in Hispanic American males. *American Journal of Family Therapy, 11,* 33-44.

Parker B, McFarlane J, Soeken K. (1994). Abuse during pregnancy: Effects of maternal complications and birthweight in adult and teenage women. *Obstetrics and Gynecology, 84,* 323-328.

Parnas RI. (1993). Criminal justice responses to domestic violence. In LE Ohlin & FJ Remington (Eds.). *Discretion in Criminal Justice: The Tension Between Individualization and Uniformity* (pp. 175-210). Albany: State University of New York Press.

Pate AM, Hamilton EE. (1992). Formal and informal deterrents to domestic violence: The Dade County spouse assault experiment. *American Sociological Review, 57,* 691-697.

Patterson GR. (Ed.). (1990). Depression and Aggression in Family Interaction. Hillsdale, New Jersey: Lawrence Erlbaum.

Paymar M. (2000). *Violent No More: Helping Men End Domestic Abuse.* Alameda, California: Hunter House Publishers.

Pearlman CL. (1984). Machismo and change in indigenous Mexico: A case study from Oaxaca. *Quarterly Journal of Ideology, 8,* 53-59.

Peled E, Davis D. (1995). *Groupwork with Children of Battered Women: A Practitioner's Manual.* Thousand Oaks, California: Sage.

Pellegrino ED, Thomasma DC. (1988). *For the Patient's Good: The Restoration of Beneficence in Health Care.* New York, New York: Oxford University Press.

Pence E. (1983). The Duluth domestic abuse intervention project. *Hamline Law Review, 6,* 247-275.

Pendleton G. (1997). Relief for women and children suffering abuse. In R.P. Murphy ed. *1997-98 Immigration and Nationality Law Handbook,* vol. 2 (pp. 482-512). Washington, D.C.: American Immigration Lawyers Association.

People v. Aris, 264 Cal. Rptr. 167 (Cal. App. 1989).

People v. Humphrey, 56 Cal. Rptr. 2d 142 (1996).

People v. Scott, 424 N.E.2d 70 (Ill. App. 1981).

People v. White, 414 N.E.2d 196 (Ill. App. 1980).

Peplau LA. (191). Lesbian and gay relationships. In JC Gonsiorek & JD Weinrich (Eds.). *Homosexuality: Implications for Public Policy* (pp. 177-196). Newbury Park, California: Sage.

Perilla JL, Bakeman R, Norris FH. (1994). Culture and domestic violence: The ecology of abused Latinas. *Violence and Victims, 9,* 325-339.

Pernanen K. (1976). Alcohol and crimes of violence. In B Kissin, H Bagleitor (Eds.). *The Biology of Alcoholism, vol. 4. Social Aspects of Alcoholism* (pp. 351-444). New York: Plenum.

Peters v. Peters, 634 P.2d 586 (Haw. 1981).

Pfouts JH. (1978). Violent families: Coping responses of abused wives. *Child Welfare,* 101-110.

Phelan J, Link BG, Moore RE, Stueve A. (197). The stigma of homelessness: The impact of the label "homeless" on attitudes towards poor persons. *Social Psychology Quarterly, 60,* 323-337.

Piepert JF, Domagalski LR. (1994). Epidemiology of adolescent sexual assault. *Obstetrics and Gynecology, 84,* 867-871.

Pirog-Good MA, Stets-Kealey JE. (1985). Male batterers and battering prevention programs: A national survey. *Response, 8,* 8-12.

Piven FF. (1981). Deviant behavior and the remaking of the world. *Social Problems, 28,* 489-508.

Pleck E. (1987). *Domestic Tyranny: The Making of American Social Policy Against Family Violence from Colonial Times to the Present.* New York: Oxford University Press.

Polsby DD. (1992). Suppressing domestic violence with law reforms. *Journal of Criminal Law and Criminology,* 83, 250-253.

Potter SH. (1977). *Family Life in a Northern Thai Village.* Berkeley, California: University of California Press.

Prasad BD. (1994). Dowry-related violence: A content analysis of news in selected newspapers. *Journal of Comparative Family Studies, 25,* 71-89.

Pratt CC, Koval JE, Lloyd S. (1983). Service workers' responses to abuses of the elderly. *Social Casework, 64,* 147-153.

Prochaska JO, DiClemente CC, Norcross, CC. (1992). In search of how people change: Applications to addictive behaviors. *American Psychologist, 47,* 1102-1104.

Procter-Smith M. (1995). 'Reorganizing victimization': The intersection between liturgy and domestic violence. In CJ Adams, MM Fortune (Eds.). *Violence Against Women and Children: A Christian Theological Sourcebook.* New York: Continuum.

PROFAMILIA. (1990). *Encuestra de Prevalencia, Demografia y Salud* [Demographic and Health Survey]. Bogota, Colombia: PROFAMILIA.

Prus RC. (1975). Labeling theory: A reconceptualization and a prepositional statement on typing. *Sociological Focus, 8,* 79-96.

Ptacek J. (1988). Why do men batter their wives? In K Yllo, M Bograd (Eds.). *Feminist Perspectives on Wife Abuse* (pp. 133-157). Beverly Hills, California: Sage.

Quay HC, Peterson DR. (1979). *Manual for the Behavior Problem Checklist.* Coral Gables, Florida: University of Miami. Cited in JR Kolbo (1996). Risk and resilience among children exposed to family violence. *Violence and Victims, 11,* 113-128.

Quesada GM. (1976). Language and communication barriers for health delivery to a minority group. *Social Science and Medicine, 10,* 323-327.

Quillian JP. (1996). Screening for spousal or partner abuse in a community health setting. *Journal of the American Academy of Nurse Practitioners,* 8, 155-160.

Racusin RJ, Copans SA, Mills P. (194). Characteristics of families of children who refuse post-divorce visits. *Journal of Clinical Psychology, 50,* 792-801.

Rahman N. (1996). Caregivers' sensitivity to conflict: The use of the vignette methodology. *Journal of Elder Abuse & Neglect, 8,* 35-47.

Randall T. (1991). AMA, joint commission urge physicians to become part of solution to family violence epidemic. *Journal of the American Medical Association, 266,* 2524-2527.

Randall T. (1990). Domestic violence intervention calls for more than treating injuries. *Journal of the American Medical Association, 264,* 939-940.

Rath GD, Jarratt LG, Leonardson G. (1989). Rates of domestic violence against adult women by men partners. *Journal of the American Board of Family Practice, 2,* 227-233.

Raybeck D. (1991). Hard versus soft deviance: Anthropology and labeling theory. In M Freilich, D Raybeck, T Savishinsky (Eds.). *Deviance: Anthropological Perspectives* (pp. 51-72). New York: Bergin and Garvey.

Reese WA II, Katovich MA. (1989). Untimely acts: Extending the interactionist conception of deviance. *Sociological Quarterly, 30,* 159-184.

Reifler CB, Howard J, Lipton MA, Lipzin MB, Widmann DE. (1971). Pornography: An experimental study of effects. *American Journal of Psychiatry, 128,* 575-582.

Reiss AJ Jr., Roth JA eds. (1993). *Understanding and Preventing Violence. Panel on the Understanding and Control of Violent Behavior, Committee on Law and Justice, National Research Council.* Washington, D.C.: National Academy Press.

Renzeti C. (1992). *Violent Betrayal: Partner Abuse in Lesbian Relationships.* Newbury Park, California: Sage.

Renzetti C. (1999). Women's use of violence in intimate relationships. In S Lamb (Ed.). *New Versions of Victims: Feminists Struggle with the Concept* (pp. 42-56). New York: New York University Press.

Reynolds S. (1993). Emergency physicians have made an effort to learn about domestic violence. *Emergency Department Management, 5,* 20-23.

Rigakos GS. (1995). Constructing the symbolic complainant: Police subculture and the nonenforcement of protection orders for battered women. *Violence and Victims, 10,* 227- 247.

Roberts AR, Roberts BS. (1990). A comprehensive model for crisis intervention with battered women and their children. In AR Roberts (Ed.). *Crisis Intervention Handbook* (pp. 105-123). Belmont, California: Wadsworth Publishing Company.

Rodriguez CE. (1994). A summary of Puerto Rican migration to the United States. In C Lamberty, CG Coll (Eds.). *Puerto Rican Women and Children: Issues in Health, Growth, and Development* (pp. 11-28). New York: Plenum Press.

Rodriguez MA, Bauer HM, Flores-Ortiz Y, Szkupinski-Quiroga S. (1998). Factors affecting patient-physician communication for abused Latina and Asian immigrant women. *Journal of Family Practice, 47*, 309-311.

Rodriguez MA, Craig AM, Mooney DR, Bauer HM. (1998). Patient attitudes about mandatory reporting of domestic violence: Implications for health care professionals. *Western Journal of Medicine, 169*, 337-341.

Rohner RP. (1975). *They Love Me, They Love Me Not: A Worldwide Study of the Effects of Parental Acceptance and Rejection.* New Haven: HRAF.

Roscoe B, Kelsey T. (1986). Dating violence among high school students. *Psychology, 23*, 53-59.

Rosecrance J. (1985). Compulsive gambling and the medicalization of deviance. *Social Problems, 32*, 275-284.

Rosenbaum A, O'Leary KD. (1981). Children: The unintended victims of marital violence. *American Journal of Orthopsychiatry, 51*, 692-699.

Rosenfeld R. (1989). Robert Merton's contributions to the sociology of deviance. *Sociological Inquiry, 59*, 453-466.

Rossi P, Waite E, Bose C, Berk R. (1974). The seriousness of crimes: Normative structures and individual differences. *American Sociological Review, 39*, 224-237.

Rounsaville B. (1978a). Battered wives: Barriers to identification and treatment. *American Journal of Orthopsychiatry, 48*, 487-494.

Rounsaville B. (1978b). Theories in marital violence: Evidence from a study of battered women. *Victimology, 3*, 11-31.

Rouse LP, Breen R, Howell M. (1988). Abuse in intimate relationships: A comparison of married and dating students. *Journal of Interpersonal Violence, 3*, 414-429.

Roy DF. Sex in the factory: Informal heterosexual relations between supervisors and work groups. In CD Bryant (Ed.). *Deviant Behavior: Occupational and Organizational Bases* (pp. 44-66). Chicago: Rand McNally.

Roy M. (1977). A research project probing a cross-section of battered women. In M Roy (Ed.). *Battered Women: A Psychosociological Study of Domestic Violence* (pp. 25-44). New York: Van Nostrand Reinhold Co.

Rusbult CE. (1980). Commitment and satisfaction in romantic situations: A test of the investment model. *Journal of Experimental Social Psychology*, 172-186.

Rusbult CE. (1983). A longitudinal test of the investment model: The development (and deterioration) of satisfaction and commitment in heterosexual involvements. *Journal of Personality and Social Psychology, 45*, 101-117.

Russell DEH. (1975). The prevalence and impact of marital rape in San Francisco. Presented at the Annual Meeting of the American Sociological Association, New York.

Rutter M. (1987). Psychosocial resilience and protective mechanisms. *American Journal of Orthopsychiatry, 57*, 316-331.

Rutter M. (1994). Resilience: Some conceptual considerations. *Contemporary Pediatrics, 11*, 36-48.

Saccuzzo DP. (196). How should the police respond to domestic violence: A therapeutic jurisprudence analysis of mandatory arrest. *Santa Clara Law Review, 39*, 765 -787.

Sachs CJ, Peek C, Baraff LJ, Hasselblad V. (1998). Failure of the mandatory domestic violence reporting law to increase medical facility referral to police. *Annals of Emergency Medicine, 31*, 488-494.

Sagarin E, Kelly RJ. (1982). Collective and formal promotion of deviance. In MM Rosenberg, RA Stebbins, A Turoetz (Eds.). *The Sociology of Deviance* (pp.203-225). New York: St. Martin's Press.

Salas v. Carpenter, 980 F.2d 299 (5th Cir. 1992).

Salzman E. (1994). Note, The Quincy district court domestic violence prevention program: A model legal framework for domestic violence intervention. *Boston University Law Review, 74*, 329-364.

Sameroff A. (1995). General systems theories and developmental psychopathology. In D Cicchetti, D Cohen (Eds.). *Developmental Psychopathology: Vol. 2: Risk, Disorder, and Adaptation* (p. 659-695). New York: Wiley.

Sangiacomo M. (1999, Oct. 17). Immigrant contesting deportation. *Plain Dealer*, B-1, 4.

Sarkar J. (1993). Till death do us part. *Far Eastern Economic Review, 156*, 40-42.

Saunders DG. (1995). The tendency to arrest victims of domestic violence: A preliminary analysis of officer characteristics. *Journal of Interpersonal Violence*, 10, 147-158.

Saunders DG. (1992). A typology of men who batter: Three types derived from cluster analysis. *American Journal of Orthopsychiatry, 62*, 264-275.

Saunders DG, Kindy P. (1993). Predictors of physicians' responses to woman abuse: The role of gender, background, and brief training. *Journal of General Internal Medicine, 8*, 606-609.

Savishinsky J. (1991). Free shows and cheap thrills: Staged deviance in the Arctic and the Bahamas. In M Freilich, D Raybeck, J Savishinsky (Eds.). *Deviance: Anthropological Perspectives* (pp. 73-88). New York: Bregin and Garvey.

Sawicki v. Village of Ottawa Hills, 525 N.E.2d 468 (Ohio 1988).

Schafer J, Caetano R, Clark CL. (1998). Rates of intimate partner violence in the United States. *American Journal of Public Health, 88*, 1702-1704.

Scheff TJ. (1966). *Being Mentally Ill: A Sociological Theory*. Chicago: Aldine.

Scheff TJ. (1974). The labeling theory of mental illness. *American Sociological Review, 39*, 444-452.

Schei B, Bakketeig LS. (1989). Gynecological impact of sexual and physical abuse by spouse: A study of a random sample of Norwegian women. *British Journal of Obstetrics and Gynecology, 96*, 1379-1383.

Schei B, Sameulson SD, Bakketeig LS. (1991). Does spousal physical abuse affect the outcome of pregnancy? *Scandinavian Journal of Social Medicine, 19*, 26-31.

Schmidt JD, Sherman LW. (1993). Does arrest deter domestic violence? *American Behavioral Scientist, 36*, 601-609.

Schulman M. (1979). *A Survey of Spousal Violence Against Women in Kentucky*. Washington, D.C.:Law Enforcement Assistance Administration, United States Department of Justice.

Schulman MA. (1981). *A Survey of Spousal Violence Against Women in Kentucky*. New York: Garland Publishing Company.

Schur EM. (1965). *Crimes Without Victims*. Englewood Cliffs, New Jersey: Prentice-Hall.

Schwartz, D. (2000). *Whose Face Is In the Mirror? The Story of One Woman's Journey from the Nightmare of Domestic Abuse to True Healing*. Carlsbad, California: Hay House, Inc.

Scott CS, Shifman L, Orr L, Owen RG, Fawcett N. (1988). Hispanic and black adolescents' beliefs relating to sexuality and contraception. *Adolescence, 23*, 667-688.

Scott MB, Lyman SM. (1968). Accounts. *American Sociological Review, 35*, 46-62.

Scott RA. (1969). *The Making of Blind Men*. New York: Russell Sage.

Scull A. (1984). Competing perspectives on deviance. *Deviant Behavior, 5*, 275-289.

Serra P. (1993). Physical violence in the couple relationship: A contribution toward the analysis of context. *Family Process, 32*, 21-33.

Shamim I. (1992). Dowry and women's status: A study of court cases in Dhaka and Delhi. In E.C. Viano (Ed.). *Intimate Violence: Interdisciplinary Perspectives* (pp. 265-275). Washington, D.C.: Hemisphere Publishing Corporation.

Sheridan DJ, Taylor WK. (1993). Developing hospital-based domestic violence programs, protocols, policies, and procedures. *AWHONN's Clinical Issues in Perinatal & Women's Health Nursing, [Association of Women's Health, Obstetric & Neonatal News] 4*, 471-482.

Sherif M, Hovland C. (1961). *Social Judgement*. New Haven, Connecticut: Yale University Press.

Sherman LW, Berk RA. (1984). The specific deterrent effects of arrest for domestic assault. *American Sociological Review, 49*, 261-272.

Sherman LW, Smith DA. (1992). Crime, punishment, and stake in conformity: legal and informal control of domestic violence. *American Sociological Review, 57*, 680-690.

Sherrell v. City of Longview, 683 F. Supp. 1108 (E.D. Tex. 1987).

Shields N, Hannecke CR. (1983). Battered wives' reactions to marital rape. In D Finkelhor, RJ Gelles, GT Hotaling, MA Straus (Eds.). *The Dark Side of Families: Current Family Violence Research* (pp. 132-147). Beverly Hills, California: Sage Publications.

Shook v. Crabb, 281 N.W.2d 616 (Iowa 1979).

Short JF Jr. (1975). The natural history of an applied theory: Differential opportunity and mobilization for youth. In NJ Demerath III, O Larsen, K Schuessler (Eds.). *Social Policy and Sociology* (pp. 193-210). New York: Academic Press.

Shostak M. (1983). *Nisa*. New York: Vintage Books.

Sigelman CK, Berry CJ, Wiles KA. (1984). Violence in college students' dating relationships. *Journal of Applied Social Psychology, 14*, 530-548.

Silvern L, Karyl J, Landis TY. (195). Individual psychotherapy for traumatized children of abused women. In E Peled, PG Jaffe, JL Edleson (Eds.). *Ending the Cycle of Violence: Community Responses to Children of Battered Women* (pp. 43-76). Thusand Oaks, California: Sage.

Simmons JL. (1965). Public stereotypes of deviants. *Social Problems, 13*, 223-232.

Simon LMJ. (1996). The legal processing of domestic violence cases. In BD Sales, DW Shuman (Eds.). *Law, Mental Health & Mental Disorder* (pp. 440-463). Pacific Grove, California: Brooks/Cole Publishing.

Smith L. (1989). *Domestic Violence: An Overview of the Literature.* London: Home Office Research and Planning Unit.

Smith MD. (1987). The incidence and prevalence of woman abuse in Toronto. *Violence and Victims, 2,* 173-187.

Smith MD. (1990). Patriarchal ideology and wife beating: A test of a feminist hypothesis. *Violence and Victims, 5,* 257-274.

Smith R, Osuch JR, Linver MN. (195). A national breast cancer database. *Radiologic Clincs of North America, 33,* 1247-1257.

Snow K, (1992). The violence at home. *The Advocate, June 2,* 604.

Snyder DK, Scheer NS. (1981). Predicting disposition following a brief residence at a shelter for battered women. *American Journal of Community Psychology, 9,* 559-566.

Soble RA, Minnet MR. (1994). Spouse abuse: Imposing liability on the police for failure to respond to the victims of domestic violence. *Michigan Bar Journal, September,* 940-945.

Sonkin DJ, Durphy M. (1985). *Learning to Live Without Violence: A Handbook for Men* (2nd ed.). San Francisco: Volcano Press.

Sonkin DJ, Martin D, Walker LE. (1985). *The Male Batterer: A Treatment Approach.* New York: Springer.

Sorenson SB. (1996). Violence against women: Examining ethnic differences and commonalities. *Evaluation Review, 20,* 123-145.

Sorenson SB, Telles CA. (1991). Self-reports of spousal violence in a Mexican-American and non-Hispanic white population. *Violence and Victims, 6,* 3-15.

Sorenson SB, Upchurch DM, Shen H. (1996). Violence and injury in marital arguments: Risk patterns and gender differences. *American Journal of Public Health, 86,* 35-40.

Stalans LJ. (1996). Family harmony or individual protection? Public recommendations about how police can handle domestic violence situations. *American Behavioral Scientist, 39,* 433-448.

Stalans LJ, Lurigio AJ. (1995). Public preferences for the court's handling of domestic violence situations. *Crime & Delinquency, 41,* 399-413.

Star B. (1982). Programs for assaulters: Nationwide trends. In JF Flanzer (Ed.). *The Many Faces of Family Violence* (pp. 76-86). Springfield, Illinois: Charles C. Thomas.

Stark E. (1996). Mandatory arrest of batterers: A reply to its critics. In ES Buzawa, CG Buzawa (Eds.). *Do Arrest and Restraining Orders Work?* (pp. 115-149). Thousand Oaks, California: Sage.

Stark E. (1990). Rethinking homicide, violence, race, and politics of gender. *International Journal of Health Services, 20,* 3-26.

Stark E, Flitcraft A. (1988). Violence among intimates: An epidemiological review. In V.B. Van Hasselt, R.L. Morrison, A.S. Bellack, M. Hersen (Eds.). *Handbook of Family Violence* (pp. 293-317). New York: Plenum.

Stark E, Flitcraft A, Frazier W. (1979). Medicine and patriarchal violence: The social construction of a "private" event. *International Journal of Health Services, 9,* 461-493.

Stark E, Flitcraft A, Zuckerman D, Grey A, Robison J, Frazier W. (1981). *Wife Abuse in the Medical Setting: An Introduction for Health Personnel.* In Domestic Violence Monograph Series No. 7. Rockville, Maryland: National Clearinghouse on Domestic Violence.

Stark R, McEvoy J. (1970). Middle class violence. *Psychology Today, 4,* 107-112.

State v. Allery, 682 P.2d 312 (Wash. 1984).

State v. Anaya, 438 A.2d 892 (Maine 1981).

State v. Baker, 424 A.2d 171 (N.H. 1980).

State v. Gallegos, 719 P.2d 1268 (N.M. App. 1986).

State v. Hadinger, 573 N.E.2d 1191 (Ohio App. 1991).

State v. Hennum, 441 N.W.2d 793 (Minn. 1989).

State v. Kellogg, 542 N.W.2d 514 (Iowa1996).

State v. Kelly, 478 A.2d 364 (N.J. 1984).

State v. Koss, 551 N.E.2d 970 (Ohio 1990).

State v. Leidholm, 334 N.W.2d 811 (N.D. 1983).

State v. Linner, 665 N.E.2d 1180 (Ohio 1996).

State v. Norman, 378 S.E.2d 8 (N.C. 1989).

State v. Stewart, 763 P.2d 572 (Kan. 1988).

State v. Wanrow, 559 P.2d 548 (Wash. 1977).

Statistics Canada. (1993). The violence against women survey. *The Daily.* Statistics Canada, November 16.

Steiner S. (1974). *The Islands: The Words of the Puerto Ricans.* New York: Harper and Row.

Steinman MK. (1990). Lowering recidivism among men who batter women. *Journal of Police Science and Administration, 17,* 124-132.

Steinman SK. (1991). Coordinated criminal justice interventions and recidivism among batterers. In M Steinman (Ed.). *Woman Battering: Policy Responses* (pp. 221-236). Cincinnati: Anderson Publishing Co.

Steinmetz SK. (1978). The battered husband syndrome. *Victimology, 2,* 499-509.

Steinmetz SK. (1987). Family violence: Past, present, and future. In M.B. Sussman and S.K. Steinmetz (Eds.). *Handbook of Marriage and the Family* (pp. 725-766). New York: Plenum.

Sternberg KJ, Lamb ME, Greenbaum C, Dawud S, Cortes RM, Krispin O, Lorey F. (1993). Effects of domestic violence on children's behavioral problems and depression. *Developmental Psychology, 29,* 44-52.

Stets JE, Straus MA. (1990). Gender differences in reporting of marital violence and its medical and psychological consequences. In MA Straus, RJ Gelles (Eds.). *Physical Violence in American Families: Risk Factors and Adaptations to Violence in 8,145 Families* (pp. 151-165). New Brunswick, New Jersey: Transaction.

Stevens E. (1973). Machismo and Marianismo. *Transaction Society, 10,* 57-63.

Stokes G. (1993). *The Walls Came Tumbling Down: The Collapse of Communism in Eastern Europe.* (New York: Oxford University Press.

Stolen KA. (1991). Gender, sexuality, and violence in Ecuador. *Ethnos, 5,* 82-100.

Straus MA. (1986). Domestic violence and homicide antecedents. *Domestic Violence, 62,* 446- 465.

Straus MA. (1993). Physical assaults by wives: A major social problem. In RJ Gelles, DR Loseke (Eds.). *Current Controversies in Family Violence* (pp. 67-87). Newbury Park, California: Sage.

Straus MA. (1994). State-to-state differences in social inequality and social binds in relation to assaults on wives in the United States. *Journal of Comparative Family Studies, 25,* 7-24.

Straus MA. (1979). Measuring intrafamily conflict and violence: The Conflict Tactics Scale. *Journal of Marriage and the Family, 41,* 75-88.

Straus MA. (1983). Ordinary violence, child abuse, and wife beating: What do they have in common ? In D Finkelhor, RJ Gelles, GT Hotaling, MA Straus (Eds.). *The Dark Side of Families: Current Family Violence Research* (pp. 213-234). Beverly Hills, California: Sage.

Straus MA. (1980). Victims and aggressors in marital violence. *American Behavioral Scientist, 23,* 681-704.

Straus MA. (1978). Wife beating: How common and why? *Victimology, 2,* 443-459.

Straus MA, Gelles RJ. (1990). How violent are American families? Estimates from the National Family Violence Resurvey and other studies. In M.A. Straus, R.J. Gelles (Eds.). *Physical Violence in American Families: Risk Factors and Adaptations to Violence in 8,145 Families* (pp. 95-112). New Brunswick, New Jersey: Transaction Publishers.

Straus MA, Gelles RJ, Steinmetz S. (1980). *Behind Closed Doors: Violence in the American Family.* Garden City, New Jersey: Anchor Press.

Straus MA, Hamby SL, Boney-McCoy S, Sugarman DB. (1996). The Revised Conflict Tactics Scale (CTS2): Development and preliminary psychometric data. *Journal of Family Issues, 17,* 283-316.

Straus MA, Smith C. (1990). Family patterns and child abuse. In MA Straus and RJ Gelles (Eds.). *Physical Violence in American Families: Risk Factor Adaptations to Violence in 8,145 Families* (pp. 245-261). New Brunswick, New Jersey: Transaction Publishers.

Strube MJ, Barbour LS. (1984). Factors related to the decision to leave an abusive relationship. *Journal of Marriage and the Family, 46,* 837-844.

Sugg NK, Inui T. (1992). Primary care physicians' response to domestic violence: Opening Pandora's box. *Journal of the American Medical Association, 267,* 3157-3160.

Sutherland EH. (1956). *The Sutherland Papers.* A Cohen, A Lindesmith, K Schuessler (Eds.). Bllogton, Indiana: Indiana University Press.

Sutherland EH, Cressey DR. (1960). *Principles of Criminology,* 6th ed. Chicago: Lippincott.

Syers M, Edleson JL. (1992). The combined effects of coordinated criminal justice intervention in woman abuse. *Journal of Interpersonal Violence, 7,* 490-502.

Sykes GM, Matza D. (1957). Techniques of neutralization: A theory of delinquency. *American Sociological Review, 22,* 644-670.

Symonds A. (1979). Violence against women: The myth of masochism. *American Journal of Psychotherapy,* 33, 161-173.

Szasz TS. (1961). *The Myth of Mental Illness.* New York. Hoeber Harper.

Szasz TS. (1960). The myth of mental illness. *American Psychologist, 15,* 113-118.

Szinovacz ME. (1983). Using couple data as a methodological tool: The case of marital violence. *Journal of Marriage and the Family, 45,* 633-644.

Szymanski M. (1991). Battered husbands: Domestic violence in gay relationships. *Genre, Fall*, 32-73.
Tanner JL. (1995). Training for family-oriented pediatric care: Issues and options. *Pediatric Clinics of North America, 42*, 193-202.
Tedeschi JT, Felson RB. (1994). *Violence, Aggression, and Coercive Actions*. Washington, D.C.: American Psychological Association.
Terry RM, Steffensmeier DJ. (1988). Conceptual and theoretical issues in the study of deviance. *Deviant Behavior, 9*, 55-76.
Thibaut JW, Kelly HH. (1959). *The Social Psychology of Groups*. New York: Wiley.
Thio A. (1978). *Deviant Behavior*. Boston: Houghton Mifflin.
Thoits PA. (1985). Self-labeling processes in mental illness. *American Journal of Sociology, 91*, 221-249.
Thomas J. (1982). New directions in deviance research. In MM Rosenberg, RA Stebbins, A Turowitz (Eds.). *The Sociology of Deviance* (pp. 288-317). New York: St. Martin's Press.
Thompson WN. (1991). Machismo: Manifestations of a cultural value in the Latin American casino. *Journal of Gambling Studies, 7*, 143-164.
Thornberry TP. (1994). *Violent Families and Youth Violence* (Fact Sheet No. 21). Washington, D.C.: United States Department of Justice, Office of Juvenile Justice and Delinquency Prevention.
Thornhill R, Palmer CT. (2000). *A Natural History of Rape: Biological Bases of Sexual Coercion*. Cambridge, Massachusetts: MIT Press.
Thurman v. City of Torrington, 595 F. Supp. 1521 (D. Conn. 1984).
Tifft LL. (1993). *Battering of Women: The Failure of Intervention and the Case for Prevention*. Boulder, Colorado: Westview Press, Inc.
Tilden VP. (1989). Response of the health care delivery system to battered women. *Issues in Mental Health Nursing, 10*, 309-320.
Tittle CR, Welch MR. (1983). Religiosity and deviance: Toward a contingency theory of constraining effects. *Social Forces, 61*, 653-682.
Tolman RM. (1989). The development of a measure of psychological maltreatment of women by their male partners. *Violence and Victims, 4*, 159-177.
Tolman RM, Weisz A. (1995). Coordinated community intervention for domestic violence: The effects of arrest and prosecution on recidivism of woman abuse perpetrators. *Crime and Delinquency, 41*, 481-495.
Torres S. (1991). A comparison of wife abuse between two cultures: Perceptions, attitudes, nature, and extent. *Issues in Mental Health Nursing: Psychiatric Nursing for the 90's: New Concepts, NewTherapies, 12*, 113-131.
Tracy KK, Crawford CB. (1992). Wife abuse: Does it have an evolutionary origin? In DA Counts, JK Brown, JC Campbell (Eds.). *Sanctions and Sanctuary: Cultural Perspectives on the Beating of Wives* (pp. 19-32). Boulder, Colorado: Westview Press, Inc.
Treptow KW. (Ed.). (1996). *A History of Romania*, rev. ed. Iasi, Romania: Center for Romanian Studies.
Tully M. (1991). *No Full Stops in India*. New Delhi: Viking Penguin India.
Uba L. (1992). Cultural Barriers to Health Care for Southeast Asian Refugees. *Public Health Reports, 107*, 544-548.
Ulrich YC. (1993). What helped most in leaving spouse abuse: Implications for interventions. *AWHONN's Clinical Issues in Perinatal and Women's Health Nursing [Association of Women's Health, Obstetric & Neonatal Nurses], 4*, 385-390.
Ulrich YC. (1991). Women's responses for leaving abusive spouses. *Health Care for Women International, 12*, 465-473.
United States Agency for International Development (USAID). (1999, April 28-April 30). *Violenta Domestica: Legislatie, Interventie, Prevenire: De la Trauma de la Integritate: Femeile din Romania Isi Regasesc Identitatea* [*Domestic Violence: Legislation, Intervention, Prevention: Trauma to Integrity: Women in Romania and Regaining Identity*].
Vance CS. (1989). Pleasure and danger: Toards a politics of sexuality. In CS Vance (Ed.). *Pleasure and Danger: Exploring Female Sexuality* (pp. 1-27). London: Pandora Press.
Vaselle-Augenstein R, Ehrlich A. (1992). Male batterers: Evidence for psychopathology. In EC Viano (Ed.). *Intimate Violence: Interdisciplinary Perspectives* (pp. 139-154). Washington, D.C.: Hemisphere Publishing Corporation.
Vasquez MJT. (1994). Latinas. In L Comas-Diaz, B Greene (Eds.). *Women of Color: Integrating Ethnic and Gender Identities in Psychotherapy* (pp. 114-138). New York: Guilford Press.
Violence Against Women Act of 1994, Pub. L. No. 103-322, 108 Stat. 1902-1955, 8 U.S.C. §§ 1151, 1154, 1186a, 1254, 2245.
Vivian D, Langhinrichsen-Rohling J. (1994). Are bi-directionally violent couples mutually victimized? A gender-sensitive comparison. *Violence and Victims, 9*, 107-124.

Waaland P, Keeley S. (1985). Police decision making in wife abuse: The impact of legal and extralegal factors. *Law and Human Behavior, 9*, 355-366.

Walker LE. (1979). *The Battered Woman.* New York: Harper and Row.

Walling MK, Reiter RC, O'Hara MW, Milburn AK, Lilly G, Vincent SD. (1994). Abuse history and chronic pain in women: I. Prevalences of sexual abuse and physical abuse. *Obstetrics and Gynecology, 84*, 193-199.

Walsh K. (1995). The mandatory arrest law: Police reaction. *Pace Law Review, 16*, 97-108.

Walter JD. (1981). Police in the middle: A study of small city police intervention in domestic disputes. *Journal of Police Science and Administration, 9*, 243-260.

Ward JV. (1988). Urban adolescents' conceptions of violence. In C Gilligan, JV Ward, JM Taylor (Eds.). *Mapping the Moral Domain: A Contribution of Women's Thinking to Pyschological Theory and Education* (pp. 177-200). Cambridge, Massachusetts: Harvard University Press.

Warshaw C. (1996). Domestic violence: Changing theory, changing practice. *Journal of the American Medical Women's Association, 51*, 87-91.

Warshaw C. (1989). Limitations of the medical model in the care of battered women. *Gender and Society, 3*, 506-517.

Watson v. City of Kansas City, 857 F.2d 690 (10th Cir. 1988).

Websdale N. (198). *Rural Woman Battering and the Justice System: An Ethnography.* Thousand Oaks, California: Sage.

Weil S. (1977). Human personality. In GA Panichas (Ed.). *The Simone Weil Reader.*New York: McKay.

Weiss E. (2000). *Surviving Domestic Violence: Voices of Women Who Broke Free.* Agreka Books.

Welch DM. (1994). Comment, Mandatory arrest of domestic abusers: Panacea or perpetuation of the problem of abuse? *DePaul Law Review, 43*, 1133-1164.

Weldon, M. (1999). *I Closed My Eyes: Revelations of a Bettered Woman: Rebuilding Life After Domestic Violence.* Center City, Minnesota: Hazelden Information and Educational Services.

Welling BL, Biren A, Johnston M, Kuehl S, Dunn D. (1990). *Achieving Equal Justice for Women and Men in the Courts [Draft Report of the Judicial Council Advisory Committee on Gender Bias in the Courts].* San Francisco: Administrative Office of the Courts.

West CM, Kantor GK, Jasinski JL. (1998). Sociodemographic predictors and cultural barriers to help seeking behavior by Latina and Anglo American battered women. *Violence and Victims, 13*, 361-375.

Wexler DB. (2000). *Domestic Violence 2000: An Integrated Skills Program for Men.* New York: W.W. Norton & Company.

Whatley MA. (1993). For better or worse: The case of marital rape. *Violence and Victims, 8*, 29-39.

Wildin SR, Williamson WD, and Wilson GS. (1991). Children of battered women: Developmental and learning profiles. *Clinical Pediatrics, 30*, 299-304.

Williams OJ, Becker RL. (1994). Domestic partner abuse treatment programs and cultural competence: The results of a national survey. *Violence and Victims, 9*, 287-296.

Willigen JV, Channa VC. (1991). Law, custom, and crimes against women: The problem of dowry death in India. *Human Organization, 50*, 369-377.

Wilson M, Daly M. (1993). An evolutionary psychological perspective on male sexual proprietariness and violence against wives. *Violence and Victims, 8*, 271-194.

Windle WF. (1969). Brain damage by asphyxia at birth. *Scientific American, 216*, 77-84.

Wingood, G.M & DiClemente, R.J. (1997). The effects of an abusive primary sexual partner on the condom use and sexual negotiation practices of African-American women. *American Journal of Public Health, 87*, 1016-1018.

Wodarski . (1987). An examination of spouse abuse: Practice issues for the profession. *Clinical Social Work Journal, 15*, 172-187.

Wolak J, Finkelhor D. (1998). Children exposed to partner violence. In JL Jasinski, LM Williams (Eds.). *Partner Violence: A Comprehensive Review of 20 Years of Research* (pp. 44-111). Thousand Oaks, California: Sage.

Wolf M. (1972). *Women and the Family in Rural Taiwan.* Stanford: Stanford University Press.

Wolfe DA, Jaffe P, Wilson SK, Zak L. (1985). Children of battered women: The relation of child behavior to family violence and marital stress. *Journal of Counseling and Clinical Psychology, 33*, 657-664.

Wolfe DA, Korsch B. (1994). Witnessing domestic violence during childhood and adolescence: Implication for pediatric practice. *Pediatrics, 94*, 594-599.

Wolfgang ME, Ferracuti F. (1967). *The Subculture of Violence: Toward An Integrated Theory of Criminology.* London: Tavistock.

Women's AIDS Organization. (1992). *Draft Report of the National Study on Domestic Violence.* Kuala Lumpur, Malaysia: Women's AID Organization.

Wood JM. (1997). Risk predictors for re-abuse or re-neglect in a predominantly Hispanic population. *Child Abuse & Neglect, 21*, 379-389.

Woodin v. Rasmussen, 455 N.W.2d 535 (Minn. Ct. App. 1990).

Worcester N. (1995). Health system response to battered women: Our "successes" are creating new challenges. *Network News, October,* 20.

Wrangham R, Peterson D. (1996). *Demonic Males: Apes and the Origins of Human Violence.* Boston: Houghton Mifflin.

WrightRJ, Wright RO, Isaac NE. (197). Response to battered mothers in the pediatric emergency department: A call for an interdisciplinary approach to family violence. *Pediatrics, 99,* 186-192.

Yates A. (196). When children witness domestic violence. *Hawaii Medical Journal, 55,* 162-163.

Yegidis BL, Renzy RB. (194). Battered women's experience with a preferred arrest policy. *Affilia, 9,* 60-70.

Yllo K, Bograd M. eds. (1990). *Feminist Perspectives on Wife Abuse.* Newbury Park, California: Sage Publications.

Young TJ. (1989). Alienation and self-reported deviance. *Psychological Reports, 66,* 727-730.

INDEX

Elder abuse, 42
Ellis, D., 104
Equal protection, 99
Erikson, E., 73, 75
Erotica, 26
Ethics, 39, 157, 159
Ethnicity, 18, 43, 45, 47, 49, 55, 156
Evidence, 97, 206, 208, 209-220,
    114, 116
Evolutionary theory, 23-25, 48, 76
Examination of victim, 88, 157
Exchange theory, 31, 77, 107
Excuse, 11, 12, 47, 65, 80, 110, 111,
    119, 121-122, 144

Fagan, J., 143
Familismo, 41
Family, defined, 2
Feldberg, M., 105
Felder, R., 69, 84, 123, 127
Feldman, M., 122
Feminist theory, 22, 25, 28
Ferracuti, F., 21
Finkelhor, D., 151
Finland, 141
Fisher, E., 18
Flitcraft, A., 15, 89
Florida, 101, 102, 103
Forgetting, 119
Forgiveness, 11, 94, 95, 137, 138,
    142
Freire, P., 1
Fromm, E., 10

Gandhi, M., 5, 159
Ganley, A., 33
Gelles, R., 1, 30, 31, 77
General systems theory, 28
Georgia, 103
Ghana, 2
Gil, R., 39
Gilligan, C., 157-159
Goetting, A, 11, 140
Golant, S., 2, 8, 9, 10, 12, 124, 128
Goode, W., 31
Graham, D., 34, 135
Great Britain, 141

Hamberger, K., 91
Hannecke, C., 122
Harris, L., 33
Hart, B., 15
Harwood, A., 40
Health care workers, 83-91
Help-seeking, 103, 131, 133-134,
    143
Hembrismo, 41
Herman, J., 16, 34
Hirschi, T., 77
Hispanics, 7, 18, 19, 37-51
Ho, C., 19, 142
Hollos, M., 75
Homicide, 8, 17, 19, 88
Homophobic control, 15
Homosexuals, 13, 37
Honeymoon period, 10, 11
Hospitals, 41, 88, 89, 90
Hostility, 8, 30, 129
Hovland, C., 143
Human immunodeficiency virus
    (HIV), 16
Humilidad, 41
Hutchison, I., 136

Illinois, 101
Immigrants, 19, 104, 135
Immigration law, 97, 115-123
Immigration and Nationality Act,
    115
Incidence, 5-6, 18, 26, 37, 52, 54,
    108, 160, 161
Inclusion and exclusion, 120
India, 4, 7, 27, 138, 140
Injuries, 10, 13, 15, 54, 83-93, 98,
    102, 106, 12-114, 127, 155
Innovation,, 70-71
Investment theory, 31, 143
Iowa, 111
Isolation, 20, 23, 9, 77, 84, 125, 131,
    133, 135, 140
Israel, 31

Jacobson, N., 12
Jealousy, 9, 10, 24, 45, 47, 48, 56-58,
    89
Joint Commission for Accreditation